# BRITISH ISLES CRUISE GUIDE 2025

Your Travel Companion to Explore England, Scotland, Ireland, and Wales.

**COLE WINCHESTER**

2

*British Isles cruise guide*

# TABLE OF CONTENTS

**INTRODUCTION** .................................................................. **10**

    Overview of the British Isles ............................................... 10

    Why Cruise the British Isles? ............................................... 13

    Best Time to Cruise the British Isles .................................... 18

    Cruise Itineraries: Short & Long Voyages in the British Isles
    ..................................................................................................... **23**

    Tips for First-Time Cruisers .................................................. 30

    Tips for First-Time Cruisers: A Guide to Smooth Sailing
    ........................................................ Error! Bookmark not defined.

**PLANNING YOUR CRUISE** .............................................. **44**

    Choosing the Right Cruise Line: A Guide for Travelers ..... 44

    Different Types of British Isles Cruises ............................... 50

    Luxury vs. Budget Cruises: Which One is Right for You?. 59

    River vs. Ocean Cruises: Which One is Right for You? ..... 67

    Best Ports of Call on a British Isles Cruise ......................... 75

    How to Book Your Cruise: A Step-by-Step Guide ............. 83

    Cruise Packages: What's Included ....................................... 90

Packing Tips for Your Cruise: What to Bring for a Smooth
Sailing Experience .................................................................... 97

**PORT BY PORT GUIDE** ................................................... **105**

    London (Tilbury): A Gateway to England's Capital ......... 105

    Top Attractions in London: Tower of London, Westminster
    Abbey, and Buckingham Palace ......................................... 112

*British Isles cruise guide*

Shore Excursions: A Guide to Making the Most of Your Cruise Stops...............117

Dining & Shopping on a Cruise: What to Expect & How to Make the Most of It...............123

Top Attractions in Edinburgh: Edinburgh Castle, Holyrood Palace, and the Royal Mile...............130

Shore Excursions: How to Make the Most of Your Time in Port...............135

Dining & Shopping: Enhancing Your Travel and Cruise Experience...............142

**EDINBURGH (LEITH)**...............149

Edinburgh (Leith): Scotland's Vibrant Port and Gateway to the Capital...............149

Shore Excursions: A Guide to Making the Most of Your Time in Port...............154

Dining & Shopping: Enhancing Your Travel and Cruise Experience...............157

**DUBLIN**...............164

Top Attractions in Dublin: Trinity College, Dublin Castle, and the Guinness Storehouse...............170

Shore Excursions: Enhancing Your Cruise Experience....175

...............182

Dining & Shopping: Enhancing Your Travel and Cruise Experience...............182

**LIVERPOOL**...............189

Attractions: The Beatles Story, Liverpool Cathedral, Albert Dock...............189

5

Shore Excursions in Liverpool .......................................... **193**

Dining & Shopping in Liverpool ....................................... **195**

**GLASGOW** ................................................................................. **199**

Attraction: Kelvingrove Art Gallery, Glasgow Cathedral, George Square ....................................................................... **199**

Shore Excursions in Glasgow ........................................... **203**

Dining & Shopping in Glasgow ....................................... **205**

**BELFAST** ................................................................................... **209**

Belfast: A City of History, Culture, and Resilience .......... **209**

Top Attractions in Belfast: Titanic Belfast, Giant's Causeway, and Belfast Castle ........................................... **215**

Shore Excursions: Making the Most of Your Time in Port **220**

Dining & Shopping: Enhancing Your Travel Experience. **227**

**CORK** ......................................................................................... **233**

Cork (Cobh): Ireland's Historic and Cultural Gem .......... **233**

Top Attractions in Cork: Blarney Castle, Cork City, and Jameson Distillery ............................................................. **239**

Shore Excursions: Enhancing Your Cruise Experience .... **243**

Dining & Shopping: A Guide to Culinary and Retail Experiences Around the World ......................................... **251**

**INVERGORDON** ...................................................................... **257**

Invergordon: Gateway to the Scottish Highlands ............. **257**

Top Attractions in the Scottish Highlands: Loch Ness, Culloden Battlefield, and Inverness .................................. **263**

Shore Excursions: Enhancing Your Cruise Experience .... **268**

Dining & Shopping: A Complete Guide to Culinary and
Retail Experiences ............................................................. 275

**ISLE OF SKYE** .................................................................... 286

Top Attractions on the Isle of Skye: Fairy Pools, Old Man of
Storr, and Dunvegan Castle .............................................. 286

Shore Excursions: Enhancing Your Cruise Experience .... 290

**STORNOWAY** ..................................................................... 304

Stornoway: The Cultural Heart of the Outer Hebrides ..... 304

Top Attractions in the Outer Hebrides: Callanish Stones,
Lews Castle, and the Isle of Harris ................................... 309

Shore Excursions: Making the Most of Your Cruise
Experience ........................................................................ 314

Dining & Shopping: A Guide to Enriching Your Travel
Experience ........................................................................ 321

Other Notable Ports: Guernsey, Isle of Man, and Isles of
Scilly ................................................................................. 327

**ONBOARD EXPERIENCE** ................................................. 332

The Onboard Experience: What to Expect on a Cruise .... 332

Cruise Ship Activities: From Spa Days to Adventure Sports
........................................................................................... 338

Wellness and Fitness Onboard: Staying Healthy at Sea ... 343

Kids and Family-Friendly Activities in the British Isles: Fun
for All Ages ...................................................................... 349

**CULTURAL INSIGHTS** ..................................................... 356

Cultural Insights: Enriching Your Travel Experience ....... 356

British Isles History and Heritage: A Journey Through Time ...................................................................................... 361

Local Customs and Etiquette in the British Isles: A Guide for Travelers ............................................................................. 367

Festivals and Events to Experience in the British Isles: Celebrating Culture and Tradition ...................................... 373

Tasting the Best of British Cuisine: A Culinary Journey Through the Isles ....................................................................... 380

English Breakfast, Fish and Chips, Haggis, and More: Iconic Dishes of the British Isles ...................................................... 386

Regional Wines, Beers, and Spirits of the British Isles .... 392

## SHORE EXCURSION AND LOCAL ADVENTURES... 399

Active Adventures: Hiking, Cycling, and Water Sports in the British Isles ........................................................................ 399

Scenic Day Trips: Castles, Gardens, and National Parks in the British Isles ................................................................... 404

Cultural Experiences in the British Isles: Museums, Music, and Arts ................................................................................ 411

Hidden Gems: Off-the-Beaten-Path Destinations in the British Isles ........................................................................ 417

## CRUISE TIPS & PRACTICAL INFORMATION: NAVIGATING YOUR VOYAGE WITH EASE .............. 424

Currency and Payment Methods in the British Isles: A Traveler's Guide .................................................................. 430

Language and Basic Phrases for Traveling the British Isles ................................................................................................. 436

Staying Connected: Wi-Fi and Communication While Traveling the British Isles .................................................... 442

Health and Safety Tips for Traveling the British Isles ...... 448

Travel Insurance and Emergencies: Essential Tips for a Safe Journey in the British Isles .................................. 455

Sustainable Cruising Practices: Navigating the Seas Responsibly ........................................................................ 461

**PACKING FOR YOUR BRITISH ISLES CRUISE: A COMPLETE GUIDE ........................................................ 467**

Essentials for the British Weather: How to Pack and Prepare .................................................................................. 473

What to Pack for Excursions: A Practical Guide for Travelers .............................................................................. 480

Special Considerations for Longer Cruises: What You Need to Know ............................................................................ 485

Tips for Packing Light and Efficiently: Travel Smart, Travel Easy ..................................................................................... 492

**TESTIMONIALS & TRAVEL STORIES: MEMORABLE EXPERIENCES FROM THE BRITISH ISLES ................................................................................ 499**

Real-Life Experiences from Fellow Cruisers: Unforgettable Journeys Through the British Isles ................................... 503

Recommended Shore Excursions from Past Travelers: Must-Do Experiences in the British Isles .................................. 507

Must-See Destinations and Activities in the British Isles ..511

# INTRODUCTION

## Overview of the British Isles

The British Isles, a stunning archipelago located off the northwestern coast of mainland Europe, encompasses a rich tapestry of history, culture, and natural beauty. Comprising Great Britain, Ireland, and over 6,000 smaller islands, this region is a unique blend of ancient traditions, vibrant cities, and unspoiled landscapes. For travelers seeking an eclectic mix of modernity and history, the British Isles offers an unparalleled adventure, where every corner tells a story of centuries past and vibrant contemporary life.

### Geography and Layout

At the heart of the British Isles lies **Great Britain**, the largest island, divided into three countries: **England**, **Scotland**, and **Wales**. To the west, across the Irish Sea, is the island of **Ireland**, which is politically divided into the **Republic of Ireland** in the south and **Northern Ireland**, a part of the United Kingdom, in the north. The geography of the British Isles is incredibly diverse—rolling hills and dramatic coastlines in the south, rugged mountains and deep lochs in the north, and serene lakes, forests, and fields spread across the islands.

One of the most striking features of the region is its coastline, which stretches over 12,000 miles, offering stunning views, sandy beaches, and secluded coves. Visitors can experience everything from the **cliffs of Dover** to the **Giant's Causeway** in Northern Ireland, and the windswept beauty of the **Scottish Highlands** to the lush, green hills of **Wales**. The natural variety makes the British Isles a paradise for outdoor enthusiasts, with numerous trails, national parks, and areas of outstanding natural beauty waiting to be explored.

## A Rich Tapestry of History

The British Isles are a place where history comes to life. The islands have been inhabited for thousands of years, with ancient sites such as **Stonehenge** in England and the **Ring of Brodgar** in Orkney, Scotland, providing glimpses into prehistory. The islands' long and complex history also includes the Roman occupation, Viking invasions, and the formation of the British Empire. The **Norman Conquest** of 1066, the **Wars of the Roses**, and the rise of the British monarchy all shaped the region's identity.

In addition to its historical landmarks, the British Isles are home to world-renowned cultural institutions. Iconic cities like **London**, **Edinburgh**, **Dublin**, and **Cardiff** feature centuries-old architecture, museums, galleries, and theatres, all offering deep dives into the regions' past. The **Tower of London**, **Edinburgh Castle**, and **Dublin Castle** are just a few examples of majestic fortifications that transport visitors back in time.

## Cultural Diversity

While the British Isles share a common geographic location, each part has its own distinct identity, shaped by its language, traditions, and history. England is known for its cosmopolitan cities, bustling markets, and iconic landmarks like **Big Ben** and **Westminster Abbey**. Scotland, with its proud Highland heritage, is synonymous with bagpipes, tartan, and the haunting beauty of its landscapes. **Welsh** culture is alive with a rich tradition of music, literature, and myth, especially celebrated in the annual **Eisteddfod** festival. Ireland's culture is equally vibrant, with its love for storytelling, music, and dance, as well as its fascinating mythology.

### Modern Attractions

In addition to its history and culture, the British Isles offer a wealth of modern attractions. From the **London Eye** and **Harry Potter Studios** to the **Giant's Causeway** and the vibrant nightlife of **Dublin**, there's no shortage of things to do. Whether it's exploring cosmopolitan cities, enjoying scenic countryside, or experiencing unique cultural festivals, the British Isles promise a memorable experience for all travelers.

## Why Cruise the British Isles?

Cruising the British Isles offers a distinctive and enriching way to explore one of the most captivating regions in Europe. With its blend of ancient history, stunning natural beauty, and vibrant cultures, the British Isles are a treasure trove of experiences waiting to be discovered. Whether you're a history enthusiast, a nature lover, or a first-time cruiser, a journey through the British Isles offers something for everyone. But what makes a cruise the best way to experience this remarkable region?

## Unmatched Scenic Beauty

One of the biggest draws of a British Isles cruise is the spectacular natural beauty that surrounds the islands. Cruising allows you to witness dramatic coastlines, rolling hills, and picturesque landscapes that are best appreciated from the water. From the towering **Cliffs of Dover** to the pristine beaches of the **Isles of Scilly**, the British Isles boast some of the most beautiful coastlines in the world. As you sail along, you'll have unobstructed views of charming harbors, rugged fjords, and lush green islands. For those who love nature, the opportunity to witness the ever-changing seascapes while enjoying the comfort of a cruise ship is unparalleled.

## Access to Multiple Destinations

One of the main advantages of cruising the British Isles is the ability to visit multiple cities, towns, and landmarks without the hassle of constant packing and transportation.

The British Isles offer a wide range of destinations, each with its own unique appeal. On a single cruise, you could explore the vibrant streets of **London**, stroll through the medieval wonders of **Edinburgh**, discover the musical heritage of **Liverpool**, and visit the breathtaking landscapes of the **Scottish Highlands**—all without the need for multiple flights or long train journeys. Whether you're visiting the castles of **Ireland**, experiencing the history of **Cardiff**, or exploring the charming villages of **Wales**, cruising provides easy access to the region's best sights.

**Immersive Cultural Experiences**

The British Isles are rich in culture, and cruising provides a fantastic opportunity to immerse yourself in its diverse traditions and history. From the famous landmarks of **London**, like **Buckingham Palace** and **Westminster Abbey**, to the old-world charm of **Dublin** and **Edinburgh**, each stop offers a cultural experience that is deeply tied to the region's past. You can visit world-renowned museums, walk through cobbled streets lined with centuries-old buildings, and learn about the fascinating history of the

British monarchy, the Roman Empire, and Celtic traditions. Additionally, shore excursions allow you to delve deeper into local experiences such as tasting the finest **Scottish whisky** or enjoying a traditional **Welsh choir performance**.

### Convenient and Relaxing Travel

Cruising the British Isles offers a level of convenience and relaxation that is hard to beat. Unlike land-based travel, there's no need to worry about arranging accommodations, navigating unfamiliar roads, or dealing with crowded airports. Once you board your ship, everything is taken care of—luxury accommodations, gourmet dining, entertainment, and shore excursions are all provided, allowing you to simply relax and enjoy the journey. Cruising offers the perfect balance of exploration and relaxation, with plenty of time to unwind onboard between ports of call.

### Tailored Cruise Options for Every Traveler

The British Isles cater to a variety of cruising styles. Whether you prefer a luxurious, all-inclusive experience or a more casual and affordable voyage, there is a cruise line and itinerary to suit your needs. Many cruises offer specialized itineraries that focus on themes like history, architecture, or natural beauty, allowing you to curate your trip based on your interests. Additionally, cruising is ideal for travelers with varying mobility levels, as most cruise ships are equipped with accessibility features, and the ease of traveling from one port to another makes it an excellent option for those with physical limitations.

**The Uniqueness of British Island Culture**

Cruising the British Isles also provides a fascinating insight into the distinctive cultures of its regions. England, Scotland, Wales, and Ireland each have their own unique identities, shaped by centuries of history, language, and tradition. As you dock in ports, you'll encounter local festivals, traditional music, local foods, and colorful markets, all of which give you a chance to connect with the heart of the region. Whether it's sampling **Irish whiskey** in Dublin, listening to bagpipes in Edinburgh, or visiting a traditional Welsh **harbor village**, a cruise through the

British Isles offers an authentic and diverse cultural experience.

## Best Time to Cruise the British Isles

When planning a cruise through the British Isles, one of the most important considerations is choosing the best time to go. The weather, local events, and the overall cruise experience can vary significantly depending on the season. Fortunately, the British Isles are a stunning destination year-round, offering a variety of experiences. To help you make the most of your trip, here's a detailed guide to the best times to cruise the British Isles, taking into account weather patterns, crowd sizes, and unique seasonal attractions.

### Late Spring (May to Early June)

Late spring, particularly from May to early June, is widely regarded as one of the best times to cruise the British Isles. The weather during this period is generally mild, with temperatures ranging from 10°C (50°F) to 18°C (64°F). It's warm enough to enjoy outdoor activities and explore the coastline, yet not too hot to cause discomfort, especially during port visits.

This time of year, also marks the blooming of vibrant flowers and lush greenery, adding an extra layer of beauty to the landscapes. The countryside is alive with color, from the bluebells carpeting forests to the gardens in full bloom. For photographers and nature lovers, this is an ideal time to capture the natural beauty of the islands.

Crowds are relatively manageable during this time as well. While there are some tourists, the peak summer rush hasn't yet begun, allowing you to enjoy a more peaceful and intimate cruise experience. Additionally, you'll find that the major cities and attractions aren't as crowded as in the height of summer, providing a more relaxed atmosphere.

### Summer (June to August)

For those who prefer the warmest weather, summer—especially June through August—is the most popular time to cruise the British Isles. The days are long, with extended daylight hours, giving you plenty of time to enjoy the sights. Temperatures can reach a pleasant 18°C (64°F) to

22°C (72°F), making it the best time for outdoor excursions, coastal walks, and sightseeing.

Summer is also the time when many of the British Isles' festivals and events take place. From the **Edinburgh Festival Fringe** to **Royal Ascot**, there's no shortage of cultural celebrations and performances to enhance your cruise experience. This vibrant season also offers opportunities to sample local food festivals, music events, and traditional markets, giving you a deeper cultural immersion.

However, because summer is the peak tourist season, it's important to plan ahead. Cruises and popular destinations can get crowded, and prices for accommodations and excursions tend to rise. If you prefer a more social atmosphere and don't mind the crowds, summer is a great time to visit, but be prepared for a busy and bustling cruise.

### Early Autumn (September to October)

For a balance of pleasant weather and fewer crowds, early autumn (September to October) is another excellent time to cruise the British Isles. As summer fades, the temperatures remain mild, typically ranging from 14°C (57°F) to 18°C (64°F), with occasional warm spells. The weather is still comfortable enough for exploring, but it's cooler than the summer months, offering a refreshing change from the summer heat.

Autumn is also when the landscape of the British Isles transforms. The forests, gardens, and parks turn golden, red, and amber, creating a stunning display of fall foliage. This is a particularly beautiful time to visit Scotland and Ireland, where the rugged landscapes seem even more dramatic against the backdrop of autumn colors.

Another benefit of cruising during this period is the lower number of tourists. While some regions may still see an influx of visitors, the crowds are generally smaller than during peak summer, offering a more relaxed cruise experience. Additionally, many cruise lines offer more affordable rates during the autumn months, making it a great option for those looking to save while still enjoying a premium cruise experience.

## Winter (November to March)

Winter cruises in the British Isles are less common, but for those who enjoy a quieter, off-the-beaten-path experience, this season has its own appeal. The temperatures are colder, ranging from 5°C (41°F) to 8°C (46°F), and the weather can be unpredictable, with occasional rain and gusty winds. However, the lack of tourists means you'll have access to popular attractions without long queues or crowded ports.

During winter, you can experience a more intimate side of the British Isles, with many ports of call offering cozy local pubs, Christmas markets, and winter festivals. The festive season is especially magical in cities like **London**, **Edinburgh**, and **Dublin**, where Christmas lights and seasonal decorations create a warm, welcoming atmosphere. This is also the time for New Year's celebrations, particularly in Scotland, where **Hogmanay** is a famous celebration of the new year.

Cruises during the winter months tend to be less expensive, and some cruise lines offer special discounts or themed voyages. However, keep in mind that the weather can be more challenging, and certain ports may be affected by rough seas or unfavorable conditions, so it's important to check with your cruise line about potential itinerary changes.

## Cruise Itineraries: Short & Long Voyages in the British Isles

Cruising the British Isles offers a wide variety of itineraries to suit every traveler's preference, whether you're looking for a brief escape or an extensive exploration. The region's diversity in history, landscapes, and culture means that both short and long voyages provide unique opportunities to discover something new. Understanding the differences between short and long cruise itineraries can help you choose the perfect voyage, depending on the time you have available, your interests, and what you're hoping to experience.

### Short Voyages (3 to 5 Days)

For travelers with limited time or those seeking a quick getaway, short British Isles cruises offer a perfect introduction to the region's highlights. These compact itineraries typically range from 3 to 5 days, providing a manageable amount of time to explore key ports of call without feeling rushed. While shorter in duration, these cruises are still packed with stunning scenery, cultural immersion, and the opportunity to visit several different destinations.

### Typical Ports of Call on Short Cruises:

**London (Tilbury):** Many short cruises depart from Tilbury, just outside London. While the city itself is often left for a future visit, travelers can still take in the nearby historical sites like **Greenwich** and **Kew Gardens** before setting sail.

**Dover:** Known for its striking white cliffs, Dover is often a gateway for cruises heading toward **France**, but it also offers the chance to visit **Canterbury Cathedral**, one of England's most famous landmarks.

**Edinburgh (Leith):** Cruises may stop at Leith, Edinburgh's main port, where passengers can explore the city's iconic **Edinburgh Castle**, stroll along the historic

**Royal Mile**, and experience Scotland's vibrant cultural scene.

**Dublin:** Ireland's capital city, known for its friendly atmosphere and historical significance, is a regular stop on many short cruises. Visitors can tour **Trinity College**, home to the famous **Book of Kells**, or sip a pint at the **Guinness Storehouse**.

**Liverpool:** Famous for its rich musical heritage, particularly as the birthplace of The Beatles, Liverpool is a frequent stop. Cruise passengers can visit the **Beatles Story** Museum or explore the city's many galleries and landmarks.

Short cruises provide a taster of the British Isles, making them ideal for first-time cruisers or those seeking a brief but enriching experience. However, these shorter itineraries tend to focus on a few major cities or towns, with limited time for in-depth exploration of the surrounding areas.

**Advantages of Short Voyages:**

Less time commitment, perfect for a weekend or long holiday break.

Great for those new to cruising or looking to dip their toes into the British Isles.

Less expensive than long voyages, making them more accessible for budget-conscious travelers.

**Long Voyages (7 to 14 Days or More)**

For those looking to dive deeper into the British Isles, longer voyages provide the chance to explore a wide variety of destinations across the islands. These itineraries typically range from 7 to 14 days, with some even extending further, offering a comprehensive look at the British Isles, from bustling cities to remote villages and stunning coastal areas.

**Typical Ports of Call on Long Cruises:**

**London & Tilbury:** For longer voyages, these ports often serve as starting points for comprehensive cruises that cover more ground. Extended time in **London** allows for deeper exploration of the city's museums, landmarks, and neighborhoods, or even a day trip to places like **Stonehenge** or **Oxford**.

**Scotland's Highlands:** Longer itineraries frequently venture into Scotland's remote areas, including the **Scottish Highlands** and **Isle of Skye**, known for their rugged beauty, lochs, and ancient castles. These cruises may also stop at **Inverness** or **Stornoway**, where visitors can explore the **Isle of Harris** or the mysterious **Loch Ness**.

**Northern Ireland:** A longer voyage will often visit **Belfast**, where travelers can explore the **Titanic Belfast Museum** and venture out to the **Giant's Causeway**, one of the region's most remarkable natural wonders.

**Ireland's West Coast:** Cruises of this length typically explore Ireland more thoroughly, with stops at **Cork** and **Galway**, allowing time to visit famous attractions like **Blarney Castle**, **Killarney National Park**, and the **Cliffs of Moher**.

**Wales & the Isle of Man:** Longer cruises often venture along the coast of **Wales**, with stops in **Cardiff**, where you can visit the historic **Cardiff Castle**, or explore the scenic **Isle of Man**, famous for its rugged coastline and unique blend of Celtic and Viking heritage.

**Isles of Scilly:** Some extended voyages venture as far as the **Isles of Scilly**, a group of small, remote islands off the coast of Cornwall, offering a peaceful retreat with white sandy beaches, nature reserves, and exceptional wildlife watching opportunities.

Longer cruises provide the luxury of time, allowing travelers to enjoy more in-depth exploration of each destination and a broader range of ports. With more days at sea, you also have the opportunity to relax, unwind, and enjoy the full amenities of the cruise ship, whether that means indulging in world-class dining, enjoying spa treatments, or simply relaxing by the pool.

**Advantages of Long Voyages:**

Comprehensive itineraries that cover a wide range of destinations and attractions.

Ample time for excursions, including in-depth guided tours and off-the-beaten-path experiences.

The ability to visit more remote locations, like the **Scottish Highlands**, **Isle of Skye**, or **Isles of Scilly**, that are often not accessible on shorter cruises.

The chance to fully immerse yourself in the cultural heritage of the region.

**Choosing the Right Voyage**

When deciding between a short or long voyage, it all comes down to your preferences, time constraints, and the type of experience you're seeking. Short cruises are perfect for travelers who want a quick getaway or those new to cruising. On the other hand, longer voyages are ideal for those who want to dive deep into the British Isles, exploring everything from cosmopolitan cities to remote and tranquil landscapes.

Regardless of the length, a cruise through the British Isles is sure to offer stunning vistas, rich history, and unforgettable memories. Whether you choose to dip your toes into the region or immerse yourself fully, there's a cruise itinerary for every kind of explorer.

## Tips for First-Time Cruisers

Embarking on your first cruise is an exciting adventure, but it can also feel a bit overwhelming if you're not sure what to expect. Whether you're cruising through the British Isles or heading to a completely different destination, there are a few important things to know that will help you make the most of your trip. From packing tips to understanding cruise etiquette, these practical pieces of advice will ensure that your first cruising experience is smooth, enjoyable, and memorable.

### Book Early and Research the Cruise Line

One of the best things you can do to ensure a stress-free experience is to plan ahead. Cruises are in high demand, especially during peak seasons, so booking early not only guarantees better cabin choices but also often comes with discounts and special offers. Once you've chosen your destination and cruise line, take the time to research the specific cruise ship you'll be sailing on. Each cruise line offers different amenities, dining options, and onboard activities, so knowing what's available on your specific ship will help you plan your days accordingly.

**Understand the Ship Layout**

Cruise ships can be vast, with many decks, restaurants, pools, and entertainment options. To avoid feeling lost on your first day, it's helpful to study the ship's layout beforehand, either through online resources or the cruise line's app. Once onboard, take time to walk around and familiarize yourself with key areas such as the dining rooms, lounges, and emergency exits. This will make navigating the ship more comfortable and allow you to quickly find your way around, especially during busy embarkation or disembarkation times.

**Pack Smart, Not Heavy**

While it's tempting to pack for every possible scenario, cruise ships typically offer most of the essentials onboard, such as toiletries, casual clothing, and even formal wear for special nights. Pack for comfort and convenience, keeping in mind the length of your cruise, the weather, and the types of excursions you'll be doing. Essential items include:

Comfortable shoes for walking (you'll be doing more walking than you might think).

Swimsuits and sunscreen for poolside relaxation or beach excursions.

A small backpack or tote for shore excursions.

Formal attire if your cruise includes elegant evenings or formal dining.

Also, consider bringing a power strip or extra chargers, as outlets in your cabin may be limited.

**Know the Cruise Schedule and Plan Activities**

Cruise ships are full of activities, from theater shows and dance classes to cooking demonstrations and trivia games. Many cruises also offer specialized shore excursions at each port of call. Before you sail, take the time to review the daily schedule, which is usually provided in a brochure or through the cruise line's app. This will give you an idea of what to expect each day and help you plan ahead.

Prioritize the activities you're most interested in, whether it's a shore excursion to a local castle, a cooking class with the ship's chef, or a wine tasting in the evening.

Be mindful that some activities may require reservations, especially for popular shows, specialty dining, or excursions. Booking early can help you avoid missing out on experiences you're excited about.

**Be Prepared for Seasickness**

If you're prone to motion sickness, it's important to be prepared. Modern cruise ships are designed to reduce motion, but there can still be some rocking, especially when passing through open waters. To minimize discomfort, consider taking seasickness medication before the cruise, packing motion sickness bands, or using other remedies like ginger or acupressure. If you're worried about seasickness, choose a cabin located near the middle of the ship and on a lower deck, as these areas tend to experience less motion.

## Understand Dining Etiquette and Options

Cruise ships typically offer multiple dining options, from casual buffets to formal sit-down meals. The first thing to remember is that dining times can vary depending on your cruise line. Some cruise lines have assigned seating times for dinner, while others operate on an open dining system. Be sure to check your dining options ahead of time and, if necessary, make reservations for specialty restaurants or excursions that include meals.

Cruise lines also cater to various dietary restrictions, such as vegetarian, vegan, gluten-free, or kosher. If you have specific dietary needs, let the cruise line know well in advance to ensure that they can accommodate you during the voyage.

## Budget for Extra Costs

While your cruise fare covers many things—such as your cabin, meals in the main dining areas, and some onboard activities—there are additional costs you should be aware of. These include:

**Gratuities:** Most cruise lines charge daily gratuities for the crew, which are either added automatically to your bill or paid at the end of the cruise. If this isn't included in your package, make sure you budget for it.

**Excursions:** Shore excursions, which are often optional, can add up, especially if you book multiple activities at different ports of call. You may also want to set aside money for shopping or eating off the ship while on land.

**Alcohol and Specialty Dining:** While some cruise lines include drinks or specialty dining in their packages, many do not. Be prepared to pay for alcohol, bottled water, specialty coffee, and meals at upscale restaurants.

If you want to keep your costs down, check for cruise lines that offer all-inclusive packages, or stick to the free dining options and included onboard activities.

## Stay Connected (or disconnect)

Before boarding, it's important to understand how you'll stay connected while at sea. Many cruise ships now offer Wi-Fi, but it can be costly and slow, especially in remote locations. If you need to stay connected, you can usually purchase internet packages, but for many, the slower speeds and higher costs are a good excuse to disconnect and enjoy the cruise without distractions.

Alternatively, if you're planning to disconnect, make sure to let family and friends know in advance that you might not be reachable for the duration of the cruise.

### Embrace the Cruise Atmosphere

Cruising is about more than just visiting new destinations; it's about enjoying the ship and the experience. Don't be afraid to embrace the onboard atmosphere, whether that means attending a themed party, joining a group activity, or simply relaxing by the pool. Cruise ships have a wide variety of entertainment options that cater to different tastes, from Broadway-style shows to live music and comedy performances.

The people you meet on board—whether fellow travelers or crew members—are part of what makes the cruise experience unique. Strike up conversations, make new friends, and take advantage of the social atmosphere that cruises are known for.

## Have an Open Mind and Be Flexible

Finally, it's important to remember that things may not always go as planned. There may be unexpected changes in the itinerary due to weather or technical issues, and some activities may be cancelled. The key is to stay flexible, keep a positive attitude, and enjoy the experience as it unfolds.

Cruising is an incredible way to explore new destinations in comfort, and with the right preparation, your first voyage can be the start of many more incredible adventures.

## Cruise Itineraries: Short & Long Voyages in the British Isles

Cruising the British Isles is an unforgettable journey that blends history, natural beauty, and cultural richness. With its rugged coastlines, ancient castles, and vibrant cities, the region offers something for every traveler. However, choosing the right cruise itinerary is essential to making the most of your experience. Whether you prefer a short voyage for a quick getaway or a longer, more immersive adventure, understanding the different options will help you select the perfect itinerary based on your interests, schedule, and budget.

## Short Voyages (3 to 6 Days): A Taste of the British Isles

Short cruises are ideal for travelers who are new to cruising or those looking for a quick escape without a long-term commitment. These itineraries focus on a select number of ports, allowing passengers to experience key highlights of the British Isles in a limited timeframe.

### Typical Short Cruise Itineraries

**London to Dublin (3-5 Days)** Many short cruises depart from **London (Tilbury or Southampton)**, making stops in Dublin or another key port before returning. This is a great way to explore Ireland's capital, where you can visit **Trinity College**, the **Guinness Storehouse**, and historic Dublin Castle.

**Scottish Highlights (4-6 Days)** Some short itineraries focus on **Scotland**, offering stops in **Edinburgh (Leith)** and **Invergordon**, where passengers can explore the **Scottish Highlands** and search for the legendary **Loch Ness Monster**. These trips provide a brief but rewarding introduction to Scotland's dramatic landscapes and rich history.

**English and French Coastline (5-6 Days)**
A short cruise around **England's southern coast** may include stops in **Dover**, famous for its white cliffs, and **Portsmouth**, home to historic naval attractions. Some itineraries extend to **Cherbourg, France**, offering a taste of Normandy's culture and cuisine.

### Benefits of Short Voyages

**Less Time Commitment:** Perfect for travelers with limited vacation time.

**Great for First-Time Cruisers:** A shorter trip allows newcomers to experience cruising before committing to a longer itinerary.

**Lower Cost:** More affordable than extended voyages, making it a great option for budget-conscious travelers.

However, short cruises may feel rushed, and with limited stops, you may not experience the full diversity of the British Isles.

## Long Voyages (7 to 14+ Days): A Deep Dive into the British Isles

For those who want to fully immerse themselves in the history, landscapes, and culture of the British Isles, a longer cruise is the best option. These itineraries cover a wider range of destinations, from major cities to remote islands, allowing for in-depth exploration and a well-rounded travel experience.

### Typical Long Cruise Itineraries

**The Grand British Isles Tour (12-14 Days)** A comprehensive itinerary typically includes stops in **London**, **Edinburgh**, **Dublin**, **Liverpool**, **Belfast**, **Glasgow**, and **Cork (Cobh)**. This route provides an in-depth look at both major cities and charming coastal towns.

**Scottish and Irish Discovery (10-12 Days)** This itinerary focuses on **Scotland** and **Ireland**, with stops in **Edinburgh, Invergordon, Belfast, Dublin, Galway,**

and **Cork**. Travelers can explore ancient castles, rolling green landscapes, and legendary sites like **Giant's Causeway** and **Blarney Castle**.

**British Isles & French Coastline (12-14 Days)** Some extended cruises combine British and French destinations, including stops in **Plymouth, England**, **St. Peter Port in Guernsey**, and **Honfleur, France**, allowing passengers to experience both British and French coastal charm.

**Wild Scotland & Remote Isles (10-14 Days)** Some itineraries focus on the rugged and less-visited **Scottish Isles**, including **Orkney**, **Shetland**, and the **Isle of Skye**. These cruises offer breathtaking scenery, ancient ruins, and encounters with wildlife such as puffins, seals, and dolphins.

### Benefits of Long Voyages

**More Destinations:** Covers a wider range of ports, allowing for a deeper exploration of different regions. **More Time to Relax:** Passengers can enjoy more days at sea, onboard activities, and extended shore excursions.

**Cultural Immersion:** Longer itineraries allow for more authentic experiences, such as meeting locals, exploring historical sites, and attending traditional events.

However, longer cruises come with higher costs and require more time off, which may not be suitable for all travelers.

### How to Choose the Right Itinerary

When deciding between a short or long cruise, consider these factors:

### Time Availability

If you have limited vacation time, a **short cruise** (3-6 days) is a great way to explore select ports without a long commitment.

If you have the flexibility, a **longer cruise** (7-14 days) provides a more immersive experience.

### Budget

Short cruises are generally more affordable, with lower overall costs for accommodations and excursions.

Longer cruises offer more destinations but come with higher expenses, including gratuities, specialty dining, and extended excursions.

## Travel Style

If you prefer a **fast-paced** trip with fewer stops, a short cruise may be ideal.

If you enjoy **slow travel** and want to deeply explore multiple locations, a long voyage is a better fit.

## Destinations of Interest

If your priority is seeing **big cities** like **London, Edinburgh, and Dublin**, a short cruise may be sufficient.

If you want to visit **remote destinations** like the **Isles of Scilly, Orkney, or the Scottish Highlands**, you'll need a longer cruise.

# PLANNING YOUR CRUISE

## Choosing the Right Cruise Line: A Guide for Travelers

Selecting the right cruise line is one of the most important decisions when planning a cruise. Each cruise line offers a distinct experience, catering to different types of travelers, from luxury seekers and adventure enthusiasts to families and budget-conscious cruisers. To ensure you have the best possible voyage, it's essential to choose a cruise line that aligns with your travel style, preferences, and budget. Here's a detailed guide on how to pick the perfect cruise line for your journey.

### Understand Your Travel Style and Preferences

Before selecting a cruise line, consider what kind of experience you're looking for:

**Luxury & Elegance** – If you prefer an upscale experience with gourmet dining, spacious suites, and personalized service, luxury cruise lines like **Regent Seven Seas**, **Silversea**, or **Seabourn** are excellent choices.

**Adventure & Expedition** – For those who crave off-the-beaten-path destinations and immersive excursions, **Hurtigruten**, **Ponant**, and **Lindblad Expeditions** specialize in adventure travel.

**Family-Friendly Fun** – Families with children may enjoy cruise lines with onboard water parks, kids' clubs, and family activities, such as **Disney Cruise Line**, **Royal Caribbean**, or **Carnival**.

**Relaxation & Wellness** – If your priority is spa treatments, wellness programs, and relaxation, **Celebrity Cruises**, **Viking**, and **Oceania** offer excellent wellness-focused itineraries.

**Budget-Friendly & Social Atmosphere** – For those looking for affordable cruises with lively entertainment, **Carnival**, **Norwegian**, and **MSC Cruises** offer great value and fun atmospheres.

Understanding your priorities will help narrow down the options and ensure you have the best experience.

## Consider the Cruise Destination and Itinerary

Different cruise lines specialize in different regions and styles of itineraries. If you have a specific destination in mind, research which cruise lines operate in that area and what type of experience they offer.

**British Isles & Northern Europe** – **Princess Cruises**, **Cunard**, and **Holland America** offer well-rounded experiences with cultural immersion and scenic coastal explorations.

**Mediterranean & Greek Isles** – **MSC Cruises**, **Costa Cruises**, and **Celebrity Cruises** provide rich historical and culinary experiences.

**Caribbean & Bahamas** – **Royal Caribbean**, **Carnival**, and **Norwegian** offer island-hopping adventures with plenty of onboard entertainment.

**Alaska & Arctic Expeditions** – **Holland America**, **Princess Cruises**, and **Silversea** provide breathtaking glacier views and wildlife encounters.

Checking itineraries ensures the cruise line matches your preferred travel route.

### Compare Ship Size and Onboard Amenities

Cruise ships come in various sizes, and the type of ship can greatly impact your overall experience.

**Large Ships (3,000-6,000 passengers):** Offer extensive entertainment, dining options, water parks, and onboard attractions. Ideal for families and social travelers.

**Mid-Size Ships (1,000-3,000 passengers):** Strike a balance between entertainment and intimacy, with quality dining and enrichment programs.

**Small Ships (500-1,000 passengers):** Provide a more personal and relaxed experience, often focusing on cultural immersion and less crowded destinations.

**Expedition Ships (100-500 passengers):** Designed for adventure cruises, with a focus on nature, wildlife, and remote destinations.

Larger ships from **Royal Caribbean**, **Carnival**, and **Norwegian** offer endless onboard activities, while smaller luxury ships like **Viking** and **Regent Seven Seas** provide a more refined, tranquil experience.

### Look at Dining Options and Specialty Cuisine

Dining is a major part of the cruise experience, and different cruise lines cater to various culinary preferences.

**Fine Dining & Gourmet Cuisine** – **Oceania Cruises**, **Viking**, and **Regent Seven Seas** are known for their world-class chefs and diverse menus.

**Casual & Buffet Dining** – If you prefer a relaxed dining experience, cruise lines like **Carnival**, **Royal Caribbean**, and **MSC Cruises** offer excellent buffet and fast-food-style options.

**All-Inclusive Beverages & Dining** – Some luxury cruise lines include specialty dining and drinks in the fare, while mainstream cruise lines charge extra for premium dining options.

If you're a foodie, researching a cruise line's dining reputation can significantly enhance your experience.

## Budget Considerations and Hidden Costs

Cruises range from budget-friendly options to ultra-luxury experiences. While comparing fares, consider what's included in the price:

**Luxury Cruise Lines (Regent, Silversea, Seabourn):** Typically all-inclusive, covering excursions, premium dining, alcohol, and gratuities.

**Premium Cruise Lines (Celebrity, Viking, Holland America):** Higher-end experience with some inclusive perks but additional charges for specialty dining and drinks.

**Mainstream Cruise Lines (Royal Caribbean, Norwegian, Carnival):** Base fares are affordable but expect to pay extra for alcohol, Wi-Fi, excursions, and gratuities.

If you're looking for a **budget-friendly** option, consider cruises with promotions that include **free drinks, Wi-Fi, or onboard credits** to save money.

## Check Passenger Demographics and Atmosphere

Each cruise line attracts a different type of crowd:

**Cunard** – Elegant and refined, with an emphasis on tradition and afternoon tea.

**Disney Cruise Line** – Ideal for families with young children, featuring Disney-themed entertainment.

**Norwegian & Carnival** – Lively, casual atmosphere with plenty of nightlife and social events.

**Viking & Oceania** – Relaxed, sophisticated, and focused on enrichment programs (typically adult-only).

Choosing the right cruise line ensures that you'll be surrounded by like-minded travelers, whether you prefer a **party atmosphere, a romantic escape, or an educational journey**.

## Different Types of British Isles Cruises

A cruise around the British Isles is one of the most scenic and enriching ways to explore the diverse landscapes, rich history, and vibrant cultures of England, Scotland, Ireland, Wales, and beyond. However, not all British Isles cruises are the same. The type of cruise you choose will shape your experience, from the destinations you visit to the onboard atmosphere and excursions available. Whether you're looking for a luxury getaway, an adventure-filled expedition, or a budget-friendly escape, there's a British Isles cruise for every type of traveler.

## Classic British Isles Cruises

A classic British Isles cruise is the most popular type, offering a well-balanced itinerary that includes a mix of **major cities, historical landmarks, and natural wonders**. These cruises typically last **7 to 14 days**, allowing passengers to experience key destinations without feeling rushed.

**Typical Itinerary:**

**London (Tilbury or Southampton):** The starting point for many cruises, offering easy access to England's capital.

**Edinburgh (Leith):** Home to Edinburgh Castle, the Royal Mile, and Arthur's Seat.

**Dublin:** A cultural hub featuring Trinity College, the Guinness Storehouse, and lively pubs.

**Belfast:** A gateway to the Titanic Belfast Museum and the Giant's Causeway.

**Liverpool:** Known for The Beatles, maritime history, and striking architecture.

**Glasgow & Scottish Highlands:** A mix of vibrant city culture and breathtaking countryside.

**Who It's Best For:**

First-time visitors who want a well-rounded experience. History lovers and cultural enthusiasts. Travelers looking for a comfortable, well-paced journey.

## Luxury British Isles Cruises

For those seeking a **more refined and intimate experience**, luxury cruises offer **smaller ships, personalized service, and high-end amenities**. These cruises often last **10 to 14 days** and include destinations that larger ships may not be able to access.

**What Sets Luxury Cruises Apart?**

**Smaller ships** (200-700 passengers) for a more private experience.

**Gourmet dining** with Michelin-star-level cuisine.

**Exclusive excursions**, such as private castle tours, whiskey tastings, and scenic helicopter rides.

**Luxury Cruise Lines:**

**Regent Seven Seas**

**Seabourn**

**Silversea**

**Viking Ocean Cruises**

**Who It's Best For:**

Travelers who prefer high-end service and all-inclusive experiences.
Those looking for a **quiet, relaxing** atmosphere. Guests who enjoy **fine dining, spa treatments, and exclusive shore excursions**.

## Expedition & Adventure Cruises

For travelers looking to explore the **rugged coastlines, remote islands, and untouched landscapes**, expedition cruises focus on nature, wildlife, and off-the-beaten-path destinations. These smaller ships (100-500 passengers) can access areas that larger vessels cannot.

**Highlights of an Expedition Cruise:**

Exploring the **Scottish Highlands, Orkney, and Shetland Islands**.

Visiting the **Isles of Scilly**, an archipelago with white sandy beaches and stunning birdlife.

Spotting **puffins, seals, and dolphins** along the coastline.

Engaging in **guided hikes, kayaking, and nature excursions**.

**Expedition Cruise Lines:**

**Hurtigruten**

**Ponant**

**Lindblad Expeditions (in partnership with National Geographic)**

**Who It's Best For:**

Nature lovers and adventure seekers. Travelers who enjoy **wildlife spotting, photography, and active excursions**. Those looking for **small-ship exploration** and a more intimate journey.

## Themed Cruises (Cultural, Historical, & Culinary Cruises)

For travelers with specific interests, themed cruises focus on **history, culture, food, or entertainment**, offering a unique way to experience the British Isles.

**Popular Themes:**

**History & Castles:** Tours of famous sites like **Edinburgh Castle, Blarney Castle, and the Tower of London**.

**Whiskey & Wine Cruises:** Visits to famous **Scottish whiskey distilleries and Irish breweries**.

**Literary & Arts Cruises:** Inspired by authors like **Shakespeare, Jane Austen, and James Joyce**, with stops in literary hotspots.

**Music & Entertainment Cruises:** Featuring live performances and exclusive tours in **Liverpool (The Beatles), Dublin (traditional Irish music), and London's West End**.

**Who It's Best For:**

Travelers with a **passion for history, literature, or music**. Those who want **in-depth experiences beyond general sightseeing**.

Foodies and wine lovers looking for a **culinary-focused voyage**.

## Budget & Family-Friendly Cruises

Cruising the British Isles doesn't have to break the bank. Several cruise lines offer **affordable and family-friendly** options with larger ships, casual dining, and plenty of onboard entertainment.

**What to Expect on a Budget Cruise:**

Larger ships with **a relaxed, social atmosphere**.

Activities for all ages, including **kids' clubs, water parks, and family-friendly entertainment**.

**Affordable excursions**, such as walking tours, local markets, and self-guided city visits.

**Best Budget & Family-Friendly Cruise Lines:**

**Royal Caribbean** (Offers family activities, rock climbing, and Broadway-style shows).

**Norwegian Cruise Line** (Casual, fun atmosphere with flexible dining options).

**MSC Cruises** (Affordable fares with European-style cruising).

**P&O Cruises** (Great for UK-based travelers looking for budget-friendly options).

**Who It's Best For:**

Families traveling with kids or teenagers. Budget-conscious travelers who still want to experience multiple destinations. Those who enjoy a **lively, social cruise atmosphere**.

## River Cruises Around the British Isles

Although most cruises in the British Isles are **ocean cruises**, there are also **river cruises** that provide a unique way to explore England, Scotland, and Ireland from a different perspective.

**Top River Cruise Destinations:**

**The Thames River:** Stops at **Oxford, Windsor Castle, and historic London sites.**

**The Shannon River (Ireland):** Cruises through **Limerick, Galway, and medieval castles.**

**The Caledonian Canal (Scotland):** A peaceful cruise through **Loch Ness and the Scottish Highlands.**

**Who It's Best For:**

Travelers who prefer **a slower, intimate cruising experience.**

History lovers who enjoy **stopping at smaller towns and landmarks.**

Those who want **less time at sea and calmer waters.**

## Luxury vs. Budget Cruises: Which One is Right for You?

Cruising is one of the most enjoyable and hassle-free ways to explore the world, but not all cruises are the same. Some cater to those seeking **luxury, exclusivity, and high-end amenities**, while others focus on **affordability, fun, and accessibility**. Choosing between a **luxury cruise** and a **budget cruise** depends on your travel preferences, expectations, and budget. Here's a comprehensive comparison to help you decide which type of cruise suits you best.

### Price & Inclusions: What's Covered?

**Luxury Cruises: All-Inclusive Comfort**

Luxury cruises typically come with a **higher price tag**, but they also **include more amenities and services**. Many luxury cruise lines operate on an **all-inclusive basis**, meaning you don't have to worry about extra fees for dining, drinks, or gratuities.

### What's Included in a Luxury Cruise?

Spacious suites with private balconies and high-end furnishings.

Fine dining with gourmet cuisine, often prepared by world-renowned chefs.

Complimentary alcoholic beverages, specialty coffees, and premium wines.

Personalized butler or concierge service.

Included shore excursions (e.g., private guided tours, exclusive experiences).

Gratuities, Wi-Fi, and premium entertainment at no extra charge.

Popular luxury cruise lines: **Regent Seven Seas, Silversea, Seabourn, and Viking Ocean Cruises**.

### Budget Cruises: Affordable and Flexible

Budget cruises are designed for travelers looking for **a great experience at a lower cost**. The base fare covers

**accommodation, standard meals, and entertainment**, but many extras require an additional fee.

### What's Included in a Budget Cruise?

Comfortable cabins, though usually smaller than luxury suites.

Buffet and casual dining options (specialty restaurants may cost extra).

Free entertainment, including shows, live music, and onboard activities.

Access to pools, fitness centers, and kids' clubs.

**Additional Costs on Budget Cruises:**

Alcoholic beverages, soft drinks, and specialty coffee.

Shore excursions, spa treatments, and specialty dining.

Wi-Fi (often slow and expensive).

Gratuities (often added daily to your onboard account).

Popular budget cruise lines: **Carnival, Royal Caribbean, MSC Cruises, and Norwegian Cruise Line**.

## Accommodations & Ship Size

**Luxury Cruises: Spacious & Elegant**

Luxury cruise ships are generally **smaller (500-1,000 passengers)**, offering a **more intimate and exclusive atmosphere**.

**Cabins are often suites** with private balconies, marble bathrooms, and plush furnishings.

Many luxury ships have **no inside cabins**, ensuring ocean views for all guests.

Fewer passengers mean **more personal space** and no overcrowding at restaurants or pools.

**Budget Cruises: Functional & Comfortable**

Budget cruise ships tend to be **larger (2,000-6,000 passengers)** with a wide variety of cabin options.

**Inside cabins** (no windows) are the cheapest, while balcony cabins cost more.

Rooms are **smaller and more basic**, but still comfortable.

Large ships mean **more crowds** in public spaces, pools, and dining areas.

## Dining Experience & Culinary Options

**Luxury Cruises: Gourmet, World-Class Cuisine**

**Michelin-star-level chefs** and **multi-course fine dining** experiences.

Specialty dining included in the cruise fare (French, Italian, sushi, etc.).

**No buffets**—everything is prepared fresh and served elegantly.

**Wider variety of dining venues**, including intimate restaurants and alfresco options.

**Budget Cruises: Variety & Casual Dining**

Large buffets and **main dining rooms with fixed menus**.

Specialty restaurants available, but at an extra cost.

More casual and **family-friendly dining**, with options like pizza, burgers, and fast food.

If you're a **foodie**, luxury cruises offer **exceptional culinary experiences**, while budget cruises provide **a more relaxed and varied dining scene**.

## Entertainment & Onboard Activities

**Luxury Cruises: Cultural & Enriching**

Luxury cruises focus on **intellectual and immersive experiences**, such as:
**Classical music performances, jazz clubs, and opera nights.**
**Guest lecturers, wine tastings, and art auctions.**
**Wellness programs, meditation classes, and luxury spas.**
**Smaller, more intimate lounges for sophisticated entertainment.**

**Budget Cruises: High-Energy & Family-Friendly**

Budget cruises are designed for **fun and entertainment for all ages**:
**Broadway-style shows, comedy clubs, and karaoke nights.**
**Water slides, rock climbing walls, and go-kart tracks on**

**mega-ships.**

**Dance parties, casinos, and lively nightclubs. Kids' clubs, themed play areas, and arcade rooms.**

If you prefer **a quiet and refined cruise**, luxury lines are ideal. If you want **non-stop entertainment and social activities**, budget cruises are a better fit.

### Shore Excursions & Destinations

**Luxury Cruises: Exclusive & Unique Experiences**

Luxury cruise lines offer **private, small-group excursions** that go beyond typical sightseeing tours.

Private wine tastings at **historic vineyards**.

Exclusive **castle tours with VIP access**.

Helicopter rides over **Scottish Highlands or Irish cliffs**.

Cultural deep-dives, including private museum tours and cooking classes.

**Budget Cruises: Traditional & Group Tours**

Budget cruises offer **affordable shore excursions**, but they are often **large-group tours** with limited flexibility.

**Walking tours** of major cities like London, Edinburgh, and Dublin.

Visits to popular landmarks like **Blarney Castle, the Giant's Causeway, and Buckingham Palace**.

Excursions can be booked through the cruise line or independently for better pricing.

If you want a **personalized, in-depth experience**, luxury cruises are better. If you **don't mind group tours and are on a budget**, a mainstream cruise line works well.

### Which Cruise Type is Right for You?

**Choose a Luxury Cruise If You:**

Prefer **all-inclusive pricing** with no hidden costs. Value **privacy, exclusivity, and five-star service**. Enjoy **fine dining, enrichment programs, and relaxed onboard experiences**. Want to visit **more remote or unique destinations with premium excursions**.

**Choose a Budget Cruise If You:**

Are looking for an **affordable vacation with flexible spending options**.
Enjoy **lively entertainment, water parks, and fun activities**.
Don't mind **paying extra for drinks, Wi-Fi, and excursions**.
Prefer **larger ships with diverse dining and social opportunities**.

## River vs. Ocean Cruises: Which One is Right for You?

Cruising is one of the most relaxing and immersive ways to travel, offering a unique perspective of destinations from the water. However, not all cruises are the same. While **ocean cruises** take you across vast seas to explore coastal cities and exotic islands, **river cruises** provide a more intimate journey through scenic waterways and historic towns. Choosing between the two depends on your travel preferences, desired pace, and the kind of experience you seek. Let's explore the key differences between river and ocean cruises to help you decide which one is right for you.

## Destinations & Itineraries

**Ocean Cruises: Exploring the World's Coastlines**

Ocean cruises travel across **seas and oceans**, covering vast distances and connecting travelers to major coastal cities, islands, and resort destinations. Popular ocean cruise routes include:

**Mediterranean Cruises** – Stops in Spain, Italy, Greece, and Turkey.
**Caribbean Cruises** – Visits to Jamaica, the Bahamas, and St. Thomas.
**Alaska Cruises** – Scenic views of glaciers and wildlife.
GB **British Isles Cruises** – Exploring England, Scotland, Ireland, and Wales.

Because ocean cruises operate on **large bodies of water**, they offer access to **far-flung destinations** that would be difficult to reach by land.

**River Cruises: Slow-Paced Cultural Exploration**

River cruises move through **smaller waterways**, offering an immersive experience in cities, villages, and rural areas.

Unlike ocean cruises, river cruises focus on **inland exploration**, bringing travelers **right to the heart of a destination**. Popular river cruise routes include:

**Danube River** (Germany, Austria, Hungary) – Historic castles and medieval towns.
**Seine River** (France) – Paris, Monet's gardens, and Normandy.
**Nile River** (Egypt) – Ancient temples, pyramids, and vibrant culture.
**Thames River** (England) – London, Windsor Castle, and Oxford.

River cruises allow for **shorter distances between ports**, meaning you spend more time **exploring destinations and less time at sea.**

## Ship Size & Onboard Experience

**Ocean Cruises: Large Ships with Endless Amenities**

Ocean cruise ships vary in size, but **mainstream cruise lines** operate **large vessels that carry thousands of passengers**. These ships come packed with:

Multiple dining venues (buffets, fine dining, casual eateries).

Theaters with Broadway-style shows and live entertainment.

Swimming pools, water slides, and onboard sports facilities.

Casinos, shopping malls, and nightclubs.

The size of ocean cruise ships allows for **a wide variety of onboard activities**, making them ideal for travelers who enjoy **entertainment, nightlife, and social experiences**.

### River Cruises: Smaller Ships, Intimate Setting

River cruise ships are **much smaller**, typically accommodating **100 to 200 passengers**. While they lack the mega-resort feel of ocean liners, they offer:

Fine dining with locally inspired cuisine.

Enrichment programs, such as lectures and cooking classes.

No inside cabins—every room typically has a window or balcony.

A quiet, relaxed atmosphere with **no crowds or long lines**.

River cruises focus more on **personalized service and cultural immersion**, rather than onboard entertainment.

### Pace & Travel Style

**Ocean Cruises: Fast-Paced, More Sea Days**

Ocean cruises often **sail overnight** between ports, giving travelers **full days to explore destinations**.

Some itineraries include **multiple sea days**, where passengers can relax onboard.

Ocean cruises allow for **bigger, more diverse excursions**, such as snorkeling in the Caribbean or glacier hiking in Alaska.

**River Cruises: Slow-Paced, More Port Time**

River cruises usually dock in **the heart of a city**, allowing passengers to step off the ship and explore **immediately**.

These cruises have **minimal sea days**, meaning you spend **most of your time sightseeing** rather than sailing.

River cruises are ideal for **history lovers and cultural travelers**, as they focus on museums, castles, and historic landmarks.

## Motion & Seasickness

### Ocean Cruises: Can Be Rocky in Open Waters

Because ocean cruises travel across **large bodies of water**, **motion sickness** can be a concern, especially in rough seas.

Modern ocean ships have stabilizers, but travelers prone to motion sickness may need **medication or sea bands**.

**Cabin location matters** – mid-ship, lower-deck cabins tend to experience less movement.

### River Cruises: Smooth & Stable

River cruises **don't experience large waves**, making them **ideal for travelers prone to seasickness**.

Ships travel **slowly on calm inland waterways**, ensuring a smooth ride.

If **motion sickness is a major concern**, a river cruise is the better choice.

## Cost & Value

**Ocean Cruises: More Budget-Friendly Options**

Ocean cruises offer **a wide range of price points**, from budget-friendly to ultra-luxury. Mainstream cruise lines **(Carnival, Royal Caribbean, MSC)** provide **affordable fares**, but many extras come at an additional cost:

Alcoholic beverages & specialty dining. Shore excursions & onboard Wi-Fi. Gratuities & premium activities.

Because of the **larger passenger capacity**, there are **more deals and discounts** available, making ocean cruises a great option for **budget-conscious travelers**.

**River Cruises: More Expensive but More Inclusive**

River cruises tend to be **more expensive upfront**, but they **include** many perks that ocean cruises charge extra for:

Complimentary shore excursions. Free wine, beer, and soft drinks with meals. Gratuities and Wi-Fi.

While river cruises **cost more**, they offer **greater value for travelers who prefer an all-inclusive experience**.

### Best for Families vs. Adults

**Ocean Cruises: Great for Families & Groups**

Ocean cruises cater to **families, multi-generational travelers, and large groups**. Many cruise lines offer: Kids' clubs and water parks. Broadway-style entertainment. Game rooms, zip lines, and adventure activities.

**River Cruises: Ideal for Adults & Culture Lovers**

River cruises have **a quieter, more relaxed atmosphere**, attracting **mature travelers, couples, and history buffs**.

**Few to no children** (some river cruises are adults-only).

A focus on **cultural enrichment rather than entertainment**.

A **peaceful, slow-paced** experience with fewer crowds.

If you're **traveling with kids**, ocean cruises offer **more excitement**. If you **prefer quiet elegance and cultural immersion**, a river cruise is better suited.

## Best Ports of Call on a British Isles Cruise

A British Isles cruise offers a spectacular journey through some of the most **historic, picturesque, and culturally rich** destinations in the world. With its mix of **cosmopolitan cities, charming coastal towns, and breathtaking natural landscapes**, the region provides an unforgettable cruising experience. Each port of call has its own unique attractions, from medieval castles and UNESCO heritage sites to vibrant local pubs and scenic countryside. Here's a guide to some of the **best ports of call** on a British Isles cruise and what makes each one special.

### Edinburgh (Leith), Scotland

The Scottish capital is a highlight on any British Isles cruise, offering a mix of history, culture, and breathtaking views.

**Top Attractions:**

**Edinburgh Castle** – Home to the **Scottish Crown Jewels** and offering panoramic views of the city. **The Royal Mile** – A historic street lined with medieval buildings, shops, and lively pubs. **Holyrood Palace** – The official residence of the British monarch in Scotland. **Arthur's Seat** – A hike to this extinct volcano provides **stunning views of the city**.

**Why It's a Must-Visit:**

Edinburgh combines **rich history, vibrant culture, and stunning architecture**, making it one of the most **captivating ports of call** in the British Isles.

### Dublin, Ireland

Dublin is a city of **literature, lively pubs, and deep-rooted history**. A stop here offers a mix of Irish charm, historic sites, and legendary hospitality.

**Top Attractions:**

**Trinity College & The Book of Kells** – A must-visit for book lovers and history buffs.
**Guinness Storehouse** – Learn about Ireland's most famous beer and enjoy a pint with a view.
**Dublin Castle** – A fascinating blend of medieval and modern architecture.
**Temple Bar District** – Famous for **live Irish music, pubs, and a vibrant atmosphere**.

**Why It's a Must-Visit:**

Dublin's **combination of history, literature, and pub culture** makes it a lively and unmissable destination on any cruise itinerary.

### Belfast, Northern Ireland

Belfast is a city of **resilience and renewal**, known for its connection to the **Titanic**, stunning natural wonders, and political history.

**Top Attractions:**

**Titanic Belfast Museum** – An award-winning interactive museum dedicated to the ship's history. **Giant's Causeway** – A UNESCO World Heritage Site with unique **hexagonal rock formations**. **Political Murals & Peace Walls** – A thought-provoking look into **Northern Ireland's past conflicts**. **Carrickfergus Castle** – One of the best-preserved medieval castles in Ireland.

**Why It's a Must-Visit:**

Belfast offers a mix of **maritime history, stunning landscapes, and cultural depth**, making it a fascinating stop.

### Liverpool, England

Liverpool is a vibrant port city with a **rich musical heritage, maritime history, and thriving arts scene**.

**Top Attractions:**

**The Beatles Story** – A museum dedicated to **the world's most famous band**. **Albert Dock & Merseyside Maritime Museum** – A historic waterfront area with excellent museums. **Liverpool Cathedral** – One of the **largest cathedrals in Europe**, offering spectacular views. **Anfield Stadium** – A must-visit for football fans and home to **Liverpool FC**.

**Why It's a Must-Visit:**

Liverpool's **connection to music, maritime history, and sports culture** makes it an exciting and diverse port of call.

### Invergordon, Scotland (Gateway to the Highlands)

For those seeking **rugged landscapes, mysterious legends, and ancient castles**, Invergordon is a gateway to **Scotland's Highlands**.

**Top Attractions:**

**Urquhart Castle & Loch Ness** – Visit the ruins of this iconic castle and search for **Nessie, the Loch Ness Monster**.
**Culloden Battlefield** – The site of the famous 1746 battle that shaped Scotland's history.
**Whisky Distillery Tours** – Experience **Scotland's famous**

single malt whiskies.

**The North Coast 500** – A scenic drive featuring **dramatic coastal landscapes**.

**Why It's a Must-Visit:**

Invergordon provides **an authentic Scottish experience**, with breathtaking scenery, castles, and legendary tales.

## Guernsey, Channel Islands

Guernsey is a **hidden gem**, offering **mild weather, stunning beaches, and a fascinating WWII history**.

**Top Attractions:**

**St. Peter Port** – A charming harbor town with cobbled streets and boutique shops.
**Castle Cornet** – A **13th-century fortress** with spectacular ocean views.
**Cobo Bay** – One of the most **beautiful beaches in the Channel Islands**.
**German Occupation Museum** – A deep dive into Guernsey's **WWII history**.

**Why It's a Must-Visit:**

Guernsey is **peaceful and picturesque**, making it a relaxing and historically intriguing stop.

## Cork (Cobh), Ireland

Cobh is a **picturesque town with strong maritime ties**, famously known as the **last port of call for the Titanic**.

**Top Attractions:**

**Titanic Experience Cobh** – A museum dedicated to the **Titanic's last voyage**. **Blarney Castle & Blarney Stone** – Kiss the legendary stone for the "gift of eloquence." **St. Colman's Cathedral** – A stunning neo-Gothic cathedral overlooking the harbor. **Local Pubs & Live Music** – Experience authentic **Irish hospitality and traditional music**.

**Why It's a Must-Visit:**

Cobh's **Titanic connection, stunning scenery, and friendly atmosphere** make it a charming and historically significant stop.

## Isle of Skye, Scotland

The Isle of Skye is a **wild, untamed paradise** known for its **rugged cliffs, mystical landscapes, and Gaelic heritage**.

**Top Attractions:**

**The Old Man of Storr** – A dramatic rock formation with **stunning views**.
**Dunvegan Castle** – The seat of **Clan MacLeod for over 800 years**.
**Fairy Pools** – Crystal-clear waterfalls set in a magical landscape.
**Wildlife Watching** – Spot **seals, dolphins, and eagles**.

**Why It's a Must-Visit:**

Skye's **otherworldly beauty and rich history** make it one of the most breathtaking ports in the British Isles.

# How to Book Your Cruise: A Step-by-Step Guide

Booking a cruise is an exciting process, but with so many options available, it can feel overwhelming—especially for first-time travelers. From selecting the right itinerary to finding the best deals, every step plays a crucial role in ensuring you get the most out of your cruise experience. Whether you're planning a **luxury voyage through the British Isles** or a **budget-friendly getaway**, this guide will walk you through everything you need to know about **how to book your cruise smoothly and effectively**.

### Choose Your Destination and Itinerary

The first step in booking a cruise is deciding **where you want to go** and how long you want to travel. Popular cruise destinations include:

**British Isles & Northern Europe** – Explore the historic cities of **London, Edinburgh, Dublin, and Belfast**.

**Mediterranean** – Visit sunny ports like **Barcelona, Rome, and Santorini**.

**Caribbean** – Relax on **white-sand beaches in the Bahamas, Jamaica, and St. Lucia**.

**Alaska** – Witness **glaciers, wildlife, and breathtaking fjords**.

Consider how much time you have available:

**Short cruises (3-5 days)** are great for first-time cruisers.

**Longer cruises (7-14 days)** offer a deeper exploration of multiple destinations.

**Tip:** Check different itineraries to ensure the cruise stops at the ports you're most interested in visiting.

## Select the Right Cruise Line

Each cruise line caters to a different type of traveler. Choosing the right one ensures a **comfortable and enjoyable experience**.

**Luxury & All-Inclusive: Regent Seven Seas, Silversea, Viking Ocean Cruises**.

**Family-Friendly & Entertainment-Focused: Disney Cruise Line, Royal Caribbean, Norwegian**.

**Budget-Friendly & Social Atmosphere: Carnival, MSC Cruises, P&O Cruises.**

**Small Ship & Expedition Cruises: Hurtigruten, Ponant, Lindblad Expeditions**.

**Tip:** If you're looking for a specific type of experience—such as adventure cruises, themed sailings, or cultural enrichment—make sure the cruise line specializes in those offerings.

## Choose Your Cabin Type

Your choice of cabin can impact your comfort and budget. Most cruise ships offer:

**Inside Cabins** – No windows, most affordable option.

**Oceanview Cabins** – A window or porthole with natural light.

**Balcony Cabins** – Private outdoor space, perfect for scenic cruises.

**Suites** – Spacious, luxurious, with exclusive amenities.

**Consider these factors when selecting a cabin:**

If you're **prone to seasickness**, choose a **mid-ship, lower-deck cabin** for more stability.

If you plan to **spend time on your balcony**, an **oceanview or suite** is worth the splurge.

If you just need a place to **sleep and shower**, an **inside cabin** is a budget-friendly choice.

### Compare Prices and Look for Deals

Cruise prices fluctuate based on **season, demand, and special promotions**. Here's how to find the best deals:

**Book early** – Many cruise lines offer **early-bird discounts** and better cabin selection.

**Look for last-minute deals** – If your schedule is flexible, you can save money on unsold cabins.

**Use a travel agent** – They often have access to **exclusive discounts, onboard credits, and perks**.

**Check for bundled packages** – Some deals include **free Wi-Fi, drink packages, or shore excursions**.

**Sign up for cruise line newsletters** – Be the first to hear about promotions and flash sales.

**Tip:** If you're booking a cruise in the **peak season (summer, holidays), prices will be higher**, so planning ahead can help secure the best rate.

## Decide How to Book: Direct vs. Travel Agent vs. Online

There are three main ways to book your cruise:

### Booking Directly Through the Cruise Line

Best for those who know exactly what they want. Access to the cruise line's promotions and loyalty rewards.

### Using a Travel Agent

Great for first-time cruisers or those looking for **expert advice**.

Agents can find **better deals and exclusive perks**. Helpful if you're booking **group travel or special events** (e.g., honeymoon, anniversary).

**Booking Through Online Travel Websites**

Websites like **Expedia, Cruise Critic, and Priceline** offer **comparison tools** to find the best prices. You can read **passenger reviews** before booking. Good for **last-minute discounts** and promotional offers.

**Tip:** Always check **cancellation policies** and **refund options** before booking.

### Plan Your Shore Excursions and Onboard Activities

Once your cruise is booked, it's time to plan **what you'll do in each port**. You can:

**Book excursions through the cruise line** (easy but often more expensive).

**Arrange private tours** (often cheaper and more personalized).

**Explore independently** (great for experienced travelers comfortable with local transport).

Popular excursions include: **Kayaking in Scottish lochs** (Invergordon). **Touring castles in Edinburgh or Dublin**.

**Guinness Storehouse visit in Dublin. Titanic Museum in Belfast.**

**Book excursions early**, as popular tours fill up quickly.

### Prepare for Departure

As your cruise date approaches, follow this checklist:

**Check required documents:** Ensure you have a **valid passport or visa** if needed. **Pack smart:** Bring **comfortable clothes, formal attire, and essentials like sunscreen and medications**. **Download the cruise line's app:** Many cruise lines offer apps to **manage reservations, daily schedules, and onboard purchases**. **Plan transportation to the port:** Arrive **at least one day early** to avoid travel delays. **Set a budget for onboard expenses:** While many amenities are included, extras like **alcohol, Wi-Fi, and specialty dining** can add up.

## Cruise Packages: What's Included

Booking a cruise is an exciting way to travel, but understanding what's included in your **cruise package** is essential to avoid unexpected costs. While cruises are often marketed as **all-inclusive vacations**, the reality is that different cruise lines offer varying levels of inclusivity. Some packages cover almost everything, while others require additional purchases for specialty services. Knowing what's included in a standard cruise fare—and what might come with extra charges—can help you plan your trip more effectively and budget accordingly.

### What's Typically Included in a Cruise Package?

Most cruise packages cover the **essentials for a comfortable vacation**, including accommodation, meals, entertainment, and select activities. Here's what you can expect in most standard cruise fares:

**Accommodation**

Your cruise fare includes your **stateroom or cabin**, with options ranging from:

**Inside cabins** (no windows, most affordable).

**Oceanview cabins** (with a porthole or window).

**Balcony cabins** (private outdoor space).

**Suites** (luxurious, with extra perks like concierge services).

Even in budget cabins, housekeeping services, clean linens, and toiletries are provided.

**Dining & Food**

Most cruise fares include:

**Buffet and main dining room meals** (breakfast, lunch, and dinner).

**Casual eateries** like pizzerias, burger joints, and sandwich bars.

**Basic coffee, tea, juice, and water** at mealtimes.

However, **specialty dining** (steakhouse, sushi bars, fine dining) often comes with an extra fee.

**Onboard Entertainment**

Most cruises include:

**Broadway-style theater shows** and live performances.

**Comedy clubs, movie nights, and musical acts.**

**Dance classes, trivia games, and cooking demonstrations.**

Luxury and premium cruises may offer **guest lectures, wine tastings, and cultural experiences** as part of their package.

**Pools, Fitness Centers, and Basic Activities**

**Access to pools, whirlpools, and sun decks** is included.

**Fitness centers** with free weights, treadmills, and cardio equipment.

Some **fitness classes** (yoga, Pilates, spin) may require an additional fee.

**Kids' Clubs & Family Activities**

Most family-friendly cruise lines offer:

**Supervised kids' clubs** for different age groups.

**Teen lounges** with video games and social activities.

**Family-friendly entertainment**, such as character meet-and-greets.

### Port Stops & Basic Shore Access

Your cruise package includes docking at **various ports**, but it does **not** cover shore excursions. You can explore ports independently for free, but guided tours cost extra.

### What's NOT Included in Most Cruise Packages?

While cruise packages cover the basics, many amenities come at an additional cost. Here's what to expect:

### Alcohol & Specialty Beverages

Most cruise lines **do not** include alcohol, soft drinks, or premium coffee in the base fare.

Beverage packages are available for purchase (ranging from **$10-$100 per day**, depending on the cruise line).

### Specialty Dining

High-end **steakhouses, sushi bars, and celebrity chef restaurants** charge an extra fee.

Prices range from **$20 to $100 per meal**, depending on the cruise line and restaurant.

### Wi-Fi & Internet Access

Basic cruise fares **do not** include Wi-Fi.

Internet packages range from **$10 to $30 per day**, depending on speed and data limits.

Some luxury cruises include **free Wi-Fi**.

### Shore Excursions & Guided Tours

While you can explore ports independently, cruise-organized excursions (city tours, snorkeling, cultural experiences) cost extra.

Prices range from **$50 to $500 per person**, depending on the excursion type.

### Spa & Wellness Treatments

Massages, facials, and salon services are available but **not included** in standard cruise fares.

Expect to pay **$50 to $300 per treatment**, depending on the cruise line.

## Gratuities & Service Charges

Most mainstream cruise lines **automatically charge gratuities** (around **$15 to $20 per person per day**).

Some luxury cruise lines include gratuities in the fare.

## Upgraded & All-Inclusive Cruise Packages

Some cruise lines offer **all-inclusive or upgraded packages** that bundle extras into one price. These may include:

**Unlimited drinks** (alcohol and specialty coffee). **Specialty dining** at fine restaurants. **Excursions & private tours**. **Wi-Fi & onboard credits** for shopping or spa treatments. **Prepaid gratuities**.

Examples of **premium cruise lines that offer more inclusions**:

**Regent Seven Seas & Silversea** – Almost everything is included (excursions, drinks, specialty dining, Wi-Fi, and gratuities).

**Celebrity Cruises & Viking Ocean Cruises** – Offer "always included" packages with **free drinks, Wi-Fi, and gratuities**.

Mainstream cruise lines like **Royal Caribbean, Norwegian, and Carnival** offer **optional packages** for those who want more inclusions.

### How to Choose the Right Cruise Package for You

**For Budget Travelers:**

Stick to **main dining and buffet meals** (avoid specialty restaurants).

Skip **beverage packages** if you don't drink alcohol.

Use **free onboard entertainment** instead of paid activities.

Explore ports independently to save money on excursions.

**For Luxury Travelers:**

Consider **all-inclusive cruise lines** to avoid hidden costs.

Look for **suite perks** that include dining, drinks, and priority access.

Book **upgraded Wi-Fi and spa packages** if you enjoy premium amenities.

**For Families:**

Choose a cruise line with **free kids' clubs and family-friendly activities**.

Buy a **non-alcoholic beverage package** for kids who love sodas and specialty drinks.

Look for **discounted or included shore excursions** that cater to families.

# Packing Tips for Your Cruise: What to Bring for a Smooth Sailing Experience

Packing for a cruise requires careful planning to ensure you have everything you need while avoiding overpacking. Unlike a traditional vacation, a cruise has unique requirements, such as **formal nights, port excursions, and shipboard essentials**. Since space in cruise cabins is often limited, it's important to pack efficiently while including all the necessary items for a comfortable and enjoyable voyage. Here's a **detailed and practical guide** on what to bring and how to pack for your cruise.

## Essential Documents & Travel Necessities

Before you even think about clothing, make sure you have the **essential documents** required for your cruise.

**Passport or Government ID** – Ensure your passport is valid for at least **six months** after your return date.
**Boarding Pass & Cruise Documents** – Print your e-tickets and luggage tags.
**Travel Insurance Policy** – In case of unexpected cancellations, medical emergencies, or lost luggage.
**Credit Cards & Local Currency** – While cruise ships are cashless, you may need cash for tips or purchases in port.
**Emergency Contact Information** – Have a copy of important phone numbers, including the cruise line's emergency contacts.

**Tip:** Keep all important documents in a **waterproof travel organizer** for easy access.

## Clothing: What to Wear on a Cruise

When packing clothes, consider the cruise **destination, weather, and dress codes**.

**Daytime Casual Wear**

Lightweight **T-shirts, tank tops, and shorts** for warm-weather cruises.

**Comfortable jeans or leggings** for cooler destinations.

**Swimsuits and cover-ups** for pool and beach days.

**Light sweater or jacket** for breezy evenings.

**Evening Attire & Formal Wear**

**Casual Evenings:** Nice **blouses, polo shirts, skirts, or sundresses**.

**Formal Nights:** A **cocktail dress, gown, or suit/tuxedo** (some cruises require formal attire for special dinners).

**Smart Casual:** Slacks, collared shirts, and elegant dresses for upscale dining.

**Tip:** Check your cruise line's **dress code**—some require **formal attire**, while others allow **relaxed resort wear**.

### Footwear: The Right Shoes for Every Occasion

**Comfortable Walking Shoes** – Essential for **shore excursions and exploring ports**.
**Flip-Flops or Sandals** – For **poolside lounging or beach days**.
**Dress Shoes** – Needed for **formal evenings or upscale dining**.
**Waterproof Hiking Shoes** – If your cruise includes **adventure excursions** (Alaska, Norway, etc.).

**Tip:** Bring **shoe bags** to keep dirty shoes separate from your clothes.

### Packing for Excursions & Activities

For port days and shore excursions, pack:

**Daypack or Foldable Backpack** – For carrying **water bottles, cameras, and essentials**.
👓 **Sunglasses & Hat** – Protect yourself from **sun exposure** during outdoor activities.

**Sunscreen & Bug Spray** – Essential for **tropical destinations and nature excursions**.
**Waterproof Phone Case** – Keeps your phone dry during **beach and water activities**.
**Reusable Water Bottle** – Stay hydrated during excursions.

**Tip:** A **dry bag** is great for keeping valuables safe from water and sand.

### Toiletries & Medications

While cruise ships provide basic toiletries, bringing your own ensures **comfort and quality**.

**Travel-sized shampoo, conditioner, and body wash** (cruise lines often provide basic ones, but they may not suit your preference).
**Toothbrush, toothpaste, floss, and mouthwash**.
**Deodorant & Perfume/Cologne**.
**Hairbrush, styling tools, and hair ties**.
**Moisturizer & lip balm** (ocean air can be drying).
**Razor & shaving cream**.
**Makeup & skincare essentials**.

**Medications & First Aid**

**Seasickness medication** (Dramamine, sea bands, or motion sickness patches).

**Pain relievers (Tylenol, ibuprofen, aspirin)**.

**Band-aids & blister pads** for walking-heavy excursions.

**Prescription medications** (pack extra in case of delays).

**Tip:** Pack medications in your **carry-on bag**, as checked luggage may be delayed.

### Electronics & Gadgets

**Power Strip (Cruise-Approved)** – Many cabins have limited outlets. Ensure its **non-surge protected** (required by most cruise lines).
**Smartphone & Charger** – For photos, onboard apps, and communication.
**Noise-Canceling Headphones or Earbuds** – For flights or noisy environments.
**Camera or GoPro** – Capture your cruise memories.
**E-Reader or Book** – Relax on deck with a good read.
**Small Flashlight** – Useful in case of **cabin power outages**.

**Tip:** Download **offline maps, travel guides, and cruise apps** before departure.

## Miscellaneous Cruise Essentials

**Laundry Bag** – Keep dirty clothes separate.
**Magnetic Hooks** – Great for extra storage on **metal cabin walls**.
**Ziplock Bags** – Store wet swimsuits, snacks, or small essentials.
**Foldable Tote Bag** – Useful for **souvenirs or extra belongings**.
**Luggage Tags & Locks** – Protect your bags and ensure easy identification.

## What NOT to Pack (Prohibited Items)

Most cruise lines **prohibit** the following:
**Irons & Steamers** – Fire hazard (use onboard laundry services).
**Surge-Protected Power Strips** – Not allowed on most ships.
**Candles & Incense** – Fire safety restrictions.
**Drugs & Illegal Substances** – Strictly prohibited and

enforced.

**Weapons or Sharp Objects** – Including **pocket knives and large scissors**.

**Tip:** Always check your cruise line's **official packing restrictions** before departure.

# PORT BY PORT GUIDE

## London (Tilbury): A Gateway to England's Capital

London (Tilbury) is one of the **most significant cruise ports in the United Kingdom**, serving as a gateway to **London and Southeast England**. Located on the northern bank of the **River Thames**, approximately **25 miles (40 km) east of central London**, Tilbury Cruise Terminal is a key stop for British Isles and European cruises. While it is often overshadowed by the grandeur of London, Tilbury itself has a rich maritime history and offers **convenient access to some of England's most famous landmarks**.

Whether you're embarking on a cruise, arriving for a port call, or planning a pre- or post-cruise stay, here's everything you need to know about **London (Tilbury) as a cruise destination**.

### The Importance of Tilbury Cruise Terminal

**A Historic Port with Modern Facilities**

Tilbury has been a key maritime hub since the 16th century and played a vital role in England's naval and trade history. The **London Cruise Terminal**, housed in a **Grade II-listed building**, was originally constructed in 1930 and has welcomed thousands of passengers over the decades, including **post-war immigrants aboard the famous Empire Windrush** in 1948.

Today, the terminal serves as an embarkation and disembarkation point for **regional and international cruises**, with ships from lines such as **Fred. Olsen Cruise Lines, Ambassador Cruise Line, and Viking Cruises** frequently calling at the port.

**Facilities at Tilbury Cruise Terminal**

**Check-in & Immigration Services** – Efficient and straightforward for cruise passengers.

**Luggage Handling & Security** – Well-organized baggage drop-off and collection areas.

**Cafés & Rest Areas** – Small but functional amenities for waiting passengers.

**Transportation Links** – Easy access to **London and surrounding areas via train, taxi, and private transfers**.

**Tip:** Since Tilbury Cruise Terminal is smaller than major cruise ports like **Southampton**, it offers a **less crowded and more relaxed** embarkation experience.

### How to Get from Tilbury to London

Although Tilbury is not in central London, it has **excellent transport links** that allow visitors to reach the capital quickly.

**By Train (Fastest & Most Convenient)**

The nearest train station is **Tilbury Town Station**, about **2 miles (3 km) from the cruise terminal**.

Take a short **taxi or shuttle ride** to the station.

From Tilbury Town, **c2c trains** run to **London Fenchurch Street Station** in **40–50 minutes**.

Tickets cost around **£10-£15 ($12-$18) per person** one way.

**By Taxi or Private Transfer**

A taxi from Tilbury to central London costs **£60-£100 ($75-$125)** depending on traffic.

Private transfer services can be booked in advance for **a more comfortable journey**.

**By Coach or Cruise Shuttle**

Some cruise lines offer **pre-arranged shuttle buses** to London.

Public buses are available but take longer and require transfers.

**Tip:** If you have **luggage**, a taxi or private transfer is the **easiest option**.

## Things to Do in Tilbury Before or After Your Cruise

While many travelers head straight to London, Tilbury itself has a **few historical and cultural sites worth exploring**:

**Tilbury Fort**

A **16th-century fortress** built by **Henry VIII** to defend the Thames from invasion.

Famous for **Queen Elizabeth I's speech in 1588** before the battle against the Spanish Armada.

Offers **panoramic views of the river and fascinating military history exhibits**.

**Coalhouse Fort & Park**

A **Victorian-era defense fort** surrounded by green parkland.

Features underground tunnels, cannons, and scenic walking trails.

**Gravesend Ferry**

A short ferry ride from Tilbury to **Gravesend**, a historic town with connections to **Pocahontas**, the Native American figure buried there.

Offers **charming riverside walks and local pubs**.

## Top Attractions in London (Easily Accessible from Tilbury)

For those with **a full day in port**, London offers an incredible selection of world-class attractions:

**Historic Landmarks & Palaces**

**Buckingham Palace** – The official residence of the **British monarchy**.

**Tower of London & Tower Bridge** – Home to the **Crown Jewels** and centuries of history.

**Westminster Abbey & Big Ben** – Iconic landmarks near the Houses of Parliament.

**Culture & Museums**

**British Museum** – A world-class collection of artifacts, including the **Rosetta Stone and Egyptian mummies**.

**National Gallery** – Masterpieces by **Van Gogh, Da Vinci, and Rembrandt**.

**The West End** – London's famous **theatre district** with Broadway-style shows.

**Scenic Views & Shopping**

**The London Eye** – A **giant observation wheel** offering breathtaking city views.

**Covent Garden & Oxford Street** – Perfect for **shopping, dining, and people-watching**.

**River Thames Cruises** – A relaxing way to see **London from the water**.

### Best Tips for Cruisers Visiting London (Tilbury)

**Plan Your Transport in Advance** – London is **a big city**, so allocate **extra travel time** to return to the port before your cruise departure.
**Book Skip-the-Line Tickets** – For top attractions like the **Tower of London and the London Eye**, buy tickets online to **avoid long queues**.
**Use Contactless Payments** – London's public transport system accepts **contactless debit/credit cards and Oyster cards** for easy travel.
**Stay Overnight for More Exploration** – If possible, **arrive a day early or stay an extra night** to fully enjoy London before or after your cruise.

## Top Attractions in London: Tower of London, Westminster Abbey, and Buckingham Palace

London is a city steeped in history, home to some of the world's most **iconic landmarks and royal residences**. Among its most famous attractions are the **Tower of London, Westminster Abbey, and Buckingham Palace**—each offering a unique glimpse into Britain's monarchy, heritage, and architecture. Whether you're fascinated by **medieval castles, royal ceremonies, or historical artifacts**, these three sites are must-visit destinations for anyone exploring the heart of England.

**Tower of London: A Fortress, Prison, and Home to the**

The **Tower of London**, a UNESCO World Heritage Site, is one of the most **important historical landmarks in the UK**. Founded by **William the Conqueror in 1066**, the fortress has served many roles over the centuries, including a **royal palace, prison, armory, and treasury**. It is most famously known for housing the **Crown Jewels** and being the site of numerous high-profile executions.

## Top Highlights

**The Crown Jewels** – A dazzling collection of **royal regalia**, including the **Imperial State Crown and the Sovereign's Sceptre**.

**The White Tower** – The oldest part of the complex, home to the **Royal Armouries collection** and medieval weaponry.

**The Bloody Tower** – Associated with the mystery of the **Princes in the Tower**, two royal children who disappeared in the 15th century.

**Yeoman Warders (Beefeaters)** – The ceremonial guards who give **entertaining guided tours**, sharing stories of the Tower's dark past.

**Ravens of the Tower** – Legend says that **if the ravens ever leave the Tower, the kingdom will fall**.

## Visitor Tips

**Best Time to Visit:** Arrive early to avoid crowds, especially at the **Crown Jewels exhibit**.

**How to Get There:** Nearest Underground station – **Tower Hill**.

**Tickets & Entry:** Prices start around **£30 for adults**, and booking online can save time.

**Westminster Abbey: The Nation's Coronation Church**

Westminster Abbey is **one of the most significant religious and historical buildings in the UK**. Founded in **960 ADS**, it has been the site of **every British coronation since 1066** and is the final resting place of many monarchs, poets, and scientists. This stunning **Gothic cathedral** is also famous for hosting **royal weddings**, including **Prince William and Kate Middleton's** in 2011.

**Top Highlights**

**The Coronation Chair** – Used for the crowning of British monarchs for over **700 years**. **Poets' Corner** – The burial place of literary greats like **Geoffrey Chaucer, Charles Dickens, and Jane Austen**. **Royal Tombs** – Includes **Queen Elizabeth I, Mary Queen of Scots, and King Henry V**. **The Nave & Stained Glass Windows** – Features breathtaking architecture and historical memorials.

**The Abbey Choir** – Famed for its performances during **royal services and special events**.

### Visitor Tips

**Best Time to Visit: Early morning or late afternoon** to avoid peak crowds.

**How to Get There:** Nearest Underground station – **Westminster**.

**Tickets & Entry:** Standard admission is around **£27 for adults**; attending a service is free.

### Buckingham Palace: The Official Residence of the Monarch

Buckingham Palace is **one of the most famous royal residences in the world** and the official home of **King Charles III**. Originally built as **Buckingham House in 1703**, it was transformed into a royal palace by **King George III** in the 18th century. Today, it serves as the **administrative headquarters of the British monarchy** and a major tourist attraction.

**Top Highlights**

**Changing of the Guard** – A spectacular military ceremony where the **King's Guard**, dressed in their iconic red uniforms and bearskin hats, take over duties.
**The State Rooms** – Open to visitors during **summer tours**, these lavish rooms feature priceless **art, chandeliers, and grand furniture**.
**The Royal Gardens** – The **largest private garden in London**, home to a lake, rare flowers, and the **Queen's Garden Parties**.
**The Queen's Gallery** – A rotating exhibition of treasures from the **Royal Collection**, including paintings by **Rembrandt and Van Dyck**.

## Visitor Tips

**Best Time to Visit: July to September**, when the **State Rooms are open to the public**.
**How to Get There:** Nearest Underground station – **Green Park** or **Victoria**.
**Tickets & Entry:** General admission for **State Rooms**

**tours is around £30**; Changing of the Guard is **free to watch**.

## Shore Excursions: A Guide to Making the Most of Your Cruise Stops

Shore excursions are a **key highlight of any cruise**, offering travelers the opportunity to explore new destinations, experience different cultures, and participate in exciting activities. Whether you're visiting **historic cities, scenic coastlines, or exotic islands**, shore excursions allow you to make the most of your time in port. With so many options available, from guided tours to independent explorations, it's important to plan ahead to ensure you choose the best experience for your interests and budget.

### Types of Shore Excursions

Shore excursions vary widely depending on the **destination and type of experience you're looking for**. Here are some of the most popular types:

**Historical & Cultural Tours**

Perfect for history buffs and those who love learning about **local heritage and architecture**.

Common activities include **castle visits, city walking tours, and museum trips**.

Example: Exploring **Edinburgh Castle in Scotland**, the **Colosseum in Rome**, or the **Acropolis in Athens**.

**Scenic & Nature Tours**

Ideal for travelers who enjoy **breathtaking landscapes and outdoor adventures**.

Includes visits to **national parks, waterfalls, mountains, and coastal cliffs**.

Example: Taking in the **Cliffs of Moher in Ireland**, **Norwegian fjord cruises**, or **Alaska's glaciers**.

**Adventure & Active Excursions**

Best for thrill-seekers and those looking for **hands-on experiences**.

Includes **snorkeling, scuba diving, zip-lining, ATV rides, and hiking**.

Example: **Snorkeling in the Caribbean**, **kayaking in Alaska**, or **hiking in Santorini**.

**Food & Wine Experiences**

Great for food lovers who want to explore **local cuisine and traditions**.

Activities include **wine tasting, cooking classes, and street food tours**.

Example: **Whiskey tasting in Scotland**, **Italian pasta-making in Rome**, or **wine tours in Bordeaux**.

**Beach & Relaxation Excursions**

Designed for those who prefer a **laid-back day by the sea**.

Activities include **swimming, sunbathing, and spa treatments**.

Example: **Enjoying private beach resorts in the Caribbean** or **lounging on the Greek Islands**.

## Booking a Shore Excursion: Cruise Line vs. Independent Tours

There are two main ways to book shore excursions: **through the cruise line** or with an **independent tour operator**. Each option has its pros and cons.

### Booking Through the Cruise Line

**Convenience** – All arrangements are handled by the cruise staff.

**Guaranteed Return to Ship** – If your tour runs late, the ship will wait for you.

**Pre-vetted Tour Operators** – Ensures **safety and reliability**.

**More Expensive** – Cruise-sponsored excursions tend to cost **more than independent tours**.

**Large Groups** – Some excursions **lack a personal touch** due to big tour sizes.

### Booking with Independent Tour Operators

**Lower Prices** – Often **30-50% cheaper** than cruise line excursions.

**Smaller Groups & Personalized Experiences** – More **flexibility and customization**.

**Unique & Off-the-Beaten-Path Activities** – Access to **hidden gems** not included in cruise tours.

**Risk of Missing the Ship** – If an independent tour runs late, the **ship won't wait**. **More Planning Required** – You'll need to research **reputable tour companies** in advance.

**Tip:** If booking independently, choose tours that **guarantee timely return to port** or aim to be back **at least two hours before departure**.

### Tips for Choosing the Best Shore Excursion

**Consider Your Interests** – Choose an excursion that matches your **personal travel style** (adventure, relaxation, culture, etc.).

**Check Activity Level & Mobility Requirements** – Some tours involve **long walks, steep climbs, or uneven terrain**. If you have mobility concerns, look for **accessible excursions**.

**Read Reviews & Ratings** – Check **TripAdvisor, Cruise Critic, or Viator** for **honest reviews from fellow travelers**.

**Compare Prices** – Don't assume the **cruise line's tour is the best deal**—compare prices with **local operators**. **Book Early for Popular Excursions** – Some tours **sell out quickly**, especially in high-demand destinations like **Rome, Santorini, and Alaska**. **Check Cancellation Policies** – Make sure you understand the **refund policy** in case plans change.

### Packing Essentials for a Shore Excursion

Bringing the right items can make your excursion **more enjoyable and hassle-free**. Here's what to pack:

**Daypack** – Lightweight bag for carrying essentials.
**Sunglasses & Hat** – Protect yourself from **sun exposure**.
**Sunscreen & Bug Spray** – Essential for **beach and jungle excursions**.
**Camera or Smartphone** – Capture memorable moments.
**Reusable Water Bottle** – Stay hydrated.
**Local Currency & Credit Card** – Some small shops **don't accept cards**.
**Printed Itinerary & Contact Info** – Just in case your phone dies.

### Can You Explore the Port on Your Own?

Yes! In many destinations, you can **explore independently** instead of booking an organized excursion. This works best in:

**Walkable cities** like **Barcelona, Venice, and Dubrovnik.**

Ports with **good public transport**, like **Amsterdam and Copenhagen.**

Destinations with **hop-on-hop-off buses**, such as **London and Sydney.**

However, in remote locations or areas with limited transport, an **organized tour is recommended.**

## Dining & Shopping on a Cruise: What to Expect & How to Make the Most of It

One of the best parts of cruising is the opportunity to **indulge in world-class dining** and **explore diverse shopping options**—all while sailing across breathtaking destinations. Cruise ships offer a **variety of dining experiences**, from **buffet-style meals to fine dining** prepared by award-winning chefs, as well as **duty-free**

**shopping, luxury boutiques, and souvenir stores.** Knowing what's available and how to make the most of it can enhance your cruise experience, whether you're a **food lover, a bargain hunter, or simply looking for a memorable keepsake.**

### Dining Options on a Cruise: What's Available?

Cruise ships offer a wide range of **dining venues**, catering to different tastes, budgets, and experiences.

### Main Dining Room (MDR) – Classic Cruise Experience

Included in your cruise fare, the **Main Dining Room** offers **multi-course meals** in an elegant setting.

Serves **breakfast, lunch, and dinner** with a rotating menu.

Features **a mix of international cuisine, seafood, steaks, and vegetarian options**.

Guests can choose between **set dining times** (early or late seating) or **flexible dining options** (depending on the cruise line).

### Buffet Restaurants – Casual & Convenient

Open for **all-day dining**, offering **a variety of dishes**, including **salads, pastas, seafood, and international cuisines**.

Great for **quick meals and flexible dining times**.

Perfect for families or travelers who prefer **a relaxed, informal atmosphere**.

**Specialty Restaurants – Fine Dining at Sea**

Offer **premium dining experiences** for an additional fee.

Includes options like **steakhouses, sushi bars, French bistros, and Italian trattorias**.

Some cruises feature **celebrity chef restaurants**, such as **Gordon Ramsay's Hell's Kitchen (Norwegian Cruise Line) or Nobu's Sushi (Crystal Cruises)**.

Advance reservations are recommended, as these venues fill up quickly.

**Room Service – Private Dining in Your Cabin**

Available **24/7 on most cruise lines**, though some charge a **service fee for late-night orders**.

Ideal for **a relaxed breakfast on your balcony** or a quiet night in.

**Themed Dining & Experiences**

Some cruises offer **exclusive dining events**, like **lobster nights, wine-pairing dinners, or chef's table experiences**.

**Afternoon tea, chocolate buffets,** and **BBQ nights on deck** are also popular on luxury cruises.

**Tip:** Check your cruise's **daily schedule for dining themes and special events**, as they can be limited to specific nights.

**Drinks & Beverage Packages**

While **water, coffee, tea, and basic juices** are free in main dining areas, **alcoholic beverages and premium coffees** cost extra.

**Beverage packages** (unlimited drinks) are available, covering **wine, cocktails, beer, and specialty coffee**.

Prices range from **$50 to $100 per day**, depending on the cruise line.

Some cruise lines **allow you to bring your own wine or champagne**, but corkage fees may apply.

**Tip:** If you enjoy **wine with dinner or morning lattes**, a **drink package** can save you money.

### Shopping on a Cruise: What to Expect?

Cruise ships feature a **variety of onboard shops**, offering everything from **luxury goods to souvenirs and duty-free items**.

### Duty-Free Shopping – Tax-Free Savings

Many cruise ships have **duty-free stores**, where you can purchase **perfume, cosmetics, liquor, cigarettes, and designer accessories** at lower prices than on land.

Popular brands include **Gucci, Michael Kors, TAG Heuer, and Swarovski**.

Best savings are often on **alcohol, high-end cosmetics, and watches**.

### Souvenirs & Cruise Line Merchandise

Many ships have **gift shops selling branded cruise memorabilia**, such as **t-shirts, mugs, and collectibles**.

Great for picking up **destination-themed souvenirs** if you don't shop at port.

### Jewelry & Luxury Boutiques

Some cruises feature **exclusive jewelry collections** from brands like **Effy, Cartier, and Tiffany & Co.**

Special events, such as **watch raffles, gemstone showcases, and designer trunk sales**, often take place onboard.

### Convenience Stores & Essentials

Forgot something? Ships have small stores selling **toiletries, sunscreen, travel accessories, and medications**.

Prices for basics (like toothpaste or sunscreen) are often **higher than on land**, so pack wisely.

**Tip: Duty-free shopping is only available in international waters**, so expect stores to close when docked.

### Shopping in Port: What to Buy & Where to Go

If you prefer shopping on land, **ports of call offer great opportunities** to find unique gifts and locally made products.

**Popular Souvenirs & Local Products:**

**British Isles: Scottish whiskey, Irish wool, and English tea.**
**Caribbean: Handmade crafts, rum, cigars, and spices.**
IT **Italy: Leather goods, ceramics, and fine wines.**
JP **Japan: Silk kimonos, green tea, and electronics.**

**Tips for Shopping in Port:**

**Bargain at local markets** – Many vendors expect negotiation.
**Look for locally owned shops** – Support small businesses and avoid mass-produced souvenirs.
**Be mindful of customs regulations** – Some items (like

Cuban cigars or fresh produce) may not be allowed back on board.

**Money-Saving Tips for Dining & Shopping**

**ake advantage of free dining** – Stick to the **main dining room, buffet, and included venues** to save money. **Use loyalty programs** – Frequent cruisers can earn **discounts on specialty dining and onboard purchases**. **Wait for last-day sales** – Shops often offer **big discounts on jewelry and souvenirs** near the end of the cruise. **Check daily promotions** – Look for **happy hour drink specials and onboard sales events** in the cruise's daily newsletter.

### Top Attractions in Edinburgh: Edinburgh Castle, Holyrood Palace, and the Royal Mile

Edinburgh, Scotland's historic and cultural capital, is home to some of the most **iconic landmarks in the United Kingdom**. Visitors to this charming city are transported back in time as they walk through its **medieval streets, royal palaces, and towering castles**. Three of the most famous attractions—**Edinburgh Castle, Holyrood**

Palace, and the Royal Mile—offer an unforgettable journey into Scotland's royal history, architectural grandeur, and vibrant heritage. Whether you're fascinated by **monarchy, medieval battles, or Scottish traditions**, these sites are must-visit destinations.

### Edinburgh Castle: Scotland's Most Iconic Fortress

Perched high on **Castle Rock**, Edinburgh Castle dominates the city's skyline and is one of **Scotland's most visited landmarks**. Dating back to the **12th century**, the castle has played a crucial role in **Scotland's history**, serving as a **royal residence, military fortress, and prison**. Over the centuries, it has witnessed **battles, sieges, and political power struggles**, making it a symbol of **Scotland's resilience and independence**.

### Top Highlights

**The Crown Jewels of Scotland** – Includes the **Scottish Crown, Sceptre, and Sword of State**, used in royal coronations.

**The Stone of Destiny** – An ancient **symbol of Scottish kingship**, once taken by the English and returned in 1996.

**St. Margaret's Chapel** – The **oldest surviving building in Edinburgh**, built in the 12th century. **One O'Clock Gun** – A **daily cannon firing tradition**, dating back to 1861, used to help ships set their timepieces. **The Great Hall & National War Museum** – Displays **medieval weapons, armor, and Scottish military history**.

**Visitor Tips**

**Best Time to Visit:** Arrive early to avoid crowds, especially during **summer and festival season**. **How to Get There:** Located at the **top of the Royal Mile**, easily accessible by foot or bus. **Tickets & Entry:** Standard entry costs **£19-£22 for adults**; booking online saves time.

## Holyrood Palace: The Royal Residence in Scotland

At the opposite end of the **Royal Mile**, Holyrood Palace (or **Palace of Holyroodhouse**) is the **official residence of the British monarch in Scotland**. Originally a **medieval abbey**, the site was transformed into a palace in the **16th century** and has been home to **Scotland's kings and**

**queens**, including **Mary, Queen of Scots**. Today, it remains a **working royal palace**, where **King Charles III** stays when visiting Edinburgh.

**Top Highlights**

**The State Apartments** – Lavish rooms filled with **tapestries, chandeliers, and royal portraits**.
**The Great Gallery** – Features **portraits of Scottish monarchs**, including legendary figures like **Robert the Bruce**.
**The Ruins of Holyrood Abbey** – A **stunning medieval abbey**, founded in 1128, offering a glimpse into Scotland's monastic past.
**Mary, Queen of Scots' Chambers** – Step inside the private rooms of one of **Scotland's most tragic queens**, including the site where her secretary **David Rizzio was murdered**.
**The Palace Gardens** – Beautiful royal gardens with **views of Arthur's Seat**, a famous hill overlooking Edinburgh.

**Visitor Tips**

**Best Time to Visit:** The palace is **closed when the King is in residence**, so check schedules in advance. **How to Get There:** At the **end of the Royal Mile**, a **10-minute walk from Edinburgh Waverley train station**. **ickets & Entry:** Standard entry costs **£18-£20 for adults**, and guided audio tours are available.

## The Royal Mile: Edinburgh's Historic Heart

The **Royal Mile** is Edinburgh's most **famous street**, connecting **Edinburgh Castle** to **Holyrood Palace**. This historic stretch, about **one mile long**, is lined with **centuries-old buildings, traditional pubs, shops, and museums**. It has been at the center of **Scottish life for hundreds of years**, hosting everything from **royal processions to public executions**.

**Top Highlights**

**Traditional Scottish Shops** – Buy **kilts, cashmere, and handmade Celtic jewelry**. **Whisky Tasting Experiences** – Visit the **Scotch Whisky Experience** to learn about and sample **Scotland's national drink**.

**Real Mary King's Close** – **A hidden underground street**, revealing the **mysteries and ghost stories** of Edinburgh's past.

**St. Giles' Cathedral** – A stunning **Gothic church** known for its **crown-shaped spire and beautiful stained glass windows**.

**Gladstone's Land** – A **17th-century merchant's house**, offering a glimpse into Edinburgh's past.

**Visitor Tips**

**Best Time to Visit:** Morning or evening for fewer crowds; **August is busiest** due to the **Edinburgh Festival**. **How to Get There:** Easily accessible by foot from **Edinburgh Waverley train station**. **Events to Watch For:** The **Edinburgh Fringe Festival** in August transforms the **Royal Mile into a stage for street performers and artists**.

## Shore Excursions: How to Make the Most of Your Time in Port

Shore excursions are one of the most exciting parts of a cruise, allowing travelers to **explore new destinations,** experience different cultures, and participate in unique activities. Whether you're visiting **historical landmarks, stunning landscapes, or vibrant markets**, a well-planned shore excursion can enhance your cruise experience. However, with so many options available, it's important to understand the different types of excursions, how to book them, and how to get the most value for your time in port.

## Types of Shore Excursions

Shore excursions vary widely depending on the **destination, activity level, and personal preferences**. Here are the most common types:

### Historical & Cultural Tours

Best for history lovers and those interested in **architecture, museums, and heritage sites**.

Typically includes guided tours of **castles, ancient ruins, or UNESCO World Heritage Sites**.

Example: Visiting the **Tower of London**, the **Colosseum in Rome**, or **Mayan ruins in Mexico**.

### Scenic & Nature Excursions

Perfect for travelers who love **natural beauty, wildlife, and photography**.

Includes **national parks, waterfalls, fjord cruises, and eco-tours**.

Example: Exploring **Alaska's glaciers**, the **Norwegian fjords**, or the **Cliffs of Moher in Ireland**.

**Adventure & Active Excursions**

Ideal for thrill-seekers looking for **physical activities and outdoor adventures**.

Includes **zip-lining, ATV riding, scuba diving, kayaking, and hiking**.

Example: **Snorkeling in the Caribbean**, hiking **Santorini's volcano**, or **zip-lining in Costa Rica**.

**Culinary & Wine Experiences**

Great for food lovers who want to **sample local cuisine and beverages**.

Includes **wine tastings, cooking classes, and street food tours**.

Example: **Whiskey tasting in Scotland**, **pasta-making in Italy**, or **seafood feasts in Greece**.

**Beach & Relaxation Excursions**

Ideal for those who want to **unwind and enjoy the coastal scenery**.

Includes **private beach resorts, snorkeling, and spa days**.

Example: Relaxing at a **Caribbean beach club**, **swimming in the Mediterranean**, or **sunbathing in Hawaii**.

## Booking a Shore Excursion: Cruise Line vs. Independent Tours

There are two main ways to book a shore excursion:

**Booking Through the Cruise Line**

**Convenient & Hassle-Free** – The cruise staff arranges everything for you.
**Guaranteed Return to Ship** – If a cruise-sponsored tour is delayed, the ship will wait.
**Well-Vetted Operators** – Ensures safety and quality.

**More Expensive** – Cruise-sponsored excursions often cost **30-50% more** than independent tours.
**Larger Groups** – Some tours feel crowded, limiting the experience.

### Booking with Independent Tour Operators

**Lower Cost & Smaller Groups** – Often cheaper and more personalized.

**Unique & Off-the-Beaten-Path** – Offers **more diverse and customized experiences**.

**More Flexible Schedules** – You can design an excursion based on your interests.

**Risk of Missing the Ship** – If the tour runs late, the cruise won't wait for you.

**More Planning Required** – You need to research **reputable tour companies**.

**Tip:** If booking independently, choose excursions that **guarantee a return to the port at least 2 hours before departure**.

## Tips for Choosing the Best Shore Excursion

**Consider Your Interests** – Pick an excursion that matches your **preferences and energy level**. **Check Activity Levels** – Some tours involve **long walks or physical activity**—choose wisely based on mobility. **Read Reviews** – Look at ratings on **TripAdvisor, Cruise Critic, or Viator** to ensure quality. **Compare Prices** – Don't assume the cruise line's tour is the best deal—**compare with independent operators**. **Book Early for Popular Tours** – Some **high-demand excursions sell out quickly**, especially in **Alaska, Europe, and the Caribbean**. **Check Cancellation Policies** – Ensure you understand the **refund policy in case plans change**.

## Packing Essentials for a Shore Excursion

To ensure a smooth excursion, pack these essentials:

**Daypack** – Lightweight and secure for carrying your items.
**Sunglasses & Hat** – Protect yourself from **sun exposure**.
**Sunscreen & Bug Spray** – Essential for **beach and jungle**

excursions.

**Camera or Smartphone** – Capture memorable moments.

**Reusable Water Bottle** – Stay hydrated.

**Local Currency & Credit Card** – Some small shops don't accept cards.

**Printed Itinerary & Contact Info** – Just in case your phone battery dies.

## Can You Explore the Port on Your Own?

Yes! In some destinations, **self-guided exploration** is just as rewarding as a guided tour.

**Great for Independent Exploration:**

**Barcelona, Spain** – Walk **Las Ramblas**, visit **La Sagrada Familia**, and explore **local tapas bars**.

**Venice, Italy** – Wander through **St. Mark's Square**, ride a **gondola**, and visit **Murano's glass factories**.

**Dubrovnik, Croatia** – Stroll through the **Old Town**, walk the **city walls**, and enjoy **seafood by the harbor**.

**Best for Guided Tours:**

**Alaska** – Glacier hikes and wildlife spotting are **best with experts**.

**Iceland** – Geothermal pools and volcano excursions require **proper transportation**.

**South America** – Some areas **require safety precautions and guided tours**.

**Tip:** If exploring independently, **download offline maps** and check public transport options.

## Dining & Shopping: Enhancing Your Travel and Cruise Experience

Dining and shopping are essential elements of any travel experience, giving you the opportunity to **immerse yourself in local cultures, savor authentic cuisine**, and bring home **unique souvenirs and gifts**. Whether you're exploring bustling city markets, enjoying gourmet cuisine on a cruise ship, or discovering hidden gems at local restaurants and boutiques, dining and shopping can shape your memories of a destination.

Here's a guide to **making the most of dining and shopping** during your travels, with tips for cruise-goers and independent explorers alike.

## Dining: Savoring Local and Onboard Cuisine

Food is a powerful way to connect with a culture, as every dish tells a story about a **region's history, climate, and traditions**. When traveling or cruising, dining experiences range from **street food stalls to world-class fine dining establishments**.

## Onboard Cruise Dining Options

Cruise ships offer a variety of **dining venues**, from casual eateries to specialty restaurants. Here are the main types:

**Main Dining Rooms** – Multi-course meals included in your cruise fare, often with international menus.

**Buffet Restaurants** – Casual, flexible, and offering a wide range of options.

**Specialty Restaurants** – Fine dining experiences for an additional fee, including **steakhouses, sushi bars, and French bistros**.

**Poolside or Snack Bars** – Great for **quick bites**, such as burgers, pizza, and ice cream.

**Room Service** – Ideal for those who want **breakfast in bed or a private meal** on their balcony.

**Dining at Local Destinations**

Dining in port or at a travel destination is an opportunity to sample **authentic flavors and local specialties**. Examples include:

**Traditional Irish Stew in Dublin, Ireland.**

**Paella and tapas in Barcelona, Spain.**

**Fresh seafood in the Caribbean Islands.**

**Street food like tacos in Mexico or dumplings in Hong Kong.**

To get an authentic experience, consider: Visiting **family-owned restaurants** instead of touristy spots.

Joining **culinary walking tours** for local insight and hidden gems.

Trying **signature dishes** even if they are outside your comfort zone.

**Tip:** Always check for **restaurant reviews**, especially if you're visiting an unfamiliar area, and make **reservations for popular spots** in advance.

**Shopping: Bringing Home Unique Finds**

Shopping is a great way to **connect with a destination**, offering travelers a chance to bring home **souvenirs, artisanal products, and luxury items**. Shopping opportunities vary by destination, ranging from street markets to high-end boutiques and duty-free stores.

**Duty-Free Shopping on Cruises**

Duty-free shopping is popular among cruise travelers because it allows for **tax-free purchases of certain goods**, including:

**Alcohol and liquor.**

**Perfumes and cosmetics.**

**Designer brands** like **Michael Kors, Gucci, and TAG Heuer.**

**Luxury watches and jewelry**.

**Tip:** Duty-free items are often available only **while the ship is at sea**, so plan your purchases accordingly.

**Shopping at Local Destinations**

Shopping in local markets and stores offers a more **authentic and personal experience**. Common items to look for include:

**Handcrafted jewelry** and **artisan-made goods**.

**Traditional clothing** or accessories, such as **kilts in Scotland** or **panama hats in Ecuador**.

**Local delicacies**, including **spices, chocolates, and specialty wines**.

Here are some **tips for shopping abroad**: **Research Local Specialties** – Know what the region is famous for to guide your purchases. **Negotiate Prices in Markets** – In many regions, bargaining is expected and part of the shopping culture. **Support Small Businesses** – Seek out **local artisans and**

**family-owned shops**, which often offer **unique items** and help boost the local economy.

### Tips for a Successful Dining & Shopping Experience

**Budget Wisely**

Set a **daily budget** for both **dining and shopping**.

Avoid impulse purchases unless it's **something you truly love**.

Some countries charge **VAT (Value Added Tax)** on goods, so inquire about **tax refunds for tourists**.

**Plan Ahead**

Research **local markets and restaurants** before your trip.

Make **dining reservations** for popular spots to avoid long waits.

Look for **cultural events or seasonal markets**, which often showcase **authentic products and dishes**.

**Be Aware of Customs Regulations**

Check **your country's import rules** before buying items like **alcohol, tobacco, or plant-based products**.

Keep **receipts and proof of purchase** for customs declarations.

**Stay Safe and Be Smart**

Use **contactless payment methods** where possible, as many destinations now accept **mobile wallets**.

Avoid using **large amounts of cash** and beware of **pickpockets in busy areas**.

# EDINBURGH (LEITH)

## Edinburgh (Leith): Scotland's Vibrant Port and Gateway to the Capital

Edinburgh (Leith) is the **primary cruise port for Scotland's capital**, offering visitors a seamless gateway to the **historic and cultural wonders of Edinburgh**. Located just **three miles north of the city center**, Leith is a destination in its own right, with a rich maritime heritage, a thriving food scene, and unique attractions. Whether you're arriving by cruise ship or exploring the area before heading into Edinburgh, Leith provides a **fascinating blend of history, modern charm, and waterfront beauty**.

### Leith: Edinburgh's Historic Port

Leith has been a major **Scottish port for centuries**, serving as Edinburgh's main maritime hub since **the 14th century**. It played a key role in **Scotland's trade, naval history, and royal connections**, welcoming famous visitors such as **Mary, Queen of Scots** in 1561. Over the years, Leith has transformed from an **industrial dockland** into a **trendy waterfront district**, known for its **restaurants, cultural attractions, and lively atmosphere**.

Today, **Leith Cruise Terminal** accommodates **small to mid-sized ships**, offering visitors an easy connection to **Edinburgh's top landmarks**, including **Edinburgh Castle, the Royal Mile, and Holyrood Palace**.

### Things to Do in Leith

While many travelers head straight into Edinburgh, Leith has **plenty to offer** for those who wish to explore its waterfront charm.

**The Royal Yacht Britannia**

One of the most famous attractions in Leith, **The Royal Yacht Britannia** was the official **royal yacht of Queen Elizabeth II** for over 40 years. Now permanently docked in Leith, the yacht allows visitors to explore its **lavish state rooms, crew quarters, and the royal deck tea room**. **Highlights:** The **Queen's bedroom, the elegant state dining room, and the Royal Deck Tea Room**.

**Tickets:** Entry costs around **£18 per adult**, with guided audio tours available.

### Leith's Culinary Scene

Leith is a **food lover's paradise**, boasting some of the best restaurants in Scotland, including **two Michelin-starred establishments**:

**The Kitchin** – Run by celebrity chef **Tom Kitchin**, offering **Scottish cuisine with French influences.**

**Restaurant Martin Wishart** – A Michelin-starred fine dining experience featuring **local seafood and modern Scottish dishes.** For a more casual experience, visitors can explore **charming waterfront pubs, seafood restaurants, and stylish cafés.**

### Leith's History & Culture

**Trinity House Maritime Museum** – A hidden gem showcasing **Leith's rich naval history and shipbuilding heritage.**

**The Shore** – A **picturesque waterfront district** lined with **historic buildings, cobbled streets, and charming bridges**.

**Leith Market** – A great place to shop for **local crafts, Scottish cheeses, and artisanal goods**.

### Getting from Leith to Edinburgh

For those looking to explore **Edinburgh's historic center**, there are several **easy transportation options**:

**By Tram:** The **Edinburgh Trams** line now connects **Leith to the city center**, with a journey time of around **20 minutes**.

**By Bus:** Several Lothian Buses (**services 16, 22, and 35**) run frequently to **Princes Street** and the **Royal Mile**.

**By Taxi or Ride-Sharing:** A taxi ride to central Edinburgh takes **10-15 minutes** and costs around **£10-£15**.

**Tip:** If you have limited time, consider **booking a guided tour from the cruise terminal**, which includes transportation and visits to **Edinburgh Castle, Holyrood Palace, and the Royal Mile**.

## Top Attractions in Edinburgh (Easily Accessible from Leith)

Once in Edinburgh, visitors can explore some of **Scotland's most iconic landmarks**:

**Edinburgh Castle** – A historic fortress perched on **Castle Rock**, home to the **Scottish Crown Jewels**. **The Royal Mile** – The city's most famous street, filled with **shops, restaurants, and historic sites**. **Holyrood Palace** – The official **residence of the British monarch in Scotland**. **The Edinburgh Festival** – If visiting in August, don't miss the **world's largest arts festival**, featuring theatre, comedy, and music.

### Best Time to Visit Leith & Edinburgh

The best time to visit is **between May and September**, when Scotland experiences its **mildest weather**.

**Summer (June–August):** Warmest months, ideal for **outdoor sightseeing and festivals**.

**Spring & Autumn (April–May & September–October):** Fewer crowds and pleasant weather.

**Winter (November–February): Colder and quieter**, but magical during **Edinburgh's Christmas markets**.

**Tip:** Be prepared for **unpredictable Scottish weather** by bringing **a waterproof jacket and comfortable walking shoes**.

## Shore Excursions: A Guide to Making the Most of Your Time in Port

Shore excursions are one of the best ways to explore new destinations while on a cruise, allowing travelers to experience **local culture, historic landmarks, stunning landscapes, and adventure activities**. Whether you prefer guided tours, independent explorations, or thrilling outdoor adventures, a well-planned shore excursion can significantly enhance your cruise experience. Here's everything you need to know about **choosing, booking, and maximizing your time on shore excursions**.

## Types of Shore Excursions

Shore excursions cater to different interests and activity levels. Here are the most popular types:

### Historical & Cultural Tours

Ideal for those who enjoy **exploring ancient sites, castles, museums, and historic landmarks**.

Often includes **guided city tours, palace visits, or UNESCO World Heritage Sites**.

Example: Touring **Edinburgh Castle in Scotland, the Colosseum in Rome, or the Mayan ruins in Mexico**.

### Scenic & Nature Tours

Perfect for travelers who love **breathtaking landscapes, national parks, and wildlife experiences**.

Includes **sightseeing cruises, fjord explorations, and visits to scenic coastal cliffs**.

Example: **The Cliffs of Moher in Ireland, the Norwegian fjords, or glacier trekking in Alaska**.

### Adventure & Active Excursions

Designed for **thrill-seekers and outdoor enthusiasts**.

Activities include **zip-lining, hiking, snorkeling, scuba diving, and ATV rides**.

Example: **Snorkeling in the Great Barrier Reef, zip-lining in Costa Rica, or dune bashing in Dubai.**

**Culinary & Wine Tours**

Best for food lovers looking to explore **local cuisine, wine, and traditional cooking techniques**.

Includes **wine tastings, market visits, and hands-on cooking classes**.

Example: **Whiskey tasting in Scotland, pasta-making in Italy, or street food tours in Thailand.**

**Beach & Relaxation Excursions**

Ideal for travelers looking to **unwind by the sea**.

Includes **private beach clubs, snorkeling, and spa treatments**.

Example: **Relaxing on the beaches of the Bahamas, Santorini, or Bora Bora.**

## Booking a Shore Excursion: Cruise Line vs. Independent Tours

There are two main ways to book a shore excursion:

**Booking Through the Cruise Line**

**Convenience** – The cruise staff handles all arrangements.
**Guaranteed Return to Ship** – The ship will wait if a cruise-sponsored excursion runs late.
**Pre-vetted Operators** – Ensures **safety and reliability**.

**More Expensive** – Cruise line excursions often cost **30-50% more**

## Dining & Shopping: Enhancing Your Travel and Cruise Experience

Dining and shopping are two of the most enjoyable aspects of any travel experience, offering opportunities to **explore local flavors, discover unique souvenirs, and indulge in luxury goods**. Whether you're **on a cruise, visiting a bustling city, or exploring a historic town**, knowing where and how to dine and shop can make your journey even more memorable. Here's a guide to **making the most** of **dining and shopping during your travels**, with insights into cruise ship options and local markets.

## Dining: Savoring Local and Onboard Cuisine

Dining while traveling offers a **taste of local culture**, allowing visitors to experience regional specialties and traditional dishes. When on a cruise, the **variety of onboard dining venues** ensures that every traveler finds something to suit their tastes.

### Onboard Cruise Dining Options

Cruise ships feature a range of **dining venues**, catering to different preferences:

**Main Dining Room (MDR)** – Included in the cruise fare, offering multi-course meals with a variety of options.

**Buffet Restaurants** – Casual, self-service dining with international cuisine.

**Specialty Restaurants** – Fine dining experiences featuring **steakhouses, sushi bars, Italian trattorias, and French bistros** (often at an additional cost).

**Poolside & Quick Service** – Offering fast, casual food like burgers, pizza, and fresh salads.

**Room Service** – Available on most cruise lines, allowing guests to enjoy meals in their cabin.

**Dining at Local Destinations**

Exploring local cuisine in ports is a highlight of travel, as each destination offers **distinct flavors and culinary traditions**.

**Street Food & Markets** – Ideal for sampling authentic dishes, such as **tapas in Spain, dumplings in China, or fresh seafood in Greece**.

**Traditional Restaurants** – Great for experiencing **regional specialties like pasta in Italy or curry in India**.

**Food & Wine Tours** – Many cities offer guided experiences to **vineyards, distilleries, and local food tastings**.

**Tips for Dining Abroad**

**Try local specialties** – Be adventurous and order dishes unique to the region.

**Make reservations** – High-end restaurants and popular eateries often require advance booking. **Check for dietary options** – Many places accommodate vegetarian, vegan, or gluten-free diets.

**Shopping: Finding the Best Deals & Unique Souvenirs**

Shopping is an integral part of travel, offering opportunities to **buy local handicrafts, designer goods, and duty-free products**. Whether you're looking for **authentic souvenirs or luxury items**, knowing where to shop ensures a rewarding experience.

**Duty-Free Shopping on Cruises**

Many cruise ships offer **tax-free shopping**, making them great places to purchase:

**Luxury watches and designer jewelry** (Cartier, Bulgari, TAG Heuer).

**Fragrances and skincare products** (Chanel, Dior, Estée Lauder).

**Alcohol and tobacco** – Cheaper than most land-based stores.

**Tip: Duty-free items are only available in international waters**, so shops may close while docked.

**Shopping at Local Destinations**

Different destinations specialize in unique products:

**Scotland** – Whisky, cashmere scarves, and Celtic jewelry.

**Italy** – Leather goods, Murano glass, and handmade ceramics.

**Japan** – Silk kimonos, green tea, and fine electronics.

**Best Places to Shop**

**Local Markets** – Perfect for finding handmade crafts, spices, and authentic souvenirs.

**Luxury Boutiques** – Found in major cities like **Paris, Milan, and Dubai**, featuring high-end fashion and accessories.

**Shopping malls & Outlets** – Ideal for travelers looking for international brands at discounted prices.

**Tips for Smart Shopping**

**Compare prices** – Prices in tourist areas are often higher, so shop around.

**Bargain in markets** – Negotiation is expected in many cultures (e.g., Morocco, India, and Thailand).

**Check customs regulations** – Some items, like alcohol or rare antiques, may have import restrictions.

### Budgeting for Dining & Shopping

To make the most of dining and shopping experiences while staying within budget, consider these tips:

**Setting a Budget**

**Allocate funds** separately for food, souvenirs, and luxury items.

Check if **gratuities, taxes, or service charges** are included in dining bills.

Look for **meal deals and tasting menus** at restaurants.

**Credit Cards vs. Cash**

Use **credit cards for major purchases**, but carry some **local currency for markets and small shops**.

**Check exchange rates and foreign transaction fees** before using a card abroad.

**Tax Refunds for Tourists**

Many countries offer **VAT refunds** on large purchases—**save your receipts and ask about tax-free shopping**.

**Dining & Shopping: A Memorable Part of Travel**

Dining and shopping add excitement to any trip, allowing travelers to **experience new flavors, collect unique souvenirs, and indulge in luxury goods**. Whether you're enjoying **a five-star meal on a cruise, exploring a lively street market, or shopping for handcrafted treasures**, these experiences become lasting memories.

By **planning ahead, setting a budget, and being open to new experiences**, you can maximize your **dining and shopping adventures** while making your travels even more enjoyable.

# DUBLIN

**Dublin: A City of History, Culture, and Irish Charm**

Dublin, the vibrant capital of Ireland, is a city rich in **history, culture, and lively atmosphere**. Located on the east coast of the island, Dublin is a **blend of old and new**, where **medieval castles stand alongside modern architecture**, and where **literary greats, traditional pubs, and historic landmarks** come together to create a unique and unforgettable experience. Whether you're interested in **exploring Ireland's Viking past, enjoying its famous pub culture, or discovering world-class museums**, Dublin offers something for every traveler.

**The History and Heritage of Dublin**

Founded by the Vikings in **841 ADS**, Dublin has grown into one of Europe's most dynamic capitals. The city played a pivotal role in Ireland's **fight for independence**, and today, its historic landmarks tell the story of Ireland's **struggles, triumphs, and cultural evolution**. From the grandeur of **Dublin Castle** to the solemn history of

**Kilmainham Gaol**, Dublin is a city that brings the past to life.

## Must-See Historical Sites

**Dublin Castle** – Once the seat of British rule in Ireland, today it is a symbol of Ireland's independence. Visitors can explore the **State Apartments, medieval towers, and the Gothic Chapel Royal**.

**Kilmainham Gaol** – One of the most historically significant sites in Ireland, this former prison housed many **Irish revolutionaries, including leaders of the 1916 Easter Rising**.

**Trinity College & The Book of Kells** – Ireland's most prestigious university is home to the world-famous **Book of Kells**, a beautifully illuminated manuscript dating back to the **9th century**.

## Dublin's Lively Pub and Music Scene

No visit to Dublin is complete without experiencing its famous **pub culture**. The city is home to some of the world's most historic and atmospheric bars, where you can enjoy a **pint of Guinness, live Irish music, and friendly conversations with locals**.

**Best Pubs & Nightlife Spots**

**Temple Bar** – Dublin's most famous pub district, known for its **lively nightlife, cobbled streets, and traditional Irish music**.

**The Brazen Head** – Ireland's oldest pub, dating back to **1198**, offering great food, drinks, and live music.

**The Cobblestone** – A must-visit for lovers of **traditional Irish folk music**, with nightly live performances.

For whiskey enthusiasts, a visit to the **Jameson Distillery Bow St.** or the famous **Guinness Storehouse** is a must. At the Guinness Storehouse, you can learn about the brewing process and enjoy a **perfectly poured pint with panoramic views of the city**.

### Culture, Museums, and Literary Legacy

Dublin has a strong literary heritage, being the birthplace of **James Joyce, W.B. Yeats, Oscar Wilde, and Samuel Beckett**. The city's museums and cultural attractions offer insight into **Ireland's artistic, literary, and historical achievements.**

## Top Cultural Attractions

**The Dublin Writers Museum** – A celebration of Dublin's literary greats.

**The Little Museum of Dublin** – Showcasing **the city's history through fascinating exhibits.**

**National Museum of Ireland** – Featuring **archaeological treasures, including Viking artifacts and the famous Tara Brooch.**

For those who love theatre, a visit to the **Abbey Theatre**, founded by W.B. Yeats, is a great way to experience Dublin's **thriving performing arts scene.**

## Shopping and Dining in Dublin

Dublin offers excellent shopping, from **luxury brands to local crafts**, and a food scene that has gained international recognition.

**Where to Shop**

**Grafton Street** – Dublin's premier shopping street, featuring high-end brands, local boutiques, and **street performers**.

**George's Street Arcade** – A **Victorian-style indoor market** with unique shops selling Irish crafts, jewelry, and antiques.

**Powerscourt Centre** – A historic Georgian building converted into a **boutique shopping and dining hub**.

**Best Places to Eat**

Dublin's food scene has evolved beyond **traditional Irish stews** to include Michelin-star restaurants and modern fusion cuisine.

**Chapter One** – A Michelin-starred restaurant offering **modern Irish fine dining**.

**The Winding Stair** – A charming bookshop-turned-restaurant with **views of the River Liffey**.

**The Boxty House** – Specializing in traditional **Irish potato pancakes (boxty)** and hearty stews.

For an authentic Dublin experience, **try a full Irish breakfast**, which includes **sausages, bacon, eggs, black pudding, baked beans, and soda bread**.

### Best Time to Visit Dublin

Dublin is a **year-round destination**, but the best time to visit depends on your preferences:

**Spring (March–May)** – Mild temperatures, fewer crowds, and the famous **St. Patrick's Day celebrations**.

**Summer (June–August)** – The warmest weather and the **busiest tourist season**.

**Autumn (September–November)** – Fewer tourists and a **great time for cultural festivals**.

**Winter (December–February)** – Colder temperatures but a **magical Christmas atmosphere**.

**Tip:** Always bring **a rain jacket and layers**, as Dublin's weather can be **unpredictable**.

## Top Attractions in Dublin: Trinity College, Dublin Castle, and the Guinness Storehouse

Dublin, the lively capital of Ireland, is filled with **rich history, stunning architecture, and cultural treasures**. Among its most famous attractions are **Trinity College, Dublin Castle, and the Guinness Storehouse**—each offering a unique glimpse into the city's past and present. Whether you're fascinated by **Ireland's literary heritage, royal history, or iconic beer culture**, these must-visit landmarks provide an unforgettable experience in the heart of Dublin.

### Trinity College & The Book of Kells

Founded in **1592, Trinity College Dublin** is Ireland's most prestigious university and a key landmark in the city. With its **cobblestone courtyards, historic buildings, and intellectual legacy**, the college has been a center of learning for centuries. It is home to one of the world's most famous literary treasures—**The Book of Kells**—as well as the breathtaking **Long Room Library**.

## Top Highlights

**The Book of Kells** – A beautifully illuminated **medieval manuscript**, created by Irish monks around **800 AD**. The intricate designs and vivid colors make it one of the finest examples of early Christian art.
**The Long Room Library** – A **majestic 65-meter-long library hall** lined with **over 200,000 rare books**, including ancient texts and first editions. The high, arched ceilings and wooden bookshelves create an awe-inspiring atmosphere.
**The Brian Boru Harp** – An **iconic Irish harp**, displayed in the Long Room, which serves as the official emblem of Ireland.

## Visitor Tips

**Best Time to Visit:** Arrive early or book tickets online to avoid long queues.
**How to Get There:** Located in central Dublin, within walking distance of other major attractions.
**Tickets & Entry:** Prices start around **€18 per adult** for

entry to the **Book of Kells Exhibition and Long Room Library**.

## Dublin Castle: A Symbol of Ireland's History

Dublin Castle has been at the heart of Irish history for **over 800 years**. Originally built as a **Viking fortress** in the 10th century, it later became the **seat of British rule in Ireland** until 1922. Today, it serves as a government building and a historical attraction, offering insight into **Ireland's medieval and colonial past**.

**Top Highlights**

**State Apartments** – Lavishly decorated rooms used for **official ceremonies, banquets, and state functions**.
**The Throne Room** – A grand chamber featuring the **gilded throne of King George IV**, symbolizing British rule over Ireland.
**The Medieval Undercroft** – Hidden beneath the castle, this area reveals the **original Viking-era defenses and remains of medieval structures**.
**Dubh Linn Garden** – A tranquil space behind the castle,

once the site of **a Viking settlement** and now a peaceful public garden.

**Visitor Tips**

**Best Time to Visit:** Visit early in the day for **quieter tours and better photo opportunities**. **How to Get There:** Located in the city center, near **Temple Bar and Christ Church Cathedral**. **Tickets & Entry:** Guided tours cost around **€8-€12 per adult**, offering a deeper insight into the castle's history.

## Guinness Storehouse: The Home of Ireland's Most Famous Beer

A trip to Dublin wouldn't be complete without visiting the **Guinness Storehouse**, an attraction dedicated to **Ireland's world-famous stout**. Located in the **St. James's Gate Brewery**, where Guinness has been brewed since **1759**, this multi-story visitor experience takes guests through the **history, production, and culture of Guinness beer**.

**Top Highlights**

**The Guinness Brewing Process** – Interactive exhibits explain how Guinness is made, from **water, barley, hops, and yeast** to the final pint.
**The 9,000-Year Lease** – Arthur Guinness famously signed a **9,000-year lease** for the brewery site in 1759—an extraordinary commitment to brewing.
**Guinness Advertisements** – A fascinating look at **Guinness's iconic marketing campaigns**, including the famous **"Guinness is Good for You"** ads.
**The Gravity Bar** – The experience ends with **a complimentary pint of Guinness** at the **Gravity Bar**, which offers **stunning panoramic views of Dublin.**

**Visitor Tips**

**Best Time to Visit:** Early morning or late afternoon to avoid peak crowds.
**How to Get There:** A short walk or bus ride from **Dublin city center**.
**Tickets & Entry:** Prices start at **€22 per adult**, including a free pint of Guinness.

## Shore Excursions: Enhancing Your Cruise Experience

Shore excursions are an essential part of any cruise, offering passengers the chance to **explore new destinations, experience local cultures, and participate in exciting activities** beyond the ship. Whether you prefer **historical sightseeing, outdoor adventures, culinary experiences, or relaxing beach days**, shore excursions provide a way to make the most of your time in port. Carefully selecting and planning your excursions ensures a **memorable and hassle-free experience**.

### Types of Shore Excursions

### Historical & Cultural Tours

Perfect for travelers interested in **heritage sites, ancient ruins, and local traditions**. These excursions often include:

Guided visits to **castles, cathedrals, and UNESCO World Heritage Sites**.

Walking tours of historic **old towns and archaeological sites**.

Museum visits showcasing **local art, artifacts, and history**.

**Example:** Touring **Edinburgh Castle in Scotland**, exploring **Pompeii in Italy**, or visiting **the Acropolis in Greece**.

**Scenic & Nature Excursions**

Ideal for those who appreciate **stunning landscapes, national parks, and wildlife**. Activities may include:

Scenic drives along **coastal cliffs, fjords, or mountain ranges**.

Exploring **rainforests, waterfalls, and nature reserves**.

Wildlife watching, including **dolphins, whales, penguins, or exotic birds**.

**Example:** A **Norwegian fjord cruise**, a visit to **Alaska's glaciers**, or a **safari in South Africa**.

**Adventure & Outdoor Activities**

Designed for thrill-seekers looking for **high-energy experiences**. Popular options include:

**Zip-lining, parasailing, bungee jumping, and rock climbing.**

**Snorkeling, scuba diving, kayaking, and white-water rafting.**

**Hiking, ATV rides, and off-road safaris.**

**Example: Snorkeling in the Great Barrier Reef, zip-lining in Costa Rica, or dune bashing in Dubai.**

**Culinary & Wine Experiences**

Great for food lovers who want to explore **local flavors and culinary traditions**. These excursions may include:

**Wine and whiskey tastings** at vineyards and distilleries.

**Cooking classes** featuring traditional recipes.

**Market tours** sampling regional delicacies.

**Example: Whiskey tasting in Scotland, pasta-making in Italy, or a street food tour in Bangkok.**

**Beach & Relaxation Excursions**

Perfect for travelers looking to **unwind and enjoy the coast**. These excursions typically include:

**Private beach resorts** with loungers and water activities.

**Spa and wellness retreats** with massages and ocean views.

**Snorkeling and paddleboarding in crystal-clear waters**.

**Example: Relaxing in the Maldives, swimming in Santorini, or enjoying a beach club in the Caribbean**.

## Booking a Shore Excursion: Cruise Line vs. Independent Operators

**Booking Through the Cruise Line**

**Convenient & Secure** – The cruise line handles all arrangements.

**Guaranteed Return to Ship** – The ship won't leave without you.

**Pre-vetted Operators** – Ensures safety and quality service.

**More Expensive** – Costs can be **30-50% higher** than independent tours.

**Larger Groups** – Less personalized experiences.

**Booking with Independent Tour Operators**

**Lower Prices & Smaller Groups** – Often cheaper and more intimate.

**Unique & Off-the-Beaten-Path Options** – Customizable experiences.

**Direct Communication with Local Guides** – More personalized service.

**Risk of Missing the Ship** – Independent tours don't guarantee a return on time.

**More Planning Required** – Research and advance booking needed.

**Tip:** If booking independently, ensure your tour returns **at least two hours before departure**.

**Tips for Choosing the Best Shore Excursion**

**Consider Your Interests** – Choose excursions that align with **your travel style** (adventure, history, food, relaxation, etc.).

**Check Activity Levels** – Some excursions require **long walks, steep climbs, or water activities**—choose accordingly.

**Read Reviews** – Check **TripAdvisor, Cruise Critic, or Viator** for honest feedback from previous travelers.

**Compare Prices** – Sometimes, **local operators offer better deals** than cruise-sponsored excursions.

**Book Early** – Popular excursions **sell out quickly**, especially in high-demand ports.

**Understand Cancellation Policies** – Some tours allow refunds, while others do not.

## Packing Essentials for a Shore Excursion

**Daypack or Small Backpack** – For carrying essentials comfortably.

**Sunglasses & Hat** – Protect yourself from **sun exposure**.

**Sunscreen & Bug Spray** – Essential for **tropical or outdoor excursions**.

**Camera or Smartphone** – Capture **memorable moments**.

**Reusable Water Bottle** – Stay hydrated.

**Local Currency & Credit Card** – Some vendors **don't accept cards**.

**Printed Itinerary & Contact Info** – Just in case your phone **dies**.

**Comfortable Walking Shoes** – Essential for **city tours and hiking**.

### Can You Explore a Port Without an Excursion?

Yes! Some ports are easy to explore on your own.

**Great for Independent Exploration:**

**Barcelona, Spain** – Walk **Las Ramblas**, visit **La Sagrada Familia**, and enjoy local tapas.

**Venice, Italy** – Wander through **St. Mark's Square**, ride a **gondola**, and visit Murano's glass factories.

**Dubrovnik, Croatia** – Walk the famous **Old City Walls** and relax at a **beachfront café**.

**Best for Guided Tours:**

**Alaska** – Glacier hikes and wildlife spotting require **experienced guides**.

**Iceland** – Geothermal pools and volcano excursions need **proper transportation**.

**South America** – Some areas require **safety precautions and guided experiences**.

**Tip:** If exploring on your own, **download offline maps and research public transport options**.

## Dining & Shopping: Enhancing Your Travel and Cruise Experience

Dining and shopping are two of the most enjoyable aspects of travel, offering opportunities to **savor local cuisine, explore unique markets, and purchase souvenirs or luxury goods**. Whether you're on a **cruise, visiting a historic city, or exploring a vibrant cultural hub**, dining and shopping allow you to immerse yourself in the local lifestyle and traditions. Here's a guide to making the most of your **dining and shopping experiences**, whether on land or at sea.

## Dining: A Taste of Local and International Cuisine

Food is an essential part of travel, as it reflects a destination's **history, culture, and traditions**. Whether indulging in **street food, fine dining, or traditional home-cooked meals**, every dish tells a story.

### Onboard Cruise Dining Options

Cruise ships offer a variety of **dining experiences**, catering to all tastes and preferences:

**Main Dining Room (MDR)** – Serves multi-course meals and is included in most cruise fares.

**Buffet Restaurants** – Offer a wide selection of **international dishes, fresh seafood, and comfort food.**

**Specialty Restaurants** – Feature **steakhouses, sushi bars, Italian trattorias, and Michelin-star chef collaborations** (usually at an extra cost).

**Casual Dining & Poolside Eateries** – Great for **quick meals like burgers, pizzas, and sandwiches.**

**Room Service** – Allows passengers to enjoy **private dining in their cabin or on the balcony.**

**Dining at Local Destinations**

Exploring a destination's **local food scene** is an unforgettable part of travel.

**Street Food Markets** – Try authentic dishes like **paella in Spain, dumplings in China, or tacos in Mexico**.

**Traditional Restaurants** – Enjoy regional specialties like **haggis in Scotland, pasta in Italy, or curry in India**.

**Food & Wine Tours** – Participate in **culinary experiences, cooking classes, or wine tastings**.

**Tips for Dining Abroad**

**Try local dishes** – Step out of your comfort zone and sample authentic cuisine.
**Make reservations** – Popular restaurants fill up quickly, so book ahead.
**Check dietary options** – Many restaurants cater to vegetarian, vegan, and gluten-free diets.
**Be mindful of tipping customs** – Some countries include service charges, while others expect tips.

**Shopping: Finding the Best Deals & Unique Souvenirs**

Shopping while traveling allows you to **discover handcrafted goods, luxury brands, and unique souvenirs** that capture the essence of a destination.

**Duty-Free Shopping on Cruises**

Most cruise ships feature **duty-free shops**, where passengers can purchase tax-free goods such as:

**Luxury watches and designer jewelry** (Cartier, Rolex, Bulgari).

**Perfumes, cosmetics, and skincare products** (Dior, Chanel, Estée Lauder).

**Liquor and fine wines** – Often **cheaper than in regular stores**.

**Tip:** Duty-free items are only available **while the ship is at sea**, so check store hours.

**Shopping at Local Destinations**

Each destination has **its own unique products** that reflect its culture and craftsmanship.

**Scotland** – Whisky, cashmere scarves, and Celtic jewelry.

**Italy** – Leather goods, Murano glass, and handmade ceramics.

**Japan** – Silk kimonos, green tea, and high-quality electronics.

**Mexico** – Silver jewelry, tequila, and Mayan handicrafts.

**Best Places to Shop**

**Local Markets** – Great for **handmade crafts, artisan goods, and street food.**

**Luxury Boutiques** – Found in cities like **Paris, Milan, and Dubai,** featuring high-end fashion and accessories.

**Shopping malls & Outlets** – Offer a mix of **international brands and local retailers.**

**Tips for Smart Shopping**

**Compare prices** – Tourist areas often charge higher prices, so shop around.

**Bargain in markets** – Negotiation is expected in some cultures (e.g., Morocco, Thailand).

**Check for authenticity** – Be cautious of counterfeit goods, especially in street markets.

**Know customs regulations** – Some items, like alcohol or rare antiques, may have import restrictions.

### Budgeting for Dining & Shopping

To avoid overspending, set a clear **budget for food and shopping** during your travels.

### Setting a Budget

**Allocate funds** separately for **dining, souvenirs, and luxury items**.

**Look for meal deals** – Many restaurants offer **fixed-price lunch menus**, which can be more affordable than dinner.

**Use discount apps and coupons** – Some destinations have shopping and dining discounts for tourists.

### Credit Cards vs. Cash

**Use credit cards for major purchases**, but carry local currency for small shops and markets.

**Highlights**

**The Cavern Club Replica** – A recreation of the iconic venue where The Beatles first gained fame.

**Rare Memorabilia** – Original instruments, handwritten lyrics, and personal belongings of **John, Paul, George, and Ringo**.

**Interactive Exhibits** – Featuring audio guides narrated by **John Lennon's sister, Julia Baird**, alongside personal stories and archive footage.

**The Fab4D Experience** – A unique **3D animated show** celebrating the music of The Beatles.

**Tickets & Visitor Tips**

**Admission:** Prices start at **£19 per adult** (discounts for children and families).

**Best Time to Visit:** Arrive early to avoid crowds, especially during weekends and summer.

**Location:** Easily accessible in **Albert Dock**, near other top attractions.

## Liverpool Cathedral

Liverpool Cathedral, also known as the **Cathedral Church of Christ**, is **Britain's largest cathedral** and an architectural masterpiece. Completed in **1978**, it is a stunning example of **Gothic Revival architecture** and offers breathtaking views of the city.

### Highlights

**The Tower Experience** – Climb to the top for a **360-degree panoramic view of Liverpool** and beyond.

**The Grand Organ** – Home to one of the **largest church organs in the world**, featuring over **10,000 pipes**.

**Stained Glass Windows** – Beautifully designed windows that **tell the story of Liverpool's religious heritage**.

**Sir Giles Gilbert Scott's Design** – The renowned architect also designed London's famous **red telephone box**.

### Tickets & Visitor Tips

**Admission:** Free, but donations are welcome. Tower Experience costs **£6 per adult**.

**Best Time to Visit:** Late afternoon for **stunning sunset views from the tower**.

**Nearby Attractions:** Liverpool's **Chinatown** and St. James' Mount Gardens are a short walk away.

## Albert Dock

Albert Dock is **the heart of Liverpool's waterfront**, a historic dockland area transformed into a **lively cultural hub**. This **UNESCO World Heritage Site** is home to **museums, restaurants, shops, and picturesque waterfront views**.

### Highlights

**Merseyside Maritime Museum** – Showcasing Liverpool's **seafaring history**, including exhibits on the **Titanic and the Battle of the Atlantic**.

**Tate Liverpool** – A contemporary art gallery featuring **works by Picasso, Warhol, and modern British artists**.

**The Pumphouse Pub** – A historic dockside pub offering **traditional British ales and pub fare**.

**Boat Tours & Cruises** – Enjoy a **ferry ride on the River Mersey**, offering a unique perspective of the city's skyline.

**Tickets & Visitor Tips**

**Admission:** Free entry to the dock; some museums have **separate ticket prices**.

**Best Time to Visit:** Evenings are particularly charming with **dockside lights reflecting on the water**.

**Nearby Attractions:** Close to **Liverpool One shopping center** and The Beatles Story Museum.

## Shore Excursions in Liverpool

Liverpool is a **fantastic cruise stop**, offering diverse shore excursions that explore **its music heritage, maritime history, and scenic surroundings**.

### City Walking & Sightseeing Tours

**The Royal Liver Building & Three Graces** – A guided tour of Liverpool's most iconic waterfront buildings.

**St. George's Hall & Walker Art Gallery** – Discover Liverpool's grand **Victorian architecture and fine art collections**.

**Liverpool Football Club (Anfield Stadium Tour)** – Perfect for football fans to explore the **home of Liverpool FC**.

**Beatles-Themed Excursions**

**Magical Mystery Tour** – A guided bus tour of famous Beatles locations, including **Penny Lane, Strawberry Field, and the childhood homes of John Lennon and Paul McCartney**.

**The Cavern Club Experience** – Visit the legendary **live music venue** where The Beatles first gained fame.

**Liverpool Beatles Museum** – Featuring over **1,000 rare Beatles artifacts**, from guitars to concert outfits.

**River Mersey Cruise**

A **50-minute scenic boat ride** along the River Mersey, offering **panoramic views of the Liverpool skyline**.

Learn about the city's **shipping and trading past** with a **live audio guide**.

**Day Trips from Liverpool**

**Chester** – A beautiful medieval city with **Roman walls, Tudor-style architecture, and charming shops** (45 minutes away).

**The Lake District** – One of England's most breathtaking natural landscapes, perfect for **hiking and boat cruises** (1.5 hours away).

**Tip:** Book shore excursions in advance, especially for **Beatles-related tours**, as they fill up quickly!

## Dining & Shopping in Liverpool

**Best Places to Eat in Liverpool**

Liverpool's food scene offers everything from **classic British dishes to global cuisine**.

**Traditional British Food**

**The London Carriage Works** – A stylish restaurant serving **modern British cuisine with locally sourced ingredients**.

**The Philharmonic Dining Rooms** – A historic Victorian pub offering **classic fish & chips, steak pies, and Sunday roasts**.

**International Cuisine**

**Mowgli Street Food** – A popular Indian street food restaurant known for **tiffin boxes and spiced curries**.

**Lunya** – A Spanish tapas bar offering **authentic Catalan dishes**.

**Casual Dining & Cafés**

**Bold Street Coffee** – Known for **artisan coffee and freshly baked pastries**.

**The Baltic Market** – A vibrant **indoor food hall** with **street food vendors and craft beers**.

**Tip:** Try **Scouse**, Liverpool's signature dish—a hearty **stew made with beef, potatoes, and vegetables**.

## Where to Shop in Liverpool

Liverpool is a **shopper's paradise**, offering **high-end brands, local boutiques, and Beatles memorabilia**.

### Liverpool one

A massive **outdoor shopping complex** with over **170 stores**, including **John Lewis, Apple, and Michael Kors**.

### Bold Street

The go-to place for **independent boutiques, vintage shops, and unique souvenirs**.

Great for **art, books, and handmade crafts**.

### Metquarter & Cavern Walks

High-end shopping destinations with **luxury brands and designer fashion**.

### Best Places for Beatles Memorabilia

**The Beatles Shop** (near The Cavern Club) – Selling **rare vinyl, posters, and limited-edition collectibles**.

**Albert Dock Gift Shops** – Featuring **Liverpool-themed souvenirs and music-related merchandise**.

**Tip:** St. John's Market is a great spot for **local products and budget-friendly finds**.

# GLASGOW

## Attraction: Kelvingrove Art Gallery, Glasgow Cathedral, George Square

Glasgow, Scotland's largest city, is a **cultural powerhouse**, renowned for its **rich history, stunning architecture, and vibrant arts scene**. Once an industrial hub, Glasgow has transformed into a **modern metropolis**, known for its **world-class museums, thriving music scene, and warm Scottish hospitality**. Whether you're a history enthusiast, an art lover, or a foodie, Glasgow offers a **dynamic mix of experiences** for all visitors.

**Top Attractions in Glasgow**

Glasgow is home to **fascinating museums, grand cathedrals, and historic landmarks**, with some of its most famous attractions being **Kelvingrove Art Gallery, Glasgow Cathedral, and George Square**.

**Kelvingrove Art Gallery & Museum**

Kelvingrove Art Gallery & Museum is one of **Scotland's most visited attractions**, boasting an extensive collection of **art, history, and natural exhibits**. Opened in **1901**, the museum houses over **8,000 objects**, covering everything from **Renaissance paintings to ancient Egyptian artifacts**.

**Highlights**

**Salvador Dalí's "Christ of Saint John of the Cross"** – One of the museum's most famous artworks.

**The Spitfire Plane** – A real **World War II fighter aircraft**, suspended from the ceiling.

**Natural History Exhibits** – Showcasing **dinosaur fossils, taxidermy animals, and minerals**.

**The Charles Rennie Mackintosh Gallery** – Dedicated to Glasgow's most famous **architect and designer**.

**Tickets & Visitor Tips**

**Admission:** Free entry. Donations are welcome.

**Best Time to Visit:** Early morning or late afternoon to avoid crowds.

**Nearby Attractions:** Located in **Kelvingrove Park**, near **Glasgow University**.

## Glasgow Cathedral

Dating back to **the 12th century**, Glasgow Cathedral is a stunning example of **medieval Gothic architecture**. It is the **oldest building in Glasgow** and one of the few Scottish cathedrals to survive the **Protestant Reformation intact**.

### Highlights

**The Blackadder Aisle** – A beautifully decorated chapel named after **Archbishop Blackadder**.

**The Crypt of St. Mungo** – The **final resting place of Glasgow's patron saint**, St. Mungo.

**Spectacular Stained-Glass Windows** – One of the **finest collections in the UK**.

**The Necropolis** – A Victorian cemetery behind the cathedral, offering **breathtaking city views**.

### Tickets & Visitor Tips

**Admission:** Free entry, but donations are encouraged.

**Best Time to Visit:** Visit in the morning for a **peaceful experience**.

**Nearby Attractions:** The **Provand's Lordship**, Glasgow's **oldest surviving house** (built in 1471).

### George Square

Located in the **heart of Glasgow**, George Square is the city's **main public square**, surrounded by **impressive Victorian architecture** and **historic monuments**.

### Highlights

**Statues & Monuments** – Features **statues of Sir Walter Scott, Queen Victoria, and Robert Burns**.

**Glasgow City Chambers** – An architectural masterpiece and home to **Glasgow's city government**.

**Seasonal Events** – Hosts **Christmas markets, summer festivals, and political gatherings**.

### Tickets & Visitor Tips

**Admission:** Free entry.

**Best Time to Visit:** Visit in the evening for a **beautifully lit-up atmosphere**.

**Nearby Attractions: Buchanan Street**, Glasgow's premier shopping street.

## Shore Excursions in Glasgow

For cruise passengers docking at **Greenock Port**, Glasgow is a **short 45-minute journey** away and offers a variety of **shore excursions**.

**Historic & Cultural Tours**

**Stirling Castle** – One of Scotland's most significant castles, known for its **royal connections and military history**.

**The Wallace Monument** – A tribute to **William Wallace ("Braveheart")**, offering **stunning views of the Scottish countryside**.

**Riverside Museum & Tall Ship** – Glasgow's interactive transport museum featuring **vintage cars, steam trains, and a 19th-century sailing ship**.

### Scenic Countryside Excursions

**Loch Lomond & The Trossachs National Park** – A perfect escape to **Scotland's most famous loch**, featuring **boat cruises and scenic trails**.

**The West Highland Way** – A guided tour through **rolling hills, castles, and picturesque villages**.

**The Whisky Trail** – Visit **Glengoyne or Auchentoshan distilleries** for a **traditional whisky-tasting experience**.

### Self-Guided City Tours

**Explore Glasgow's Street Art** – The **Glasgow Mural Trail** features stunning urban murals across the city.

**The Merchant City Walk** – A historic district filled with **independent boutiques, trendy cafés, and architectural gems**.

**Tip:** Most tours last **4-6 hours**, allowing cruise passengers enough time to explore before returning to Greenock Port.

## Dining & Shopping in Glasgow

Glasgow is a **food lover's paradise**, offering a mix of **traditional Scottish dishes, international flavors, and award-winning restaurants**. The city also boasts **fantastic shopping districts**, from luxury brands to quirky vintage stores.

**Best Places to Eat in Glasgow**

**Traditional Scottish Cuisine**

**The Ubiquitous Chip** – A legendary restaurant serving **modern Scottish cuisine**. Try the **haggis, venison, and cranachan dessert**.

**Stravaigin** – Famous for **locally sourced seafood, Highland beef, and creative Scottish dishes**.

**Seafood & International Dining**

**Gamba** – One of Glasgow's best **seafood restaurants**, known for its **fresh oysters and langoustines**.

**Paesano Pizza** – A must-visit for **authentic Neapolitan-style pizza**.

**Casual & Vegan-Friendly**

**Mono Café Bar** – A vegan eatery with a great selection of **plant-based Scottish comfort food**.

**The Hanoi Bike Shop** – A cozy **Vietnamese restaurant** serving delicious **pho and banh mi**.

**Tip:** Don't leave Glasgow without trying **Scottish shortbread and deep-fried Mars bars!**

**Where to Shop in Glasgow**

Glasgow is known as **Scotland's shopping capital**, featuring **luxury brands, independent boutiques, and vibrant markets**.

**High-End & Designer Shopping**

**Buchanan Street** – Glasgow's **main shopping district**, home to **Harvey Nichols, House of Fraser, and high-street brands**.

**Princes Square** – A stylish shopping center with **boutiques, jewelry stores, and designer outlets**.

**Independent & Vintage Shops**

**Ashton Lane & West End** – Ideal for **quirky fashion, second-hand books, and vinyl records**.

**The Hidden Lane** – A creative shopping area filled with **local artisans, handmade crafts, and bespoke jewelry**.

**Souvenirs & Local Specialties**

**House of Scotland** – The perfect place to buy **kilts, cashmere scarves, and Celtic jewelry**.

**The Good Spirits Co.** – Specializing in **Scottish whisky and craft gin**.

**Tip:** If you're looking for **authentic Scottish souvenirs**, opt for **Harris Tweed bags, handmade pottery, or a bottle of aged Scotch whisky**.

# BELFAST

## Belfast: A City of History, Culture, and Resilience

Belfast, the capital of **Northern Ireland**, is a city that beautifully blends its **rich history, cultural vibrancy, and modern transformation**. Once known for its **shipbuilding industry and political conflicts**, Belfast has evolved into a **dynamic destination** filled with **world-class attractions, thriving arts, and a buzzing food scene**. Whether you're drawn to its **Titanic heritage, stunning landscapes, or lively atmosphere**, Belfast offers an **unforgettable experience** for all visitors.

### A City with a Rich History

Belfast's history dates back centuries, but it became a major industrial powerhouse during the **19th and early 20th centuries**, particularly in **shipbuilding, linen production, and engineering**. The city's **Harland & Wolff shipyard** famously built the **RMS Titanic**, one of the most luxurious and tragic ships in maritime history.

During the late **20th century**, Belfast was heavily affected by "The Troubles"—a period of **sectarian conflict between Nationalists and Unionists**. Today, the city has emerged as a **symbol of peace and regeneration**, with landmarks like the **Peace Walls and murals** serving as a reminder of its past while celebrating progress and unity.

### Top Attractions in Belfast

**Titanic Belfast**

Belfast's most famous attraction, **Titanic Belfast**, is a world-class museum dedicated to the history of the **Titanic and the city's shipbuilding legacy**. Located on the site where the ship was built, the museum features **interactive exhibits, original artifacts, and a full-scale replica of the Titanic's grand staircase**.

**Highlights:**

Immersive galleries detailing the **Titanic's construction, voyage, and tragic sinking**.

The **Shipyard Ride**, which recreates the experience of working at Harland & Wolff.

The **Titanic Film Archive** and real-life survivor stories.

**Tip:** Book tickets in advance to avoid long queues, especially during peak seasons.

### Giant's Causeway

A **UNESCO World Heritage Site**, the **Giant's Causeway** is one of Northern Ireland's most breathtaking natural wonders. This geological marvel consists of **40,000 hexagonal basalt columns**, formed by volcanic activity over **60 million years ago**.

**Highlights:**

The **legend of Finn McCool**, an Irish giant who is said to have created the causeway.

Stunning coastal views and **photography opportunities**.

Well-marked trails suitable for both **casual walkers and hikers**.

**Tip:** Arrive early in the morning or late in the afternoon to **avoid crowds**.

**Belfast Castle**

Perched on **Cave Hill**, Belfast Castle offers **spectacular views over the city and Belfast Lough**. Built in **1870**, the castle features **beautiful gardens, historical exhibits, and walking trails** leading up to **McArt's Fort**, a scenic viewpoint.

**Highlights:**

The **legend of the Belfast Castle Cat**, which is said to bring good luck to the castle.

**Traditional afternoon tea in the castle's restaurant.**

The **Cave Hill Country Park**, offering **nature walks and panoramic views**.

**Tip:** Wear comfortable walking shoes if you plan to explore the **hiking trails**.

## Cultural & Political Landmarks

**Belfast Murals & Peace Walls**

The **political murals of Belfast** depict the city's history, from **The Troubles to modern peace efforts**. Many murals highlight **key events, political figures, and messages of reconciliation**.

**Tip:** Take a **Black Taxi Tour** for a guided experience with a local expert who can explain the significance of the murals.

## Dining & Shopping in Belfast

### Best Places to Eat

Belfast's food scene has seen **a culinary renaissance**, offering a mix of **traditional Irish dishes, fresh seafood, and modern fine dining**.

**Mourne Seafood Bar** – Famous for **fresh oysters, mussels, and locally caught fish**.

**OX Belfast** – A Michelin-starred restaurant serving **modern Irish cuisine**.

**The Crown Liquor Saloon** – A historic pub known for **its Victorian interior and excellent Irish stew**.

**Tip:** Try an **Ulster Fry**, a traditional Irish breakfast with **sausages, bacon, eggs, soda bread, and black pudding**.

## Where to Shop

Belfast offers a great shopping experience, from **high-street brands to independent boutiques**.

**Victoria Square** – Belfast's **top shopping center**, home to **international brands and luxury stores**.

**St. George's Market** – A **historic market offering fresh produce, crafts, antiques, and handmade souvenirs**.

**Avoca Belfast** – A boutique known for **Irish fashion, homeware, and artisanal products**.

### Shore Excursions from Belfast

For cruise passengers, Belfast is an excellent base for exploring **Northern Ireland's top attractions**.

**Day Trips & Excursions**

**Giant's Causeway & Carrick-a-Rede Rope Bridge** – A **scenic coastal drive** with dramatic landscapes.

**Game of Thrones Filming Locations** – Visit **Castle Ward (Winterfell) and the Dark Hedges**.

**The Gobbins Cliff Path** – A thrilling **cliffside walkway with tunnels, bridges, and sea caves**.

### Best Time to Visit Belfast

The best time to visit Belfast is **between April and September**, when the weather is **mild and ideal for outdoor exploration**. However, if you prefer **fewer crowds**, visiting in **autumn or winter** can provide a **more relaxed experience**, especially at major attractions.

**Tip:** Always carry a **rain jacket**, as Belfast's weather can be **unpredictable**.

## Top Attractions in Belfast: Titanic Belfast, Giant's Causeway, and Belfast Castle

Belfast, the capital of **Northern Ireland**, is a city filled with **rich history, stunning landscapes, and cultural landmarks**. Among its most famous attractions are **Titanic Belfast, the Giant's Causeway, and Belfast Castle**—each offering a **unique glimpse into the city's past, natural wonders, and architectural beauty**. Whether you're fascinated by the **story of the Titanic, the geological marvels of the Causeway, or the charm of a**

**historic castle**, these must-visit sites provide an unforgettable experience.

### Titanic Belfast: The Story of a Legendary Ship

Titanic Belfast is **the world's largest Titanic Museum**, located at the exact site where the iconic **RMS Titanic** was built in **1912** by Harland & Wolff shipyard. Opened in **2012**, this state-of-the-art museum offers an **immersive and interactive experience** that takes visitors through the entire journey of the Titanic—from its **construction and maiden voyage to its tragic sinking**.

### Highlights of Titanic Belfast

**Nine Interactive Galleries** – Explore the ship's history through exhibits covering **Belfast's shipbuilding industry, Titanic's design, luxurious interiors, and final hours**.

**The Shipyard Ride** – A thrilling **virtual tour of Harland & Wolff's shipyard**, where visitors experience what it was like to build the Titanic.

**Replica Grand Staircase** – A stunning **full-scale recreation of the Titanic's first-class staircase**, perfect for photos.

**Underwater Exploration Theatre** – View **deep-sea footage of Titanic's wreck site**, captured by oceanographer **Dr. Robert Ballard**.

**Tickets & Visitor Tips**

**Admission:** Prices start at **£24 per adult**. Booking online is recommended.

**Best Time to Visit:** Arrive **early morning or late afternoon** to avoid crowds.

**Nearby Attractions:** Visit the **SS Nomadic**, the last remaining White Star Line ship, located next to the museum.

**Giant's Causeway: A Natural Wonder of Northern Ireland**

The **Giant's Causeway** is one of Northern Ireland's most famous landmarks and a **UNESCO World Heritage Site**. Formed over **60 million years ago** by volcanic activity, this site consists of **40,000 interlocking hexagonal basalt columns** stretching along the coast.

**Highlights of Giant's Causeway**

**The Legend of Finn McCool** – According to Irish mythology, the Causeway was built by the giant **Finn McCool** as a bridge to Scotland.

**The Grand Causeway** – The most famous **basalt rock formation**, where visitors can walk across the hexagonal stones.

**The Wishing Chair** – A naturally formed **rock seat** believed to bring **good luck**.

**Clifftop Trails** – Several hiking paths, including the **Red Trail for panoramic views and the Blue Trail for a coastal walk**.

**Tickets & Visitor Tips**

**Admission:** The **Causeway itself is free**, but entry to the **Visitor Centre costs £13 per adult**.

**Best Time to Visit: Early morning or late evening** for fewer crowds and stunning sunset views.

*British Isles cruise guide*

**Nearby Attractions: Carrick-a-Rede Rope Bridge**, a thrilling **rope bridge suspended over the Atlantic Ocean**.

## Belfast Castle: A Fairytale Landmark with Stunning Views

Belfast Castle, perched on **Cave Hill**, offers **breathtaking panoramic views of Belfast and Belfast Lough**. Originally built in the **12th century**, the castle was later reconstructed in **1870** in the **Scottish Baronial style**.

### Highlights of Belfast Castle

**The Castle Gardens** – Beautifully manicured **floral gardens** with stunning city views.

**The Belfast Cat Legend** – Local folklore says that **good fortune** will come to those who spot the **stone cat sculptures hidden around the castle grounds**.

**The Castle Restaurant** – Enjoy **traditional afternoon tea** or a fine dining experience with **panoramic views**.

**Cave Hill Trails** – Hiking paths leading to **McArt's Fort**, a viewpoint overlooking **Belfast and the Mourne Mountains**.

**Tickets & Visitor Tips**

**Admission:** Free entry.

**Best Time to Visit: Spring and summer** for the best weather and **blooming gardens**.

**Nearby Attractions: Belfast Zoo**, located close to the castle, is a great stop for families.

## Shore Excursions: Making the Most of Your Time in Port

Shore excursions are one of the most exciting aspects of a cruise, offering travelers the opportunity to **explore new destinations, experience local cultures, and participate in unique activities** beyond the ship. Whether you're drawn to **historical sites, outdoor adventures, cultural experiences, or simply relaxing on a scenic tour**, shore excursions enhance your journey by allowing you to discover the best of each port.

Planning and selecting the right shore excursion can make a **significant difference** in your cruise experience, ensuring you maximize your time while enjoying memorable activities.

## Types of Shore Excursions

### Historical & Cultural Tours

For history lovers and cultural enthusiasts, these excursions focus on **landmarks, ancient ruins, castles, and museums**.

**Guided city tours** visiting UNESCO World Heritage sites, cathedrals, and historic districts.

**Museum visits** showcasing artifacts, art, and regional history.

**Palace and castle explorations**, offering insight into royal heritage and architectural grandeur.

**Example:** A guided tour of **Edinburgh Castle in Scotland, the Colosseum in Rome, or the Acropolis in Greece.**

### Scenic & Nature Excursions

Ideal for those who love **breathtaking landscapes, national parks, and wildlife encounters**.

**Coastal and countryside drives** showcasing dramatic landscapes.

**Wildlife tours** featuring dolphins, whales, or exotic birds.

**Eco-tours** exploring rainforests, volcanic craters, or mountain trails.

**Example:** Visiting the **Giant's Causeway in Northern Ireland**, exploring **Alaska's glaciers**, or taking a **Norwegian fjord cruise**.

**Adventure & Outdoor Activities**

Perfect for thrill-seekers looking for **exciting, hands-on experiences**.

**Snorkeling, scuba diving, or kayaking** in crystal-clear waters.

**Zip-lining, rock climbing, or off-road ATV tours.**

**Hiking, white-water rafting, or paragliding.**

**Example: Zip-lining in Costa Rica, snorkeling in the Great Barrier Reef, or dune bashing in Dubai.**

**Food & Wine Experiences**

A must for food lovers who want to **sample local cuisine and beverages**.

**Cooking classes** led by local chefs.

**Wine and whiskey tastings** at famous vineyards and distilleries.

**Market and street food tours**, sampling authentic regional delicacies.

**Example: Whiskey tasting in Scotland, pasta-making in Italy, or tapas tours in Barcelona.**

**Beach & Relaxation Excursions**

Ideal for travelers looking to **unwind and enjoy the seaside**.

**Exclusive beach resorts** with loungers and tropical cocktails.

**Spa and wellness experiences** with ocean views.

## Packing Essentials for a Shore Excursion

**Daypack or Small Bag** – To carry your essentials.**Sunglasses & Hat** – Protection from **sun exposure.**

**Sunscreen & Bug Spray** – Crucial for **beach and jungle excursions.**

**Camera or Smartphone** – Capture memories. **Reusable Water Bottle** – Stay hydrated. **Local Currency & Credit Card** – Some places **don't accept cards.**

**Printed Itinerary & Emergency Contact Info** – Just in case **your phone dies.**

**Comfortable Walking Shoes** – Essential for **city tours and hiking.**

## Exploring Ports Without an Excursion

Yes! In some ports, **self-guided exploration** is just as rewarding.

**Great for Independent Exploration:**

**Barcelona, Spain** – Walk **Las Ramblas**, visit **La Sagrada Familia,** and explore local tapas bars.

**Venice, Italy** – Wander through **St. Mark's Square**, ride a gondola, and visit Murano's glass factories.

**Dubrovnik, Croatia** – Walk the **Old City Walls** and relax at a **beachfront café**.

**Best for Guided Tours:**

**Alaska** – Glacier hikes and wildlife spotting require **experienced guides**.

**Iceland** – Geothermal pools and volcano excursions need **proper transportation**.

**South America** – Some areas require **safety precautions and guided experiences**.

**Tip:** If exploring independently, **download offline maps** and research public transport options.

## Dining & Shopping: Enhancing Your Travel Experience

Dining and shopping are two of the most enjoyable aspects of travel, allowing visitors to **immerse themselves in local culture, discover unique flavors, and bring home memorable souvenirs**. Whether exploring a **historic European city, a tropical island, or a modern metropolis**, sampling regional cuisine and browsing local markets add depth to any journey. Understanding **where to eat, what to try, and where to shop** ensures a rewarding and enriching experience.

### Dining: A Taste of Local and International Cuisine

Food plays a **central role in travel**, offering insight into a region's **history, agriculture, and traditions**. From street food stalls to Michelin-starred restaurants, there's always something new to try.

### Traditional Cuisine & Regional Specialties

Each destination boasts **signature dishes** that reflect its culture:

**Italy:** Fresh **pasta, Neapolitan pizza, and gelato**.

**France: Croissants, escargots, coq au vin, and crème brûlée**.

**Japan: Sushi, ramen, and matcha-flavored desserts**.

**Mexico: Tacos, tamales, and churros**.

**Thailand: Pad Thai, green curry, and mango sticky rice.**

**Scotland: Haggis, black pudding, and shortbread biscuits.**

Trying these dishes not only **excites the taste buds** but also provides a deeper appreciation of **local customs and ingredients.**

**Best Places to Dine**

There are various ways to experience **authentic local food**:

**Street Food Markets** – Ideal for casual, budget-friendly eats (e.g., Bangkok's floating markets, London's Borough Market).

**Family-Run Restaurants** – Offer home-cooked, traditional meals (e.g., trattorias in Italy, tascas in Portugal).

**Fine Dining & Michelin-Starred Restaurants** – Perfect for **a luxury dining experience with innovative cuisine.**

**Food & Wine Tours** – Great for sampling **regional specialties and learning about food culture**.

**Cooking Classes** – Hands-on way to **learn how to prepare traditional dishes**.

**Dining Tips for Travelers**

**Make Reservations in Advance** – Popular restaurants fill up quickly.

**Check Local Dining Customs** – Some cultures **eat late (Spain), use chopsticks (Japan), or expect tipping (USA)**.

**Be Adventurous** – Try **local delicacies** (e.g., escargots in France, ceviche in Peru, or kimchi in Korea).

**Allergies & Dietary Preferences** – Research vegetarian, gluten-free, or halal options before dining.

## Shopping: Finding the Best Deals & Unique Souvenirs

Shopping while traveling offers the chance to **buy high-quality, one-of-a-kind items** that reflect a destination's **craftsmanship and culture**.

## Best Shopping Destinations

**Luxury Shopping:** Paris (Champs-Élysées), Milan (Via Montenapoleone), New York (5th Avenue).

**Local Markets:** Marrakech (souks), Istanbul (Grand Bazaar), Bangkok (Chatuchak Market).

**Handmade Crafts:** Peru (alpaca wool), India (silk saris), Scotland (cashmere scarves).

**Duty-Free Shopping:** Airports and cruise ports for **tax-free luxury goods**.

## Popular Souvenirs by Region

**Japan:** Hand-painted ceramics, washi paper, and green tea.

**Italy:** Handmade leather goods, Murano glass, and Limoncello.

**Mexico:** Handwoven textiles, tequila, and silver jewelry.

**Ireland:** Claddagh rings, wool sweaters, and whiskey.

**France:** Perfume, wine, and artisanal cheese.

**Shopping Tips for Travelers**

**Compare Prices** – Tourist areas may overcharge; shop around for better deals.
**Negotiate When Appropriate** – Haggling is expected in markets in **Morocco, Egypt, and Southeast Asia**.
**Check Customs Regulations** – Some items (alcohol, ivory, rare antiques) may be restricted.
**Bring a Reusable Bag** – Many countries **charge for plastic bags**.

### Dining & Shopping: A Memorable Part of Travel

By exploring **local cuisine and shopping markets**, travelers **experience a destination's culture firsthand**. Whether enjoying a **traditional meal**, finding a **one-of-a-kind souvenir**, or indulging in a **luxury shopping spree**, dining and shopping bring **excitement and authenticity** to any trip.

By **planning ahead, budgeting wisely, and being open to new experiences**, you'll create **lasting travel memories** through the flavors and treasures of the world.

# CORK

## Cork (Cobh): Ireland's Historic and Cultural Gem

Cork, often referred to as **Ireland's "Rebel City"**, is a vibrant and historic destination known for its **rich maritime history, lively culture, and stunning natural scenery**. Located in the south of Ireland, it is the country's **second-largest city** and a gateway to many of **Ireland's most famous attractions**. The nearby town of **Cobh (pronounced "Cove")** is particularly significant as it was the **last port of call for the Titanic in 1912** and a key departure point for millions of Irish emigrants. Whether you're exploring its **castles, distilleries, or scenic coastlines**, Cork and Cobh offer a **memorable Irish experience**.

### A City of History & Heritage

Cork's history dates back to the **6th century**, when it was founded as a **monastic settlement**. Over time, it grew into a **major seaport and trading hub**, playing a key role in Ireland's economic and political history. The city is known for its **rebellious spirit**, having been at the center of many conflicts, including the Irish War of Independence.

Cobh, previously called **Queenstown**, holds a special place in Ireland's maritime history. It was a **major emigration port**, where millions of Irish people boarded ships to **America, Canada, and Australia** during the **Great Famine (1845–1852)**. Today, it is home to **Titanic-related sites, colorful waterfront buildings, and beautiful cathedrals**.

## Top Attractions in Cork & Cobh

### Blarney Castle & The Blarney Stone

One of Ireland's most famous landmarks, **Blarney Castle** attracts visitors from around the world. Built in the **15th century**, it is famous for the **Blarney Stone**, which, according to legend, grants the "gift of eloquence" to those who kiss it.

**Highlights:**

**Climb the castle's ancient stone steps** for breathtaking views.

**Kiss the Blarney Stone**, located at the top of the castle.

**Explore the surrounding gardens**, including the mystical **Poison Garden**.

**Tip:** Arrive early to avoid long lines for the Blarney Stone.

**Cork City**

Cork is a lively city filled with **historic sites, charming streets, and excellent restaurants**.

**The English Market** – One of Europe's **oldest food markets**, dating back to **1788**, offering **local cheeses, meats, and artisanal products**.

**Shandon Bells at St. Anne's Church** – Climb to the top for **panoramic views of the city**.

**Fitzgerald Park & Cork Public Museum** – A peaceful escape with **beautiful gardens and historical exhibits**.

**Cobh: Titanic & Emigration History**

Cobh is best known as the **final port of call for the Titanic** before its doomed voyage.

**Titanic Experience Cobh** – A **museum located in the original White Star Line ticket office**, where visitors can learn about passengers who boarded the Titanic in Cobh.

**Cobh Heritage Centre** – Tells the story of **Irish emigration**, including those who left during the famine.

**St. Colman's Cathedral** – A stunning **neo-Gothic cathedral** with breathtaking views over Cobh's harbor.

**Tip:** Take a **harbor boat tour** for the best views of Cobh's colorful waterfront.

### Shore Excursions from Cork & Cobh

For cruise passengers docking in **Cobh**, there are many fantastic shore excursions available:

**Blarney Castle & Woollen Mills** – A half-day tour combining **history, scenic beauty, and shopping**.

**Jameson Distillery Midleton** – A tour of **Ireland's oldest whiskey distillery**, with tastings of **world-famous Jameson whiskey**.

**Kinsale & The Wild Atlantic Way** – Visit the picturesque coastal town of **Kinsale**, known for **seafood and historic forts**.

### Dining & Shopping in Cork & Cobh

**Where to Eat**

Cork is known as Ireland's **food capital**, offering everything from traditional Irish dishes to gourmet dining.

**Fishy Fishy Café (Kinsale)** – Famous for **fresh seafood and locally sourced ingredients**.

**The Farmgate Café (English Market)** – A great place to try **traditional Irish stew and soda bread**.

**Jacques Restaurant (Cork City)** – A cozy spot offering **farm-to-table Irish cuisine**.

**Shopping in Cork**

**Blarney Woollen Mills** – The best place to buy **authentic Irish wool sweaters, scarves, and linens**.

**Patrick Street (Cork City)** – The main shopping street, featuring **Irish boutiques, jewelry stores, and bookstores**.

**Cobh Craft Shops** – Great for picking up **Titanic-themed souvenirs, local art, and handcrafted gifts**.

### Best Time to Visit Cork & Cobh

The best time to visit is **between May and September**, when the weather is **mild and ideal for outdoor exploration**.

**Spring (March–May):** Fewer crowds and blooming gardens.

**Summer (June–August):** The warmest weather and festival season.

**Autumn (September–October):** A great time for **whiskey tastings and scenic drives**.

**Tip:** Always carry a **rain jacket**, as Irish weather can be unpredictable!

## Top Attractions in Cork: Blarney Castle, Cork City, and Jameson Distillery

Cork, located in **southern Ireland**, is a region rich in **history, culture, and scenic beauty**. It is home to some of Ireland's most famous attractions, including the legendary **Blarney Castle, the bustling streets of Cork City, and the historic Jameson Distillery in Midleton**. Whether you're seeking **ancient castles, charming markets, or a taste of Ireland's finest whiskey**, Cork offers something for every traveler.

### Blarney Castle: A Legendary Landmark

Blarney Castle is one of **Ireland's most famous and visited castles**, known for the **Blarney Stone**, which is said to grant the "gift of eloquence" to those who kiss it. Built in **1446** by the **McCarthy clan**, the castle is surrounded by **stunning gardens, mystical rock formations, and secret tunnels**.

### Highlights of Blarney Castle

**The Blarney Stone** – Visitors climb to the **top of the castle tower** to kiss the stone, following an age-old tradition believed to give the gift of persuasive speech.

**The Castle Ruins** – Explore the **medieval towers, dungeons, and narrow staircases**, which tell stories of the castle's history.

**The Poison Garden** – A fascinating **collection of toxic plants**, including **wolfsbane, nightshade, and hemlock**, once used in medieval medicine.

**Blarney House & Gardens** – A **19th-century mansion** set amidst **beautifully landscaped gardens and walking trails**.

**Tickets & Visitor Tips**

**Admission:** Prices start at **€20 per adult**, with discounts for children and families.

**Best Time to Visit:** Arrive **early in the morning** to avoid crowds, especially during peak seasons.

**Nearby Attractions: Blarney Woollen Mills**, the perfect place to shop for **Irish woolens, crafts, and souvenirs**.

## Cork City: The Heart of Ireland's Cultural Scene

Cork City is a lively and historic destination known for its **colorful streets, charming cafés, and a strong sense of Irish identity**. Often called **Ireland's "real capital"** by locals, the city is packed with **historic landmarks, bustling markets, and cultural attractions**.

### Highlights of Cork City

**The English Market** – One of Europe's **oldest covered markets**, dating back to **1788**, where visitors can sample **local cheeses, meats, and artisan foods**.

**Shandon Bells & St. Anne's Church** – A landmark church where visitors can **ring the famous bells** and enjoy **panoramic views of the city**.

**Fitzgerald Park & Cork Public Museum** – A peaceful riverside park with **lush gardens, art installations, and historical exhibits**.

**University College Cork (UCC)** – A stunning campus with **Gothic-style buildings, a historic observatory, and the beautiful Honan Chapel**.

**Tickets & Visitor Tips**

**Best Time to Visit: Spring and summer** are ideal for exploring Cork's **outdoor attractions and vibrant markets.**

**Nearby Attractions:** Cork is a great base for **day trips to Kinsale, Cobh, and the scenic Wild Atlantic Way.**

### Jameson Distillery Midleton: The Spirit of Ireland

Located in **Midleton, just outside Cork City**, the **Jameson Distillery** is a must-visit for whiskey lovers and history enthusiasts. The distillery, established in **1825**, is where **Jameson Irish Whiskey is made today**, using a blend of **malted and unmalted barley, triple-distilled for smoothness.**

**Highlights of Jameson Distillery Midleton**

**Guided Distillery Tour** – Learn about the **whiskey-making process**, from **malting and mashing to distillation and aging.**

**Whiskey Tasting Experience** – Compare **Jameson's smooth flavors** with Scotch and American whiskeys.

**The World's Largest Pot Still** – See the **giant copper pot still**, used for distillation, which holds **143,872 liters** of liquid.

**The Master Distiller's Cottage** – A beautifully preserved **historic building** where past distillers lived.

Tickets & Visitor Tips

**Admission:** Tours start at **€30 per adult**, including a **complimentary whiskey tasting**.

**Best Time to Visit:** Early in the day for a **quieter experience**.

**Nearby Attractions: Ballymaloe House**, a famous country estate known for its **farm-to-table dining and cookery school**.

## Shore Excursions: Enhancing Your Cruise Experience

Shore excursions are an essential part of any cruise, offering passengers the opportunity to **explore destinations, experience local cultures, and take part in exciting activities** beyond the ship. Whether you're interested in **historical sites, scenic landscapes, adventure sports, or culinary delights**, a well-planned shore excursion can transform your port stop into an unforgettable experience.

With limited time in each destination, choosing the **right shore excursion** ensures that you make the most of your visit while balancing **comfort, adventure, and cultural immersion**.

## Types of Shore Excursions

Cruise lines and independent tour operators offer a variety of shore excursions, catering to different interests and activity levels.

### Historical & Cultural Tours

Explore **ancient ruins, castles, and historic districts** with knowledgeable guides.

Visit **UNESCO World Heritage Sites** and learn about local traditions.

Take part in **museum tours, palace visits, and guided city walks**.

**Example:** Touring **Edinburgh Castle in Scotland**, visiting the **Acropolis in Greece**, or walking the **medieval walls of Dubrovnik**.

**Scenic & Nature Excursions**

Discover **breathtaking landscapes**, national parks, and protected wildlife areas.

Enjoy **coastal drives, hiking trails, or boat tours** showcasing stunning views.

Experience **wildlife encounters**, such as whale watching or safari tours.

**Example:** Exploring the **Cliffs of Moher in Ireland**, cruising through **Norwegian fjords**, or visiting **Alaska's glaciers**.

**Adventure & Outdoor Activities**

Ideal for thrill-seekers looking for **high-energy experiences**.

Options include **zip-lining, scuba diving, kayaking, dune buggy rides, and rock climbing**.

Great for those who love **water sports, off-road excursions, or aerial tours**.

**Example:** Snorkeling in the **Great Barrier Reef**, zip-lining in **Costa Rica**, or ATV riding in **Iceland's lava fields**.

**Food & Wine Experiences**

Perfect for travelers who love to **explore local cuisine and beverages**.

Includes **cooking classes, wine tastings, and farm-to-table experiences**.

Visit **local markets, distilleries, and famous food streets**.

**Example: Jameson Whiskey Distillery tour in Ireland**, wine tasting in **Bordeaux, France**, or a street food tour in **Bangkok, Thailand**.

**Beach & Relaxation Excursions**

Ideal for those looking to **unwind on pristine beaches**.

Enjoy private beach resorts with **loungers, cocktails, and water sports**.

Indulge in **spa and wellness experiences** with oceanfront views.

**Example: Relaxing in the Maldives, sunbathing in the Caribbean, or exploring Greece's Santorini beaches**.

## Booking a Shore Excursion: Cruise Line vs. Independent Operators

**Booking Through the Cruise Line**

**Guaranteed Return to Ship** – The cruise will wait if a ship-organized tour runs late.
**Reliable & Well-Vetted Operators** – Ensures **safety and quality**.
**Hassle-Free Experience** – No need to arrange transportation or logistics.

**More Expensive** – Typically costs **30-50% more** than booking independently.
**Larger Group Sizes** – Less **personalized experience** due to big tour groups.

**Booking with Independent Tour Operators**

**Lower Prices & Smaller Groups** – Often more affordable and offers a **customized experience**. **Unique, Off-the-Beaten-Path Tours** – More flexible and can visit places **not covered by cruise line excursions**. **Direct Communication with Local Guides** – Learn from locals and **support small businesses**.

**Risk of Missing the Ship** – If an independent tour runs late, the cruise **won't wait**. **Requires More Research & Planning** – You'll need to vet operators **for safety and reliability**.

**Tip:** If booking independently, choose excursions that **return at least 2 hours before departure** to avoid missing your ship.

**Tips for Choosing the Best Shore Excursion**

**Consider Your Interests & Activity Level** – Pick tours that match your preferences (e.g., **relaxing vs. adventurous**).

**Read Reviews & Compare Prices** – Use **TripAdvisor, Viator, or Cruise Critic** for recommendations.

**Book Early for Popular Tours** – Some excursions sell out quickly, especially in **high-demand ports**.
**Check Cancellation Policies** – Some tours allow refunds if your plans change.
**Be Aware of Time Zones** – Cruise ships operate on **ship time**, which may differ from **local time** in port.

### Packing Essentials for a Shore Excursion

**Small Backpack** – Carry essentials like sunscreen, snacks, and a camera.
**Sunglasses & Hat** – Protection from **sun exposure**.
**Sunscreen & Bug Spray** – Crucial for **tropical destinations**.
**Camera or Smartphone** – Capture **memorable moments**.
**Reusable Water Bottle** – Stay **hydrated throughout the tour**.
**Local Currency & Credit Card** – Some small vendors don't accept **cards**.
**Printed Itinerary & Emergency Contact Info** – In case your **phone runs out of battery**.

**Comfortable Walking Shoes** – Essential for **city tours, hikes, and long excursions**.

### Exploring Ports Without an Excursion

In some destinations, **self-guided exploration** can be just as enjoyable as a formal tour.

**Great for Independent Exploration:**

**Barcelona, Spain** – Walk **Las Ramblas**, visit **La Sagrada Familia**, and explore tapas bars.

**Venice, Italy** – Wander through **St. Mark's Square**, ride a gondola, and visit Murano's glass factories.

**Dubrovnik, Croatia** – Walk the famous **Old City Walls** and relax at a **beachfront café**.

**Best for Guided Tours:**

**Alaska** – Glacier hikes and wildlife spotting require **expert guides**.

**Iceland** – Volcanoes, geysers, and geothermal pools need **proper transportation**.

**South America** – Some areas require **safety precautions and guided experiences**.

**Tip:** If exploring on your own, **download offline maps and research public transport options**.

## Dining & Shopping: A Guide to Culinary and Retail Experiences Around the World

Dining and shopping are two of the most enjoyable aspects of travel, allowing visitors to **immerse themselves in local culture, sample authentic cuisine, and find unique souvenirs**. Whether indulging in **fine dining, exploring street food, browsing luxury boutiques, or hunting for handmade crafts**, these experiences add depth and excitement to any journey. Understanding where to **eat, what to try, and where to shop** ensures a rewarding and enriching experience.

### Dining: Savoring Local and International Cuisine

Food is a **universal language** that connects people, and every destination offers its own **signature flavors and dining customs**. Whether dining at a **Michelin-starred restaurant, a family-run café, or a bustling street

**market**, food plays a key role in understanding a place's culture and history.

**Must-Try Dishes from Around the World**

**Italy** – Fresh **pasta, Neapolitan pizza, risotto, and tiramisu**.

**France** – Croissants, escargots, coq au vin, and crème brûlée.

**Japan** – Sushi, ramen, tempura, and wagyu beef.

**Mexico** – Tacos, tamales, mole, and churros.

**Thailand** – Pad Thai, green curry, mango sticky rice, and Tom Yum soup.

**Scotland** – Haggis, black pudding, and Scotch whisky-infused dishes.

**Best Places to Dine**

**Street Food Markets** – Ideal for authentic, budget-friendly meals (e.g., **Bangkok's Chatuchak Market, Istanbul's Grand Bazaar, London's Borough Market**).

**Family-Run Restaurants** – Perfect for experiencing **home-cooked, traditional meals** in an intimate setting.

**Fine Dining & Michelin-Starred Restaurants** – For **gourmet experiences showcasing innovative cuisine**.

**Food & Wine Tours** – Combine sightseeing with **tastings of local specialties**.

**Cooking Classes** – A hands-on way to **learn traditional cooking techniques**.

**Dining Tips for Travelers**

**Make Reservations in Advance** – Especially for fine dining and popular restaurants.
**Learn Basic Dining Etiquette** – Different cultures have **unique table customs** (e.g., tipping is expected in the U.S. but not in Japan).
**Try Something New** – Be adventurous and sample **local delicacies** (e.g., escargots in France, ceviche in Peru, or fermented shark in Iceland).
**Check for Dietary Options** – Research **vegetarian, gluten-free, or halal-friendly places** if needed.

## Shopping: Finding Unique Souvenirs and Luxury Goods

Shopping while traveling is an opportunity to find **one-of-a-kind items, luxury goods, and local handicrafts** that serve as lasting mementos of a trip.

**Best Shopping Destinations**

**Luxury Shopping:** Paris (**Champs-Élysées**), Milan (**Via Montenapoleone**), New York (**5th Avenue**).

**Local Markets & Bazaars:** Marrakech (**Souks**), Istanbul (**Grand Bazaar**), Mexico City (**Mercado de Coyoacán**).

**Handmade Crafts & Artisan Goods:** Peru (**Alpaca wool scarves**), India (**Silk saris**), Ireland (**Handwoven wool sweaters**).

**Duty-Free Shopping:** Airports and cruise ports for **tax-free luxury goods**.

**Popular Souvenirs by Region**

**Japan** – Hand-painted ceramics, washi paper, green tea.

**Italy** – Handmade leather goods, Murano glass, Limoncello.

**Mexico** – Handwoven textiles, silver jewelry, tequila.

**Ireland** – Claddagh rings, Aran wool sweaters, whiskey.

**France** – Perfume, wine, artisanal cheese.

**Shopping Tips for Travelers**

**Compare Prices Before Buying** – Tourist areas often charge higher prices; explore different shops. **Negotiate When Appropriate** – Haggling is common in markets in **Morocco, Egypt, and parts of Asia**. **Check Customs Regulations** – Some items (alcohol, rare antiques, ivory) may have import restrictions. **Bring a Reusable Bag** – Many countries **charge for plastic bags** to reduce waste.

### Dining & Shopping: A Memorable Part of Travel

Exploring **local cuisine and shopping markets** is more than just an activity—it's a way to **connect with a destination, its history, and its people**. Whether you're indulging in a **traditional meal, browsing a lively**

**market, or bringing home a handcrafted souvenir**, these experiences create lasting travel memories.

By **planning ahead, budgeting wisely, and being open to new experiences**, you'll enjoy a **richer and more rewarding travel adventure**.

# INVERGORDON

## Invergordon: Gateway to the Scottish Highlands

Invergordon, a charming port town in the **Scottish Highlands**, is a popular stop for cruise passengers looking to explore Scotland's **rich history, breathtaking landscapes, and whisky heritage**. Located on the **Cromarty Firth**, Invergordon serves as a gateway to some of **Scotland's most famous attractions**, including **Loch Ness, castles, distilleries, and Highland villages**. Though small, the town itself is known for its **colorful murals, naval history, and warm Highland hospitality**.

For travelers seeking **Scottish culture, history, and scenic beauty**, Invergordon offers an unforgettable experience.

### Exploring Invergordon: A Town of Murals & Naval Heritage

Though most visitors use Invergordon as a base to explore the Highlands, the town itself has a **fascinating history** and is worth exploring.

**Invergordon Murals**

One of the most unique features of Invergordon is its **collection of murals** that decorate the town's buildings. These **hand-painted artworks** tell the story of Invergordon's **history, industries, and legends**, including:

The Royal Navy's presence in WWII.

**The Highland Clearances** and their impact on Scottish communities.

**Whisky distillation**, which remains a key industry in the region.

A self-guided **mural walking tour** is a great way to learn about the town while enjoying its charming streets.

**Naval & Industrial Heritage**

Invergordon has long been associated with the **Royal Navy** due to its **deep-water port and strategic location**. During **World War I and II**, it was a major naval base, and remnants of its military past can still be seen today. The **Invergordon Naval Museum & Heritage Centre** provides insight into the town's **naval history, shipbuilding, and oil industry**.

## Top Attractions Near Invergordon

Most visitors use Invergordon as a **launchpad for exploring the Scottish Highlands**, with several world-famous attractions located just a short drive away.

### Cawdor Castle

Famous for its connection to **Shakespeare's Macbeth**, Cawdor Castle is a **beautiful 14th-century fortress** with:

**Immaculate gardens and woodlands.**

**A well-preserved medieval interior.**

**A drawbridge, dungeons, and impressive art collections.**

### Loch Ness & Urquhart Castle

No trip to the Highlands is complete without a visit to **Loch Ness**, home to the legendary **Loch Ness Monster**. Visitors can:

Take a **boat cruise on Loch Ness** to spot "Nessie."

Explore the ruins of **Urquhart Castle**, which overlooks the loch.

Visit the **Loch Ness Centre**, which delves into the legend of the monster.

**Glenmorangie Distillery**

For whisky lovers, a visit to **Glenmorangie Distillery**, one of Scotland's most famous whisky producers, is a must. Tour highlights include:

Learning about the **whisky-making process**.

Sampling **award-winning single malts**.

Visiting the **traditional copper stills and oak casks**.

### Shore Excursions from Invergordon

Cruise passengers stopping in Invergordon can choose from a variety of **shore excursions**:

**Highland Village Tours** – Visit charming villages like **Dornoch**, known for its cathedral and historic streets.

**Dunrobin Castle** – A fairytale-like castle with **stunning gardens and falconry displays**.

**Culloden Battlefield** – The site of the infamous **Battle of Culloden (1746)**, where the Jacobite rebellion met its end.

**Wildlife Tours** – Spot **dolphins, seals, and Highland cows** in the scenic countryside.

## Dining & Shopping in Invergordon

**Where to Eat**

While Invergordon is a small town, it offers a few great spots to enjoy traditional Scottish food:

**The Ship Inn** – A cozy pub serving **fresh seafood, fish & chips, and Highland beef dishes**.

**The Crazy Horse Coffee Shop** – A charming café for **Scottish breakfasts and homemade cakes**.

**Local Whisky Bars** – Enjoy a **Highland whisky tasting experience** with traditional Scottish fare.

**Where to Shop**

Visitors looking for souvenirs can explore:

**Whisky Shops** – Featuring **Scotland's finest single malts**, including Glenmorangie and Dalmore.

**Scottish Craft Stores** – Selling **handmade tartans, wool scarves, and Celtic jewelry**.

**Local Markets** – Offering **Highland souvenirs, Scottish shortbread, and artisan crafts**.

### Best Time to Visit Invergordon

The best time to visit Invergordon is **between May and September**, when the weather is mild, and the **Highlands are in full bloom**.

**Spring (April–June):** Great for **wildflowers and fewer crowds**.

**Summer (July–August):** Best for **warm weather, long daylight hours, and festivals**.

**Autumn (September–October):** Stunning **fall foliage and quieter attractions**.

**Tip:** Always bring a **rain jacket**, as Scottish weather can be unpredictable!

# Top Attractions in the Scottish Highlands: Loch Ness, Culloden Battlefield, and Inverness

The **Scottish Highlands** are one of the most breathtaking and historically rich regions in the world, offering a blend of **myth, history, and natural beauty**. Among the most visited destinations in the Highlands are **Loch Ness, Culloden Battlefield, and Inverness**—each offering a unique experience that showcases Scotland's **legends, heritage, and scenic landscapes**. Whether you're drawn by the mystery of **Nessie, the tragic history of the Jacobites, or the cultural charm of the Highland capital**, these attractions provide an unforgettable glimpse into Scotland's past and present.

### Loch Ness: The Home of Myths and Majesty

Loch Ness, one of Scotland's most famous landmarks, is a **deep freshwater loch** stretching over **23 miles (37 km)** through the Great Glen. It is best known for the **legend of the Loch Ness Monster ("Nessie")**, a mythical creature said to inhabit the dark waters.

**Highlights of Loch Ness**

**Loch Ness Cruises** – One of the best ways to experience Loch Ness is by taking a **boat cruise**, which offers stunning views and a chance to search for **Nessie**.

**Urquhart Castle** – Overlooking the loch, this **13th-century fortress** is a major highlight. Explore its ruins, climb the tower, and take in **panoramic views of the water**.

**The Loch Ness Centre & Exhibition** – Located in **Drumnadrochit**, this museum explores the history of **Loch Ness, its geology, and the Nessie legend** through **interactive exhibits**.

**Hiking & Scenic Drives** – Surrounding the loch are **forests, waterfalls, and walking trails**, making it an excellent spot for **outdoor activities**.

**Tickets & Visitor Tips**

**Loch Ness Cruises:** Prices start from **£20 per person** for a **one-hour boat tour**.

**Best Time to Visit: Spring and summer** for **warmer weather and better visibility**.

**Nearby Attractions:** The village of **Fort Augustus** offers great **canal views and local restaurants**.

## Culloden Battlefield: The Site of Scotland's Last Battle

Culloden Battlefield is one of **Scotland's most important historical sites**, marking the location of the **Battle of Culloden (April 16, 1746)**. This was the **last battle fought on British soil**, where **Jacobite forces led by Bonnie Prince Charlie were defeated by the British army**, leading to the end of the Highland way of life.

### Highlights of Culloden Battlefield

**The Culloden Visitor Centre** – Features a **360-degree immersive battle experience**, historical artifacts, and exhibits about the Jacobite uprising.

**The Battlefield Walk** – Explore the **well-preserved battlefield**, marked by **stone memorials, mass graves, and the Leanach Cottage**, which survived the battle.

**The Memorial Cairn & Clan Stones** – These stones mark the **final resting place of the fallen Jacobite soldiers**, representing various Highland clans.

**Guided Tours** – Expert-led tours provide **detailed insight into the tactics, weapons, and impact of the battle**.

**Tickets & Visitor Tips**

**Admission:** Entry to the visitor centre costs around **£14 per adult**. The battlefield itself is **free to visit**.

**Best Time to Visit: Spring and autumn** for **fewer crowds and a peaceful atmosphere**.

**Nearby Attractions: Clava Cairns**, a **4,000-year-old prehistoric burial site**, located just **a few minutes away**.

### Inverness: The Capital of the Highlands

Inverness, often referred to as the **"Gateway to the Highlands,"** is a **charming and historic city** located along the **banks of the River Ness**. It is the **largest city in the Highlands**, offering a **mix of ancient history, modern culture, and scenic beauty**.

**Highlights of Inverness**

**Inverness Castle** – Perched above the city, this **red sandstone castle** offers stunning views. While the castle itself is not open to the public, visitors can explore the **North Tower viewpoint**.

**Inverness Museum & Art Gallery** – A great place to learn about **Highland history, the Jacobites, and Scottish culture**.

**St. Andrew's Cathedral** – A beautiful **Gothic-style cathedral** located along the **River Ness**, known for its impressive **stained-glass windows and architecture**.

**The Ness Islands Walk** – A scenic trail along the **River Ness**, perfect for a relaxing stroll or wildlife spotting.

**Tickets & Visitor Tips**

**Best Time to Visit:** Summer offers **long daylight hours**, but autumn is great for **fall colors and fewer crowds**.

**Nearby Attractions:** Inverness is a great starting point for **day trips to Glen Affric, Fort George, and whisky distilleries**.

# Shore Excursions: Enhancing Your Cruise Experience

Shore excursions are a **highlight of any cruise**, offering passengers the opportunity to **explore new destinations, experience local culture, and engage in unique activities** beyond the ship. Whether you're interested in **historical landmarks, scenic landscapes, adventure sports, or culinary experiences**, shore excursions provide a way to **make the most of your limited time in port**.

Planning ahead and choosing the right shore excursion ensures that you **maximize your experience while balancing relaxation, exploration, and comfort**.

## Types of Shore Excursions

Cruise lines and independent tour operators offer a variety of shore excursions catering to different interests and activity levels.

### Historical & Cultural Tours

For travelers who love **history and heritage**, these excursions provide insights into the region's past:

**Guided city tours** exploring ancient ruins, castles, and UNESCO World Heritage Sites.

**Museum visits**, palaces, and cathedrals showcasing local art and architecture.

**Traditional performances**, including folk dances, storytelling, and music.

**Example:** Visiting **Edinburgh Castle in Scotland**, touring the **Acropolis in Greece**, or exploring the **ruins of Pompeii in Italy**.

**Scenic & Nature Excursions**

Ideal for those who appreciate **breathtaking landscapes, national parks, and wildlife encounters**:

**Scenic drives** through coastal cliffs, fjords, and mountain ranges.

**Wildlife watching**, including dolphin and whale spotting, safaris, or birdwatching.

**Eco-tours** featuring waterfalls, volcanic craters, and rainforests.

**Example:** Taking a **Norwegian fjord cruise**, visiting the **Cliffs of Moher in Ireland**, or exploring **Alaska's glaciers**.

**Adventure & Outdoor Activities**

For thrill-seekers, these excursions provide an **active and exhilarating experience**:

**Water sports** like snorkeling, scuba diving, jet skiing, and white-water rafting.

**Hiking, zip-lining, ATV rides, and bungee jumping** for adrenaline-pumping fun.

**Kayaking, canoeing, or paddleboarding** in lakes, rivers, or coastal waters.

**Example: Zip-lining in Costa Rica, scuba diving in the Great Barrier Reef, or off-roading in Iceland**.

**Culinary & Wine Experiences**

Perfect for **food lovers**, these excursions highlight local flavors and traditions:

**Wine tastings at vineyards** and distillery tours.

**Cooking classes** featuring local ingredients and traditional techniques.

**Market tours** sampling street food and regional specialties.

**Example: Whiskey tasting in Scotland, pasta-making in Italy, or a tapas tour in Barcelona**.

### Beach & Relaxation Excursions

For those looking to **unwind**, these excursions offer the ultimate **leisure experience**:

**Private beach resorts** with loungers, cocktails, and spa treatments.

**Sailing trips** with snorkeling and sunset views.

**Thermal springs and wellness retreats**.

**Example: Relaxing in the Maldives, sunbathing in the Caribbean, or visiting Greece's Santorini beaches**.

### Booking a Shore Excursion: Cruise Line vs. Independent Operators

**Booking Through the Cruise Line**

**Guaranteed Return to Ship** – If a cruise-organized excursion runs late, the ship will wait.

**Reliable & Well-Vetted Operators** – Ensures safety and quality.

**Hassle-Free Experience** – Transportation and logistics are handled for you.

**More Expensive** – Typically costs **30-50% more** than booking independently.

**Larger Group Sizes** – Less personalized experience.

**Booking with Independent Tour Operators**

**More Affordable** – Often **cheaper** and offers **smaller group sizes**.

**Unique & Customizable** – Allows for a **more tailored experience**.

**Supports Local Businesses** – Often run by **local guides** rather than large corporations.

**Risk of Missing the Ship** – If delayed, the ship **won't wait**.

**More Research Required** – You must vet operators for safety and reliability.

**Tip:** If booking independently, choose tours that return at least **2 hours before the ship's departure**.

### Tips for Choosing the Best Shore Excursion

**Consider Your Interests & Activity Level** – Pick tours that match your **travel style** (adventure vs. sightseeing).
**Read Reviews & Compare Prices** – Use **TripAdvisor, Viator, or Cruise Critic** for recommendations.
**Book Early for Popular Tours** – Some excursions **sell out quickly**.
**Check Cancellation Policies** – Some tours allow refunds if your plans change.
**Be Aware of Time Zones** – Cruise ships operate on **ship time**, which may differ from **local time in port**.

### Packing Essentials for a Shore Excursion

**Daypack or Small Bag** – Carry your **essentials comfortably**.
**Sunglasses & Hat** – Protection from **sun exposure**.
**Sunscreen & Bug Spray** – Essential for **beach and jungle excursions**.
**Camera or Smartphone** – Capture **memorable**

moments.

**Reusable Water Bottle** – Stay **hydrated throughout the tour**.

**Local Currency & Credit Card** – Some small vendors **don't accept cards**.

**Printed Itinerary & Emergency Contact Info** – In case your phone battery dies.

**Comfortable Walking Shoes** – Essential for **city tours, hikes, and long excursions**.

## Exploring Ports Without an Excursion

In some destinations, **self-guided exploration** can be just as rewarding.

**Great for Independent Exploration:**

**Barcelona, Spain** – Walk **Las Ramblas**, visit **La Sagrada Familia**, and explore tapas bars.

**Venice, Italy** – Wander through **St. Mark's Square**, ride a gondola, and visit Murano's glass factories.

**Dubrovnik, Croatia** – Walk the famous **Old City Walls** and relax at a **beachfront café**.

**Best for Guided Tours:**

**Alaska** – Glacier hikes and wildlife spotting require **expert guides**.

**Iceland** – Volcanoes, geysers, and geothermal pools need **proper transportation**.

**South America** – Some areas require **safety precautions and guided experiences**.

**Tip:** If exploring independently, **download offline maps and research public transport options**.

## Dining & Shopping: A Complete Guide to Culinary and Retail Experiences

Dining and shopping are two of the most enjoyable aspects of travel, offering visitors a chance to **experience local culture, indulge in authentic cuisine, and take-home unique souvenirs**. Whether you're strolling through a bustling street market, savoring a gourmet meal, or browsing high-end boutiques, these activities **enhance any travel experience** by providing a deeper connection to a destination's traditions and lifestyle.

From **fine dining to casual eateries, luxury boutiques to vibrant local markets**, knowing where to eat and shop can make a trip even more memorable.

## Dining: Exploring Local & International Cuisine

Food is an **integral part of cultural identity**, and trying local dishes allows travelers to experience **authentic flavors and cooking traditions**. Whether it's a bowl of **steaming ramen in Tokyo, fresh seafood in the Mediterranean, or slow-cooked barbecue in Texas**, every meal tells a story.

**Must-Try Dishes from Around the World**

**Italy:** Handmade **pasta, Neapolitan pizza, risotto, and tiramisu**.

**France: Croissants, escargots, coq au vin, and crème brûlée**.

**Japan: Sushi, ramen, tempura, and wagyu beef**.

**Mexico: Tacos, tamales, mole, and churros**.

**Thailand: Pad Thai, green curry, mango sticky rice, and Tom Yum soup**.

**Scotland: Haggis, black pudding, and Scotch whisky-infused dishes.**

**Best Places to Dine**

**Street Food Markets** – Ideal for trying **authentic, affordable local dishes** (e.g., Bangkok's floating markets, Marrakech's night souks, London's Borough Market).

**Family-Run Restaurants** – Offer home-cooked, traditional meals in a cozy setting.

**Fine Dining & Michelin-Starred Restaurants** – Perfect for those seeking **a luxury culinary experience** with gourmet dishes.

**Food & Wine Tours** – A great way to sample **local cuisine and specialty drinks** while learning about the region's food culture.

**Cooking Classes** – Hands-on experiences that teach travelers how to prepare **regional dishes**.

**Dining Tips for Travelers**

**Make Reservations in Advance** – Popular restaurants book up quickly.

**Learn Local Dining Customs** – Tipping varies worldwide, and dining etiquette differs across cultures.

**Be Adventurous** – Try **unique local dishes**, even if they seem unfamiliar.

**Check Dietary Options** – Many restaurants accommodate **vegetarian, vegan, and gluten-free diets**.

## Shopping: Finding Unique Souvenirs and Luxury Goods

Shopping while traveling is an opportunity to find **one-of-a-kind items, handcrafted goods, and high-quality local products**. Whether it's a **handwoven rug from Morocco, a bottle of aged Scotch whisky from Scotland, or designer fashion from Milan**, shopping can be both an enjoyable activity and a way to bring home meaningful memories.

### Best Shopping Destinations

**Luxury Shopping:** Paris (**Champs-Élysées**), Milan (**Via Montenapoleone**), New York (**5th Avenue**).

**Local Markets & Bazaars:** Marrakech (**Souks**), Istanbul (**Grand Bazaar**), Mexico City (**Mercado de Coyoacán**).

**Handmade Crafts & Artisan Goods:** Peru (**Alpaca wool scarves**), India (**Silk saris**), Ireland (**Handwoven wool sweaters**).

**Duty-Free Shopping:** Airports and cruise ports for **tax-free luxury goods**.

### Popular Souvenirs by Region

**Japan:** Hand-painted ceramics, washi paper, green tea.

**Italy:** Handmade leather goods, Murano glass, Limoncello.

**Mexico:** Handwoven textiles, silver jewelry, tequila.

**Ireland:** Claddagh rings, Aran wool sweaters, whiskey.

**France:** Perfume, wine, artisanal cheese.

### Shopping Tips for Travelers

**Compare Prices Before Buying** – Tourist areas often charge higher prices.
**Negotiate When Appropriate** – Haggling is common in

markets in **Morocco, Egypt, and Southeast Asia**. **Check Customs Regulations** – Some items (alcohol, rare antiques, ivory) may have import restrictions. **Bring a Reusable Bag** – Many countries **charge for plastic bags** to reduce waste.

### Dining & Shopping: A Memorable Part of Travel

Exploring **local cuisine and shopping markets** is more than just an activity—it's a way to **connect with a destination, its history, and its people**. Whether you're indulging in a **traditional meal, browsing a lively market, or bringing home a handcrafted souvenir**, these experiences create lasting travel memories.

By **planning ahead, budgeting wisely, and being open to new experiences**, you'll enjoy a **richer and more rewarding travel adventure**.

### Isle of Skye: Scotland's Most Enchanting Island

The **Isle of Skye**, located off the west coast of Scotland, is one of the most breathtaking and **mystical destinations in the country**. Known for its **dramatic landscapes, rugged mountains, medieval castles, and charming**

**villages**, Skye offers an unforgettable experience for nature lovers, history enthusiasts, and adventure seekers. With its **rich Gaelic heritage, abundant wildlife, and stunning coastal scenery**, the Isle of Skye embodies the wild beauty of the **Scottish Highlands**.

## Spectacular Natural Scenery

**The Quiraing**

One of Skye's most famous landscapes, **The Quiraing** is a landslip on the **Trotternish Ridge**. The area features **towering cliffs, rolling green hills, and bizarre rock formations** that make it look like something out of a fantasy novel. A **hiking trail** through the Quiraing offers **breathtaking panoramic views** over the island and beyond.

**The Old Man of Storr**

Arguably Skye's most iconic landmark, the **Old Man of Storr** is a **towering rock pinnacle** formed by an ancient landslide. Located just north of **Portree**, this site is a favorite among photographers and hikers. The **steep but**

**rewarding hike** to the top provides **sweeping views of the Sound of Raasay**.

**Fairy Pools**

The **Fairy Pools**, located in **Glen Brittle**, are a series of **crystal-clear blue pools and waterfalls** fed by the Cuillin Mountains. Many visitors **hike to the pools** for scenic views, while adventurous travelers **swim in the cold waters**. The surrounding landscape adds to the site's **magical and otherworldly feel**.

## Historical and Cultural Attractions

**Dunvegan Castle**

Dunvegan Castle, home to **Clan MacLeod for over 800 years**, is **the oldest continuously inhabited castle in Scotland**. Visitors can explore:

The castle's **historic interiors**, including **clan artifacts and fine art**.

The **Fairy Flag**, a legendary relic said to grant victory in battle.

The **castle gardens**, featuring woodlands, waterfalls, and beautiful floral displays.

**Boat trips** to see the **seal colony** near the castle.

### Isle of Skye Museum of Island Life

Located in **Kilmuir**, this open-air museum showcases **traditional thatched cottages** and exhibits detailing **Skye's rural life during the 19th and early 20th centuries**. It offers a glimpse into the **island's history, crofting heritage, and Gaelic traditions**.

### Neist Point Lighthouse

One of the most scenic lighthouses in Scotland, **Neist Point Lighthouse** sits on the westernmost tip of Skye. The **clifftop walk to the lighthouse** offers stunning views of the Atlantic Ocean, making it a **perfect spot for sunset photography** and **wildlife spotting (whales, dolphins, and seabirds)**.

## Local Villages and Unique Experiences

**Portree**

Portree, the **capital of Skye**, is a charming harbor town with **colorful waterfront houses, seafood restaurants, and craft shops**. Visitors can:

Enjoy **fresh seafood** at local restaurants.

Browse **artisan shops** selling wool, pottery, and jewelry.

Use Portree as a **base for exploring the rest of Skye**.

**Talisker Distillery**

Skye's most famous whisky distillery, **Talisker**, produces **rich and peaty single malts**. A visit includes:

**Guided distillery tours**, explaining the whisky-making process.

**Tasting sessions**, featuring Talisker's signature smoky flavors.

A chance to buy **exclusive whiskies** only available at the distillery.

## Best Time to Visit & Travel Tips

**Best Season: May to September** offers mild weather and long daylight hours for exploring.

**Packing Tips: Waterproof clothing** and **sturdy hiking boots** are essential due to Skye's unpredictable weather.

**Getting There:** Accessible via **Skye Bridge from Kyle of Lochalsh** or by **ferry from Mallaig**.

# ISLE OF SKYE

## Top Attractions on the Isle of Skye: Fairy Pools, Old Man of Storr, and Dunvegan Castle

The **Isle of Skye**, located off Scotland's west coast, is renowned for its **dramatic landscapes, rugged mountains, and rich history**. Among its many breathtaking sights, three stand out as must-visit attractions: the **Fairy Pools**, a collection of crystal-clear waterfalls; the **Old Man of Storr**, a towering rock formation; and **Dunvegan Castle**, Scotland's oldest continuously inhabited castle. These locations offer a mix of **natural beauty, adventure, and historical significance**, making them essential stops on any trip to Skye.

### Fairy Pools: A Magical Natural Wonder

Nestled at the foot of the **Cuillin Mountains**, the **Fairy Pools** are a series of **stunning blue pools and cascading waterfalls** along the River Brittle. The site is one of Skye's most **photographed and visited attractions**, drawing nature lovers, hikers, and photographers alike.

## Highlights of the Fairy Pools

**Crystal-Clear Pools** – The pools are known for their **remarkable clarity and blue-green hues**, which look almost surreal against the rugged Highland landscape.

**Multiple Waterfalls** – The pools are connected by a **series of small waterfalls**, adding to the site's enchanting appeal.

**Wild Swimming** – Some visitors take a dip in the icy waters, though even in summer, the temperatures are quite cold.

**Scenic Hiking Trails** – The walk to the Fairy Pools is **moderate and scenic**, with views of the **Cuillin Mountains** in the background.

## Visitor Information & Tips

**Distance from Portree:** About **30 minutes by car**.

**Hiking Distance: 2.4 km (1.5 miles) round trip**, taking around **40 minutes**.

**Best Time to Visit: Early morning or late afternoon** to avoid crowds.

**What to Bring: Waterproof clothing** (Skye's weather is unpredictable) and **good hiking shoes**.

## Old Man of Storr: Skye's Most Iconic Landmark

The **Old Man of Storr** is one of the Isle of Skye's most **recognizable and dramatic rock formations**. Located on the **Trotternish Ridge**, this towering pinnacle is a result of ancient **landslides and volcanic activity**, creating a landscape that looks almost otherworldly.

### Highlights of the Old Man of Storr

**Towering Rock Spires** – The main pinnacle, the "Old Man," stands **over 50 meters (164 feet) tall**.

**Panoramic Views** – On a clear day, visitors can see across the **Sound of Raasay** to the mainland.

**Incredible Photography Spot** – This location has been featured in movies, travel magazines, and postcards.

**Hiking Adventure** – A moderately challenging **4.5 km (2.8 miles) round-trip hike**, taking about **1.5–2 hours** to complete.

## Visitor Information & Tips

**Distance from Portree: 15-minute drive.**

**Best Time to Visit: Early morning** for the best light and fewer crowds.

**Weather Warning:** The path can get **muddy and slippery**, so **sturdy hiking boots** are essential.

### Dunvegan Castle: A Historic Highland Fortress

Dunvegan Castle, home to **Clan MacLeod for over 800 years**, is **the oldest continuously inhabited castle in Scotland**. Overlooking **Loch Dunvegan**, this **majestic castle and gardens** offer visitors a glimpse into Scotland's noble past.

**Highlights of Dunvegan Castle**

**The Fairy Flag** – A legendary banner said to have magical properties that once protected the MacLeods in battle.

**Opulent Interiors** – The castle features **historical artifacts, fine art, and antique furniture**.

**Magnificent Gardens** – The **formal gardens and woodlands** surrounding the castle provide a peaceful retreat.

**Seal Watching Tours** – Boat trips depart from the castle to see the **local seal colony**.

**Visitor Information & Tips**

**Distance from Portree:** About **35 minutes by car**.

**Opening Times:** Open seasonally from **April to October**.

**Entry Fees:** Around **£16 per adult** (including gardens).

**Best Time to Visit: Spring and summer**, when the gardens are in full bloom.

## Shore Excursions: Enhancing Your Cruise Experience

Shore excursions are a **key highlight of any cruise**, allowing travelers to **explore new destinations, experience local culture, and participate in exciting activities** beyond the ship. Whether you're interested in **historical landmarks, scenic landscapes, adventure**

**sports, or culinary experiences**, shore excursions provide an opportunity to **maximize your time in port and create unforgettable memories**.

Planning and selecting the right shore excursion ensures you **balance relaxation, exploration, and cultural immersion** while making the most of your limited time ashore.

### Types of Shore Excursions

Cruise lines and independent tour operators offer a variety of shore excursions tailored to different interests and activity levels.

**Historical & Cultural Tours**

For travelers interested in **heritage and history**, these excursions provide **insights into ancient civilizations, royal palaces, and historical landmarks**.

**Guided city tours** of UNESCO World Heritage Sites, castles, and archaeological ruins.

**Museum visits**, including fine art galleries and historical exhibitions.

**Local cultural experiences**, such as folk performances, traditional workshops, and religious sites.

**Example:** Exploring **Edinburgh Castle in Scotland, the Colosseum in Rome, or the Acropolis in Athens**.

### Scenic & Nature Excursions

Ideal for those who appreciate **breathtaking landscapes, national parks, and wildlife encounters**.

**Scenic drives** along coastal roads, mountains, and countryside.

**Boat tours** offering views of fjords, glaciers, or tropical islands.

**Wildlife experiences**, including whale watching, birdwatching, and safaris.

**Example:** Cruising through **Norwegian fjords, visiting the Cliffs of Moher in Ireland, or spotting penguins in Antarctica**.

## Adventure & Outdoor Activities

For thrill-seekers, adventure excursions provide an **adrenaline rush** and an **immersive outdoor experience**.

**Water sports** like snorkeling, scuba diving, jet skiing, and paddleboarding.

**Hiking, zip-lining, ATV rides, and bungee jumping** in breathtaking natural settings.

**Kayaking and canoeing** in lakes, rivers, and coastal waters.

**Example: Snorkeling in the Great Barrier Reef, zip-lining in Costa Rica, or hiking to waterfalls in Iceland.**

## Culinary & Wine Experiences

Perfect for **food lovers**, these excursions focus on **local cuisine and regional specialties**.

**Cooking classes** with local chefs.

**Wine tastings and vineyard tours.**

**Street food and market tours.**

Example: **Whiskey tasting in Scotland, pasta-making in Italy, or a seafood feast in Portugal**.

**Beach & Relaxation Excursions**

For those looking to **unwind**, these excursions provide the ultimate **relaxation experience**.

**Private beach resorts** offering sun loungers, cocktails, and spa treatments.

**Sailing and catamaran cruises**.

**Hot springs and wellness retreats**.

**Example: Relaxing on the beaches of the Maldives, swimming in Santorini, or enjoying a tropical escape in the Caribbean**.

## Booking a Shore Excursion: Cruise Line vs. Independent Operators

**Booking Through the Cruise Line**

**Guaranteed Return to Ship** – If a cruise-organized excursion runs late, the ship will wait. **Reliable & Well-Vetted Operators** – Ensures safety and quality.

**Hassle-Free Experience** – Transportation and logistics are handled for you.

**More Expensive** – Typically costs **30-50% more** than booking independently.

**Larger Group Sizes** – Less personalized experience.

**Booking with Independent Tour Operators**

**More Affordable** – Often **cheaper** and offers **smaller group sizes**.

**Unique & Customizable** – Allows for a **more tailored experience**.

**Supports Local Businesses** – Often run by **local guides** rather than large corporations.

**Risk of Missing the Ship** – If delayed, the ship **won't wait**.

**More Research Required** – You must vet operators for safety and reliability.

**Tip:** If booking independently, choose tours that return at least **2 hours before the ship's departure**.

## Tips for Choosing the Best Shore Excursion

**Consider Your Interests & Activity Level** – Pick tours that match your **travel style** (adventure vs. sightseeing).
**Read Reviews & Compare Prices** – Use **TripAdvisor, Viator, or Cruise Critic** for recommendations.
**Book Early for Popular Tours** – Some excursions **sell out quickly**.
**Check Cancellation Policies** – Some tours allow refunds if your plans change.
**Be Aware of Time Zones** – Cruise ships operate on **ship time**, which may differ from **local time in port**.

## Packing Essentials for a Shore Excursion

**Daypack or Small Bag** – Carry your **essentials** comfortably.
**Sunglasses & Hat** – Protection from **sun exposure**.
**Sunscreen & Bug Spray** – Essential for **beach and jungle excursions**.
**Camera or Smartphone** – Capture **memorable moments**.
**Reusable Water Bottle** – Stay **hydrated throughout the**

tour.

**Local Currency & Credit Card** – Some small vendors don't accept cards.

**Printed Itinerary & Emergency Contact Info** – In case your phone battery dies.

**Comfortable Walking Shoes** – Essential for **city tours, hikes, and long excursions**.

## Exploring Ports Without an Excursion

In some destinations, **self-guided exploration** can be just as rewarding.

**Great for Independent Exploration:**

**Barcelona, Spain** – Walk **Las Ramblas**, visit **La Sagrada Familia**, and explore tapas bars.

**Venice, Italy** – Wander through **St. Mark's Square**, ride a gondola, and visit Murano's glass factories.

**Dubrovnik, Croatia** – Walk the famous **Old City Walls** and relax at a **beachfront café**.

**Best for Guided Tours:**

**Alaska** – Glacier hikes and wildlife spotting require **expert guides**.

**Iceland** – Volcanoes, geysers, and geothermal pools need **proper transportation**.

**South America** – Some areas require **safety precautions and guided experiences**.

**Tip:** If exploring independently, **download offline maps and research public transport options**.

### Dining & Shopping: A Guide to Culinary and Retail Experiences

Dining and shopping are two of the most exciting and immersive aspects of travel, offering visitors the chance to **experience local culture, indulge in authentic cuisine, and take-home meaningful souvenirs**. Whether you're savoring a traditional dish in a local eatery, browsing artisan markets, or shopping in high-end boutiques, these activities provide a deeper connection to a destination's **heritage, lifestyle, and economy**.

From **street food vendors to Michelin-starred restaurants, bustling markets to luxury shopping districts**, knowing where to eat and shop can make any trip more memorable.

**Dining: A Taste of Local and International Flavors**

Food is a **reflection of a place's culture and history**, and exploring local cuisine allows travelers to experience **regional flavors, traditional cooking techniques, and native ingredients**.

**Must-Try Dishes from Around the World**

**Italy:** Handmade **pasta, Neapolitan pizza, and tiramisu**.

**France: Croissants, escargots, coq au vin, and crème brûlée**.

**Japan: Sushi, ramen, tempura, and wagyu beef**.

**Mexico: Tacos, tamales, mole, and churros**.

**Thailand: Pad Thai, green curry, mango sticky rice, and Tom Yum soup**.

**Scotland: Haggis, black pudding, Cullen skink, and Scotch whisky-infused dishes**.

### Best Places to Dine

**Street Food Markets** – Affordable and authentic meals cooked fresh (e.g., Bangkok's floating markets, Istanbul's Grand Bazaar, London's Borough Market).

**Family-Run Restaurants** – Cozy eateries offering **homemade traditional meals** in a welcoming atmosphere.

**Fine Dining & Michelin-Starred Restaurants** – Ideal for those seeking **gourmet culinary experiences**.

**Food & Wine Tours** – Perfect for sampling **local specialties and learning about regional culinary traditions**.

**Cooking Classes** – A hands-on way to learn how to prepare **traditional dishes** from local chefs.

### Dining Tips for Travelers

**Make Reservations in Advance** – Especially for popular restaurants.

**Learn Local Dining Customs** – Tipping norms and table manners vary across cultures.

**Be Adventurous** – Try **unique local delicacies**, even if they seem unfamiliar.

**Check Dietary Options** – Many restaurants cater to **vegetarian, vegan, and gluten-free diets**.

## Shopping: Finding Unique Souvenirs and Luxury Goods

Shopping while traveling is an opportunity to find **handcrafted goods, high-quality local products, and luxury items** that make for great souvenirs or personal keepsakes.

**Best Shopping Destinations**

**Luxury Shopping:** Paris (**Champs-Élysées**), Milan (**Via Montenapoleone**), New York (**5th Avenue**).

**Local Markets & Bazaars:** Marrakech (**Souks**), Istanbul (**Grand Bazaar**), Mexico City (**Mercado de Coyoacán**).

**Handmade Crafts & Artisan Goods:** Peru (**Alpaca wool scarves**), India (**Silk saris**), Ireland (**Handwoven wool sweaters**).

**Duty-Free Shopping:** Airports and cruise ports for **tax-free luxury goods**.

**Popular Souvenirs by Region**

**Japan:** Hand-painted ceramics, washi paper, green tea.

**Italy:** Handmade leather goods, Murano glass, Limoncello.

**Mexico:** Handwoven textiles, silver jewelry, tequila.

**Ireland:** Claddagh rings, Aran wool sweaters, whiskey.

**France:** Perfume, wine, artisanal cheese.

**Shopping Tips for Travelers**

**Compare Prices Before Buying** – Tourist areas often charge higher prices.
**Negotiate When Appropriate** – Haggling is common in markets in **Morocco, Egypt, and parts of Asia**.
**Check Customs Regulations** – Some items (alcohol, rare

antiques, ivory) may have import restrictions. **Bring a Reusable Bag** – Many countries **charge for plastic bags** to reduce waste.

### Dining & Shopping: A Memorable Part of Travel

Exploring **local cuisine and shopping markets** is more than just an activity—it's a way to **connect with a destination, its history, and its people**. Whether you're indulging in a **traditional meal, browsing a lively market, or bringing home a handcrafted souvenir**, these experiences create lasting travel memories.

By **planning ahead, budgeting wisely, and being open to new experiences**, you'll enjoy a **richer and more rewarding travel adventure.**

# STORNOWAY

## Stornoway: The Cultural Heart of the Outer Hebrides

Stornoway, the largest town in the **Outer Hebrides** (also known as the **Western Isles**), is a vibrant port town located on the east coast of **the Isle of Lewis** in Scotland. As the administrative and cultural capital of the islands, Stornoway offers a unique blend of **Gaelic heritage, natural beauty, and modern amenities**. Known for its **historic sites, traditional music, and world-famous Harris Tweed**, the town serves as both a cultural hub and a gateway to exploring the rugged beauty of the surrounding Hebridean landscapes.

### A Glimpse into Stornoway's History and Culture

Stornoway's history stretches back over a thousand years, with roots in the **Norse period**, when Vikings established it as an important trading port. The town's name comes from the Old Norse "Stjórnavágr," meaning **"steering bay."** Over the centuries, Stornoway evolved into a vital center for **fishing, maritime trade, and Harris Tweed production**.

Today, Stornoway remains a stronghold of **Gaelic culture**, with many residents speaking **Scottish Gaelic** as their first language. The town plays a key role in preserving traditional music, dance, and crafts, making it an authentic destination for those looking to experience **Scotland's Celtic heritage**.

## Must-Visit Attractions in Stornoway

### Lews Castle

Overlooking Stornoway Harbour, **Lews Castle** is one of the town's most iconic landmarks. Built in the mid-19th century by **Sir James Matheson**, who purchased the Isle of Lewis after making his fortune in the tea trade, the castle is surrounded by extensive **woodlands and gardens**.

**Museum nan Eilean:** Located within the castle grounds, this museum showcases the history and culture of the Outer Hebrides, including the famous **Lewis Chessmen**, a set of medieval chess pieces carved from walrus ivory.

**Castle Grounds:** Covering over **270 hectares**, the grounds offer scenic walking trails with stunning views of the harbour and the island's rugged coastline.

## An Lanntair Arts Centre

**An Lanntair** (meaning "the lantern" in Gaelic) is Stornoway's **contemporary arts hub**, hosting a range of events, including **art exhibitions, live music performances, theater, and film screenings**. The center also has a popular café offering views of the harbor, making it a great spot to relax and experience local culture.

## Harris Tweed Industry

Stornoway is the heart of the **Harris Tweed industry**, producing the globally renowned fabric that is **handwoven by islanders** in their homes, using pure virgin wool. Visitors can:

Tour local **Harris Tweed workshops** to see the weaving process firsthand.

Shop for authentic **Harris Tweed jackets, bags, and accessories** in local boutiques.

### Outdoor Adventures Around Stornoway

While Stornoway itself is lively, the surrounding **Isle of Lewis** offers a wealth of outdoor experiences:

**Beaches:** The nearby beaches of **Dalmore** and **Dalbeg** feature **golden sands and turquoise waters**, perfect for scenic walks.

**Callanish Standing Stones:** Just a short drive from Stornoway, these **5,000-year-old Neolithic stones** are often compared to Stonehenge and are steeped in mystery.

**Wildlife Watching:** The Outer Hebrides are rich in wildlife, from **seals and otters** to a variety of **seabirds and eagles**.

### Local Dining and Shopping

**Dining in Stornoway**

**Stornoway Black Pudding:** A local delicacy that has achieved **Protected Geographical Indication (PGI)**

status. It's often served as part of a traditional Scottish breakfast.

**Seafood Restaurants:** Try **freshly caught scallops, langoustines, and salmon** at local eateries like **HS-1 Café Bar** and **The Boatshed**.

## Shopping

**Craft Shops:** Find unique, handmade items such as **Gaelic books, jewelry, pottery, and knitwear**.

**Local Markets:** The **Stornoway Town Hall Market** offers local produce, artisan foods, and crafts.

### Best Time to Visit Stornoway

The best time to visit Stornoway is between **May and September**, when the weather is milder, and daylight lasts longer—perfect for outdoor activities. This period also hosts festivals like:

**HebCelt Festival (July):** A vibrant celebration of **Celtic music and culture**, attracting artists and visitors from around the world.

**Royal National Mòd (rotating annually):** A festival celebrating **Gaelic language, music, and arts**.

## Top Attractions in the Outer Hebrides: Callanish Stones, Lews Castle, and the Isle of Harris

The **Outer Hebrides**, an archipelago off the west coast of Scotland, is a land of **mystical landscapes, ancient history, and Gaelic culture**. Among its most captivating destinations are the **Callanish Stones**, the grand **Lews Castle**, and the breathtaking **Isle of Harris**. These sites showcase the region's rich heritage and natural beauty, offering visitors a unique blend of **archaeological wonders, historical landmarks, and dramatic scenery**.

### Callanish Stones: Scotland's Mysterious Megaliths

The **Callanish Stones** (or **Clach an Tursa** in Gaelic) are one of Scotland's most enigmatic and iconic prehistoric monuments. Located on the **Isle of Lewis**, this **5,000-year-old stone circle** predates Stonehenge and continues to fascinate historians, archaeologists, and visitors alike.

**Highlights of the Callanish Stones**

**The Stone Circle:** Comprising **13 main standing stones** arranged in a circle with a central monolith, the site forms a **cross-shaped layout** with additional stone rows radiating outward.

**Ancient Origins:** Dating back to around **2900 BC**, the stones are believed to have been used for **rituals, astronomical observations, and ceremonial gatherings**.

**Mystical Legends:** Local folklore suggests the stones were **giants turned to stone** for refusing to convert to Christianity, adding a mystical charm to the site.

**Surrounding Stone Circles:** Nearby, visitors can explore **Callanish II and III**, smaller but equally atmospheric stone formations.

**Visitor Information & Tips**

**Callanish Visitor Centre:** Offers insightful exhibitions about the stones' history, theories about their purpose, and an onsite café.

**Best Time to Visit: Sunrise or sunset** for magical light and fewer crowds.

**Accessibility:** Easily accessible by car from Stornoway, about a **30-minute drive**.

### Lews Castle: A Window into Hebridean Heritage

Overlooking **Stornoway Harbour, Lews Castle** is an impressive 19th-century mansion built by **Sir James Matheson**, who made his fortune in the Chinese tea and opium trade. Surrounded by **beautiful woodlands and extensive grounds**, the castle is a blend of **Victorian grandeur and Gaelic heritage**.

**Highlights of Lews Castle**

**Historic Architecture:** The castle's striking design features **Gothic Revival elements**, grand staircases, and ornate interiors.

**Museum nan Eilean:** Located within the castle, this museum showcases the history and culture of the Outer Hebrides, including exhibits on **Gaelic traditions, Viking**

influences, and the famous **Lewis Chessmen**—12th-century chess pieces carved from walrus ivory.

**Castle Grounds:** Over **270 hectares** of parkland with **walking trails, gardens, and scenic viewpoints** overlooking the harbor.

**Accommodation:** Some parts of the castle have been converted into **luxury apartments**, allowing visitors to stay overnight in this historic setting.

**Visitor Information & Tips**

**Location:** In the heart of Stornoway, easily accessible on foot from the town center.

**Admission:** Entry to the museum is free, though guided tours of the castle may require a fee.

**Best Time to Visit:** Spring and summer when the gardens are in full bloom.

## Isle of Harris: A Landscape of Stunning Contrasts

The **Isle of Harris**, connected to the Isle of Lewis, is renowned for its **dramatic mountain landscapes, pristine beaches, and rich Gaelic heritage**. Despite its rugged terrain, Harris is famous for its **soft, white sands and turquoise waters**, making it one of Scotland's most beautiful natural destinations.

**Highlights of the Isle of Harris**

**Luskentyre Beach:** Voted one of the **most beautiful beaches in the world**, Luskentyre features **sweeping sands, crystal-clear waters**, and views of the nearby **North Harris hills**.

**Harris Tweed:** Harris is the birthplace of the world-famous **Harris Tweed**, a handwoven fabric made from pure virgin wool. Visitors can tour local **weaving workshops** to learn about the craft and purchase authentic Harris Tweed products.

**Harris Distillery:** Located in **Tarbert**, the distillery produces the award-winning **Isle of Harris Gin**, known for its unique infusion of **sugar kelp**. Guided tours offer insights into the distilling process, with tastings included.

**Outdoor Adventures:** Harris is a haven for outdoor enthusiasts, offering activities such as **hiking, sea**

**kayaking, wildlife watching**, and **boat trips to St. Kilda**, a remote UNESCO World Heritage site.

**Visitor Information & Tips**

**Getting There:** Harris is accessible by car from Lewis or via **ferry from Uig on the Isle of Skye**.

**Best Time to Visit:** Late Spring to early autumn, when the weather is milder and perfect for outdoor activities.

**Local Tip:** Drive the scenic **Golden Road** on Harris's east coast, known for its **rugged coastline and charming villages**.

## Shore Excursions: Making the Most of Your Cruise Experience

Shore excursions are an essential part of any cruise, offering passengers the opportunity to **explore new destinations, immerse themselves in local cultures, and engage in unique activities** beyond the ship. Whether you're interested in **historical landmarks, scenic landscapes, adventure sports, or culinary experiences**, shore excursions provide a way to make the most of your limited time in port.

Planning ahead and choosing the right shore excursion can significantly enhance your cruise, transforming a simple stop into a **memorable travel experience**.

## Types of Shore Excursions

Cruise lines and independent operators offer a variety of shore excursions tailored to different interests and activity levels. Understanding your options can help you select the perfect experience.

### Historical & Cultural Tours

Ideal for travelers who love exploring history and heritage:

**City walking tours** showcasing ancient ruins, castles, and UNESCO World Heritage Sites.

**Museum visits** that highlight local art, artifacts, and traditions.

**Cultural experiences** like traditional music performances, dance shows, and handicraft workshops.

**Example:** Touring **Edinburgh Castle in Scotland**, exploring the **Acropolis in Athens**, or visiting **Mayan ruins in Mexico**.

### Scenic & Nature Excursions

For nature enthusiasts, these excursions focus on the great outdoors:

**Scenic drives** through coastal roads, mountain passes, and picturesque countryside.

**Wildlife watching**, including dolphin tours, birdwatching, and safaris.

**Eco-tours** exploring rainforests, glaciers, waterfalls, and national parks.

**Example:** A **fjord cruise in Norway**, a **wildlife safari in Alaska**, or a visit to the **Cliffs of Moher in Ireland**.

### Adventure & Outdoor Activities

Perfect for thrill-seekers and active travelers:

**Water sports** such as snorkeling, scuba diving, jet skiing, and paddleboarding.

**Hiking, zip-lining, and ATV tours** in rugged, scenic environments.

**Kayaking, canoeing, and white-water rafting** for a dose of adrenaline.

**Example: Snorkeling in the Great Barrier Reef, hiking volcanoes in Iceland,** or **zip-lining in Costa Rica.**

### Culinary & Wine Experiences

Great for food lovers who want to indulge in local flavors:

**Cooking classes** with local chefs using traditional techniques.

**Wine and whiskey tastings** at vineyards and distilleries.

**Food tours** through bustling markets and local eateries.

**Example: Whiskey tasting in Scotland, pasta-making classes in Italy,** or a **street food tour in Bangkok.**

### Beach & Relaxation Excursions

Ideal for travelers looking to unwind:

**Private beach getaways** with loungers, cocktails, and spa treatments.

**Catamaran cruises** with snorkeling stops and sunset views.

**Hot springs and wellness retreats** for ultimate relaxation.

**Example:** Relaxing on Caribbean beaches, swimming in Santorini's crystal waters, or visiting the **Blue Lagoon in Iceland**.

## Booking Shore Excursions: Cruise Line vs. Independent Operators

**Booking Through the Cruise Line**

**Guaranteed Return to Ship:** The cruise won't leave without you if a ship-sponsored tour runs late.

**Reliability:** Tours are vetted for **safety and quality**.

**Convenience:** Transportation and logistics are handled for you.

**Cons:**

**Higher Cost:** Typically, **30–50% more expensive** than independent tours.

**Larger Groups:** Less personalized attention.

**Booking with Independent Operators**

**More Affordable:** Often cheaper with **smaller group sizes**.

**Unique Experiences:** More flexibility and off-the-beaten-path adventures.

**Local Insights:** Direct interaction with **local guides** and businesses.

**Cons:**

**Risk of Missing the Ship:** The ship won't wait if an independent tour runs late.

**More Research Required:** Need to vet operators for safety and reliability.

**Tip:** If booking independently, choose tours that return at least **2 hours before the ship's departure**.

**Tips for Choosing the Best Shore Excursion**

**Consider Your Interests & Activity Level:** Choose tours that match your preferences—whether adventurous, cultural, or relaxing.
**Read Reviews & Compare Options:** Use websites like **TripAdvisor** or **Cruise Critic** for feedback.
**Book Early for Popular Tours:** High-demand excursions sell out quickly, especially in peak season.
**Check Cancellation Policies:** Understand refund terms in case of schedule changes.
**Be Mindful of Time Zones:** Cruise ships operate on **"ship time"**, which may differ from local time.

### What to Pack for Shore Excursions

**Daypack:** Carry essentials like water, sunscreen, and snacks.
**Sunglasses & Hat:** Protect against the sun.
**Sunscreen & Insect Repellent:** Essential for tropical destinations.
**Camera or Smartphone:** Capture memorable moments.
**Reusable Water Bottle:** Stay hydrated.

**Local Currency & Credit Card:** Some small vendors don't accept cards.

**Comfortable Shoes:** Important for walking tours or hikes.

## Dining & Shopping: A Guide to Enriching Your Travel Experience

Dining and shopping are two of the most rewarding ways to immerse yourself in a new destination. Whether you're indulging in **authentic local cuisine** or discovering **unique souvenirs**, these experiences offer a deeper connection to the culture, history, and lifestyle of the places you visit. From bustling markets to fine dining establishments, the diversity in flavors and products ensures that every traveler can find something memorable to savor or take home.

### Dining: A Culinary Journey Through Culture

Food is more than just sustenance; it's a **story of tradition, history, and community**. Exploring local cuisine allows travelers to experience a destination's essence through its flavors, ingredients, and culinary techniques.

**Local Cuisine and Must-Try Dishes**

Every region boasts signature dishes that reflect its heritage:

**Italy:** Fresh **pasta**, authentic **Neapolitan pizza**, creamy **risotto**, and rich **gelato**.

**Japan:** Delicate **sushi**, flavorful **ramen**, crisp **tempura**, and tender **wagyu beef**.

**Mexico:** Vibrant **tacos**, hearty **tamales**, complex **mole sauces**, and sweet **churros**.

**Thailand:** Aromatic **Pad Thai**, spicy **green curry**, tangy **papaya salad**, and sweet **mango sticky rice**.

**Scotland:** Traditional **haggis**, hearty **Cullen skink** (smoked fish chowder), and **black pudding**.

Sampling these dishes isn't just about taste—it's about experiencing the **ingredients grown locally**, the **cooking methods passed down through generations**, and the **stories behind each recipe**.

### Where to Dine

**Street Food Markets:** Perfect for trying authentic, budget-friendly dishes. Markets like **Bangkok's Chatuchak, Istanbul's Grand Bazaar**, or **Barcelona's La Boqueria** offer fresh, flavorful bites.

**Local Cafés & Family-Run Restaurants:** Cozy settings where traditional recipes are prepared with care, often using locally sourced ingredients.

**Fine Dining:** For a more refined experience, many destinations offer **Michelin-starred restaurants** showcasing innovative culinary techniques.

**Food Tours & Cooking Classes:** Great ways to explore a city's food scene while learning about its culinary history.

### Dining Tips

**Embrace Local Customs:** Research **tipping practices**, dining etiquette, and common table manners.

**Be Adventurous:** Don't hesitate to try unfamiliar dishes—you might discover a new favorite!

**Dietary Preferences:** If you have dietary restrictions, learn key phrases in the local language or carry a translation card.

### Shopping: Discovering Unique Treasures

Shopping while traveling isn't just about souvenirs—it's about finding **authentic products that reflect a destination's culture and craftsmanship.**

**Popular Shopping Destinations**

**Local Markets & Bazaars:** Great for **handmade crafts, textiles, spices, and antiques.** Explore places like the **Marrakech Souks, Chatuchak Market in Bangkok,** or **Portobello Road Market in London.**

**Artisan Boutiques:** Discover **handcrafted jewelry, pottery, and traditional clothing** made by local artisans.

**Luxury Stores:** Cities like **Paris, Milan, and Dubai** offer high-end fashion, designer brands, and luxury goods.

**Duty-Free Shops:** Ideal for purchasing items like **perfume, liquor, and luxury watches** at tax-free prices.

**Popular Souvenirs Around the World**

**Japan:** Delicate **ceramics, kimono fabrics,** and **matcha green tea.**

**Italy: Murano glass, leather goods,** and **limoncello** from the Amalfi Coast.

**Mexico: Talavera pottery,** colorful **handwoven textiles,** and **silver jewelry.**

**Scotland:** Authentic **Harris Tweed,** whisky, and **Celtic jewelry.**

**France:** Luxurious **perfume, gourmet cheeses,** and fine **wines.**

**Shopping Tips**

**Haggling:** In many markets, especially in Asia, the Middle East, and Africa, bargaining is expected—just remember to be polite and respectful.

**Check for Authenticity:** When buying local crafts, verify authenticity to avoid mass-produced items marketed as handmade.

**Customs Regulations:** Be aware of restrictions on items like **alcohol, antiques, or animal products** when returning home.

**Payment Options:** Carry a mix of **cash and cards**, as some small vendors may not accept credit payments.

### Combining Dining & Shopping: A Perfect Pair

Many destinations seamlessly blend dining and shopping into one immersive experience. For example:

**Food Markets:** Places like **La Boqueria (Barcelona)** or **Borough Market (London)** allow you to sample local delicacies and buy fresh produce or artisanal products to take home.

**Cultural Festivals:** Events like **Oktoberfest in Germany** or **Songkran in Thailand** combine traditional foods with local crafts and souvenirs.

**Winery or Distillery Tours:** After a tasting session at a **whisky distillery in Scotland** or a **vineyard in Tuscany**, you can purchase exclusive bottles to remember your visit.

## Other Notable Ports: Guernsey, Isle of Man, and Isles of Scilly

While major cruise destinations like London and Edinburgh often steal the spotlight, the **British Isles** are dotted with **lesser-known ports** that offer unique charm, rich history, and stunning natural beauty. Among these, **Guernsey, the Isle of Man, and the Isles of Scilly** stand out as captivating stops on any British Isles cruise itinerary. Each of these ports boasts its own distinct character, from medieval fortresses and rugged coastlines to botanical gardens and ancient heritage sites.

### Guernsey: A Blend of British Charm and French Influence

Located in the **Channel Islands**, just off the coast of France, **Guernsey** offers a fascinating blend of **British heritage and French culture**. Its capital, **St. Peter Port**, is a picturesque harbor town with **cobblestone streets, colorful houses, and vibrant waterfront cafés**.

**Highlights of Guernsey:**

**Castle Cornet:** Standing guard over St. Peter Port for over **800 years**, this impressive fortress offers **panoramic views** of the harbor, **museums**, and daily **cannon-firing ceremonies** during summer.

**Hauteville House:** The former home of **Victor Hugo**, where the French author wrote *Les Misérables* during his exile. The house, filled with eclectic decor, offers a glimpse into his creative mind.

**German Occupation Museum:** Guernsey was occupied by Nazi Germany during World War II. This museum provides a sobering yet fascinating insight into the island's wartime history.

**Coastal Walks and Beaches:** Guernsey's **rugged cliffs, sandy beaches, and scenic walking trails** offer stunning views of the English Channel. Don't miss **Petit Bot Bay** and **Cobo Beach**.

**Local Tip: Sample the famous Guernsey cream tea, made with the island's rich dairy products.**

## Isle of Man: A Land of Legends and Motorsports

Situated in the **Irish Sea** between England and Ireland, the **Isle of Man** is known for its **Viking heritage, scenic landscapes, and the thrilling Isle of Man TT motorcycle race**. Its capital, **Douglas**, is a lively port with a beautiful promenade and Victorian architecture.

**Highlights of the Isle of Man:**

**Laxey Wheel:** Also known as the **"Great Laxey Wheel"**, it's the world's largest working waterwheel, built in 1854 to pump water from the island's mines.

**Snaefell Mountain Railway:** Take a historic electric train to the summit of **Snaefell**, the island's highest peak, where you can see **England, Ireland, Scotland, and Wales** on a clear day.

**Peel Castle:** A striking medieval fortress built by the Vikings, offering scenic views over the Irish Sea.

**Manx Museum:** Located in Douglas, this museum delves into the **island's Celtic and Norse heritage**, natural history, and maritime past.

**Local Tip:** Try **Manx kippers**, a traditional smoked herring dish that's a staple of the island's cuisine.

### Isles of Scilly: A Subtropical Paradise Off Cornwall

Just **28 miles off the coast of Cornwall**, the **Isles of Scilly** are a group of around **140 islands**, with only five inhabited. The largest, **St. Mary's**, serves as the main port for cruise ships. Known for their **mild climate, crystal-clear waters, and white sandy beaches**, the Isles of Scilly feel like a hidden paradise.

**Highlights of the Isles of Scilly:**

**Tresco Abbey Garden:** A stunning **botanical garden** featuring over **20,000 exotic plants** from around the world, thriving thanks to the islands' subtropical climate.

**St. Mary's Island:** Explore the **coastal path**, charming villages like **Hugh Town**, and secluded coves perfect for beachcombing.

**Historic Sites:** Visit the **Star Castle**, a 16th-century fortress, and the **Garrison Walls**, offering breathtaking views of the surrounding islands.

**Island Hopping:** Take a small boat to nearby islands like **St. Agnes** or **Bryher** for peaceful walks, wildlife spotting, and unspoiled scenery.

**Local Tip: Sample fresh Scillonian seafood, especially lobster and crab, caught daily by local fishermen.**

# ONBOARD EXPERIENCE

## The Onboard Experience: What to Expect on a Cruise

The **onboard experience** is one of the most exciting aspects of a cruise, offering passengers a perfect blend of **relaxation, entertainment, fine dining, and world-class amenities**. Whether you're embarking on a luxury voyage through the British Isles or a tropical adventure in the Caribbean, modern cruise ships are designed to be **floating resorts**, providing something for everyone—from **spa enthusiasts and foodies** to **adventure seekers and families**.

Here's what you can expect from an unforgettable onboard experience.

### Accommodation: Comfortable Cabins for Every Traveler

Cruise ships offer a variety of accommodation options, catering to different preferences and budgets:

**Interior Cabins:** Budget-friendly rooms without windows, perfect for those who spend most of their time exploring the ship.

**Oceanview Cabins:** Rooms with a window or porthole, offering natural light and sea views.

**Balcony Staterooms:** Private balconies with seating areas—ideal for enjoying **sunrises, sunsets, and fresh sea air**.

**Suites:** Spacious, luxurious accommodations with extra amenities, such as **personal butlers, priority boarding, and exclusive lounges**.

Regardless of the room type, cabins are thoughtfully designed with **comfortable beds, en-suite bathrooms, storage space, and modern conveniences**.

### Dining: A Culinary Adventure at Sea

Dining on a cruise is an experience in itself, with **diverse options to satisfy every palate**.

**Main Dining Room**

Most cruises include meals in the **main dining room**, offering a **multi-course menu** with dishes inspired by international cuisine. The atmosphere ranges from **casual breakfasts** to **elegant dinners**, often with flexible seating arrangements.

**Buffet Restaurants**

Buffets provide **casual, all-you-can-eat options**, featuring a variety of dishes from fresh salads and pastas to global favorites. They're perfect for quick meals or trying new foods without commitment.

**Specialty Restaurants**

For a more refined dining experience, specialty restaurants (usually at an extra cost) offer gourmet menus:

**Steakhouses** with premium cuts.

**Italian trattorias** serving authentic pasta and pizza.

**Sushi bars** and **Asian fusion** cuisine.

**Seafood restaurants** showcasing fresh catches.

**Cafés & Room Service**

Enjoy **24-hour room service**, poolside snacks, and cozy cafés serving specialty coffees and desserts.

### Entertainment: Endless Activities Day and Night

Cruise ships are renowned for their **world-class entertainment options**, ensuring there's never a dull moment.

**Live Shows & Performances**

**Broadway-style productions** in grand theaters.

**Comedy shows, magic acts, and acrobatic performances**.

**Live music** ranging from jazz bands to classical quartets.

**Casinos & Nightlife**

**Casinos** with slot machines, poker, blackjack, and roulette.

**Nightclubs and bars** offering themed parties, DJ sets, and dance floors.

**Piano bars and lounges** for a more relaxed evening vibe.

**Daytime Activities**

**Trivia games, cooking demonstrations, and art auctions**.

**Enrichment lectures** about destinations, history, or photography.

**Workshops** on everything from dance lessons to language classes.

## Recreation & Wellness: Relax or Rejuvenate

**Pools & Spas**

**Multiple pools** with hot tubs, water slides, and even surf simulators on some ships.

**Adults-only retreats** for peaceful sunbathing and relaxation.

**Luxury spas** offering massages, facials, saunas, and thermal suites.

**Fitness Centers & Sports**

**Fully-equipped gyms** with cardio machines and weights.

**Fitness classes** like yoga, Pilates, spinning, and Zumba.

**Sports courts** for basketball, tennis, and mini-golf.

### Family-Friendly Features

Cruises are fantastic for families, with activities designed for all ages:

**Kids' Clubs** with supervised programs based on age groups.

**Teen lounges** offering gaming consoles, music, and social events.

**Water parks and adventure zones** with slides, climbing walls, and zip lines.

### Onboard Shopping & Duty-Free Deals

From **boutiques selling luxury brands** to **duty-free shops**, cruise ships offer excellent shopping opportunities:

**Jewelry, watches, and designer clothing**.

**Souvenirs, local crafts, and gifts**.

**Duty-free liquor, perfumes, and cosmetics.**

### Connectivity & Technology

Modern ships offer **Wi-Fi packages**, allowing you to stay connected at sea. Some also have **apps** to help you navigate the ship, book activities, and manage your schedule.

## Cruise Ship Activities: From Spa Days to Adventure Sports

A cruise vacation isn't just about the destinations—it's also about the journey. Modern cruise ships are designed to be **floating resorts**, offering a wide range of activities that cater to every type of traveler. Whether you're looking to **relax and unwind** or **seek thrilling adventures**, there's something for everyone onboard. From **luxurious spa experiences** to **heart-pumping adventure sports**, here's what you can expect when it comes to cruise ship activities.

## Spa & Wellness: Ultimate Relaxation at Sea

For those seeking tranquility and rejuvenation, cruise ship spas provide a haven of **peaceful indulgence**.

**Spa Services**

Most cruise ships feature full-service spas offering:

**Massages:** From **Swedish and deep tissue** to **hot stone** and **aromatherapy**.

**Facials:** Tailored treatments for **hydration, anti-aging, and skin rejuvenation**.

**Body Wraps and Scrubs:** Detoxifying and exfoliating therapies using **seaweed, mud, or salt**.

**Thermal Suites & Hydrotherapy Pools**

Some ships offer **thermal suites** with **saunas, steam rooms, and heated loungers**, perfect for easing muscle tension. **Hydrotherapy pools** and **saltwater baths** enhance relaxation, helping to relieve stress and improve circulation.

**Beauty & Wellness Treatments**

Onboard salons offer:

**Haircuts, styling, and color treatments.**

**Manicures, pedicures, and nail art.**

**Acupuncture, teeth whitening, and even Botox on select luxury liners.**

**Mind & Body Wellness**

**Yoga and Pilates classes** for flexibility and mindfulness.

**Meditation sessions** and **wellness workshops** to promote mental well-being.

### Fitness & Recreation: Staying Active at Sea

For fitness enthusiasts, cruise ships offer state-of-the-art **gyms and sports facilities** to maintain your routine while at sea.

**Fitness Centers**

**Modern equipment:** Treadmills, elliptical machines, free weights, and resistance training machines.

**Group fitness classes: Zumba, spin classes, HIIT sessions, and circuit training** led by certified instructors.

**Personal training:** One-on-one sessions tailored to your fitness goals.

### Sports Courts & Recreation Areas

**Basketball and tennis courts** for friendly matches.

**Mini-golf courses** with ocean views.

**Running tracks** circling the upper decks for morning jogs.

## Adventure Sports: Thrills on the High Seas

For adrenaline seekers, cruise ships offer an array of **adventure activities** that push the boundaries of traditional cruising.

### Thrill Rides & Attractions

**Zip Lines:** Soar across the ship's deck with breathtaking ocean views.

**Rock Climbing Walls:** Test your skills against towering climbing walls.

**Surf Simulators:** Ride the waves on **FlowRider surf machines**, perfect for beginners and pros.

**Skydiving Simulators:** Experience the thrill of freefall in a controlled wind tunnel.

**Water Parks & Pools**

**Water slides:** Twist and turn down multi-story slides.

**Wave pools and splash zones** for family fun.

**Infinity pools** for a more serene, scenic experience.

### Unique Onboard Activities

Modern cruise lines constantly innovate to offer **one-of-a-kind experiences**:

**Ice Skating Rinks:** Yes, some ships have real ice rinks for skating shows and guest sessions.

**Virtual Reality (VR) Experiences:** Immerse yourself in VR games and simulations.

**Laser Tag Arenas:** Compete with friends in high-energy laser battles.

**Relaxation & Leisure Activities**

Not every activity has to be adrenaline-packed. For a slower pace, enjoy:

**Poolside lounging** with a cocktail in hand.

**Sunset yoga classes** or peaceful walks on deck.

**Library lounges** for quiet reading time.

**Board games and trivia contests** for social fun.

## Wellness and Fitness Onboard: Staying Healthy at Sea

Gone are the days when cruising was just about indulgent buffets and lounging by the pool. Modern cruise ships are designed with a strong focus on **wellness and fitness**, offering travelers a variety of options to maintain a healthy lifestyle while at sea. Whether you're a fitness enthusiast, a yoga lover, or someone simply looking to relax and rejuvenate, today's cruise ships provide **state-of-the-art facilities, diverse classes, and holistic wellness programs** to cater to all your health needs.

Here's what you can expect when it comes to staying fit and feeling your best onboard.

### Fitness Centers: State-of-the-Art Gym Facilities

Most cruise ships are equipped with **modern fitness centers** that rival land-based gyms. These spaces are designed to help passengers stay active, offering everything from **cardio machines** to **free weights**.

**Equipment Available:**

**Treadmills, ellipticals, and stationary bikes** with ocean-view windows.

**Rowing machines** and **stair climbers** for full-body workouts.

**Free weights, resistance machines, and kettlebells** for strength training.

**Functional training areas** with battle ropes, TRX suspension trainers, and stability balls.

Fitness centers are typically open from early morning until late at night, allowing guests to work out at their convenience.

## Group Fitness Classes: Motivation and Fun

For those who prefer **guided workouts**, cruise ships offer a variety of **group fitness classes** led by professional instructors.

## Popular Classes Include:

**Yoga & Pilates:** Great for improving flexibility, balance, and mindfulness.

**Spinning Classes:** High-energy cycling sessions with music and motivating coaches.

**Zumba & Dance Fitness:** Fun, calorie-burning workouts set to lively music.

**HIIT (High-Intensity Interval Training):** For those looking to challenge themselves with intense, fast-paced exercises.

**Aqua Aerobics:** Low-impact water workouts in the ship's pool, ideal for joint-friendly exercise.

Some classes are included in your cruise fare, while specialty classes (like Pilates reformer or TRX sessions) may carry an additional fee.

**Outdoor Fitness & Sports Activities**

If you prefer exercising in the fresh sea breeze, cruise ships offer plenty of outdoor fitness options.

**Sports Courts & Tracks:**

**Running Tracks:** Most ships have a dedicated track for jogging or walking, often with stunning ocean views.

**Basketball and Tennis Courts:** For friendly games with fellow passengers.

**Mini-Golf & Rock-Climbing Walls:** Fun ways to stay active while enjoying the scenery.

**Rope Courses & Zip Lines:** Available on some adventure-focused ships for an adrenaline rush.

Many ships also feature **open-air fitness zones** with equipment like pull-up bars, stretching areas, and balance trainers.

## Wellness & Spa Facilities: Relaxation and Rejuvenation

Wellness isn't just about breaking a sweat—it's also about relaxation and mental well-being. Most cruise lines feature **luxurious spas and wellness centers** offering a range of treatments.

### Spa Services Include:

**Massages:** Swedish, deep tissue, hot stone, aromatherapy, and more.

**Facials & Skin Treatments:** Designed to hydrate, rejuvenate, and refresh your skin.

**Body Wraps & Scrubs:** Detoxifying and exfoliating treatments using sea salt, algae, or mud.

**Acupuncture & Alternative Therapies:** Available on some luxury cruise lines for holistic wellness.

**Thermal Suites & Relaxation Areas:**

**Saunas and steam rooms** to detoxify and relax muscles.

**Heated loungers and hydrotherapy pools** for ultimate relaxation.

**Salt rooms** and **aromatherapy showers** for enhanced sensory experiences.

### Mindfulness and Mental Wellness

Cruises also cater to mental well-being through programs focused on **mindfulness, meditation, and stress reduction**.

**Mindfulness Activities:**

**Guided meditation sessions** for stress relief and mental clarity.

**Breathing workshops** to promote relaxation.

**Wellness seminars** covering topics like sleep health, nutrition, and holistic living.

Some luxury cruise lines even offer **wellness retreats** with personalized programs, private coaching, and specialized classes.

**Healthy Dining Options**

Maintaining a healthy lifestyle onboard isn't limited to the gym. Many cruise lines now offer **nutritious dining options**, including:

**Salad bars, fresh fruit stations, and plant-based menus.**

**Gluten-free, vegetarian, and low-calorie dishes** clearly labeled on menus.

**Smoothie bars** and **cold-pressed juices** for a refreshing, healthy boost.

Additionally, **nutrition workshops** and **cooking classes** are sometimes available for guests interested in healthy eating habits.

## Kids and Family-Friendly Activities in the British Isles: Fun for All Ages

The **British Isles** offer a wealth of family-friendly experiences, combining **historic landmarks, outdoor adventures, and interactive activities** that will engage both adults and kids. Whether you're exploring the

**charming streets of London**, hiking through the **Scottish Highlands**, or enjoying coastal adventures in **Ireland**, there's something for everyone in the family. Here's a guide to the top family-friendly activities across the British Isles that promise to create lasting memories for all ages.

### London – A City Full of Wonders

**Top Family-Friendly Activities:**

**The Natural History Museum:** A fantastic starting point for families with young children, the museum is filled with interactive exhibits on **dinosaurs, volcanoes**, and **space exploration**. The giant **dinosaur skeleton** in the main hall is a highlight for all ages.

**The London Eye:** A thrilling experience for families, offering **panoramic views** of London from the top of this iconic Ferris wheel. Kids will love spotting landmarks like **Big Ben**, **Buckingham Palace**, and the **River Thames** from above.

**Harry Potter Studio Tour:** A magical experience for Harry Potter fans, this studio tour gives a behind-the-scenes look at the films, featuring **sets, props**, and **costumes** from the wizarding world.

**Hyde Park and Kensington Gardens:** Let the kids run wild at the **Princess Diana Memorial Playground**, which is inspired by the **Peter Pan** story, featuring a giant pirate ship and lots of interactive play areas.

**Travel Tip:** For convenience, purchase a **London Pass** to gain entry to multiple attractions and avoid long queues.

## Edinburgh, Scotland – History and Adventure Combined

**Top Family-Friendly Activities:**

**Edinburgh Castle:** Kids will love exploring this **medieval fortress** perched atop a volcano. The castle offers interactive displays and a chance to see the **Crown Jewels of Scotland**.

**Camera Obscura & World of Illusions:** A fun and interactive museum filled with optical illusions, 3D exhibits, and a **rooftop view** of Edinburgh. It's both educational and entertaining for children of all ages.

**The Royal Botanic Garden:** A beautiful and peaceful spot to explore with kids. The **Glasshouse** features exotic plants from around the world, while **playful themed gardens** keep children engaged.

**Arthur's Seat:** For families who enjoy outdoor activities, take a hike up this ancient volcano for stunning views of the city. It's a family-friendly trek suitable for all fitness levels.

**Travel Tip:** Edinburgh's **Old Town** can be hilly and cobbled, so wear **comfortable shoes** for walking.

### Dublin, Ireland – A Family-Friendly Cultural Hub

**Top Family-Friendly Activities:**

**Dublin Zoo:** Located in **Phoenix Park**, this zoo is one of the oldest in Europe and features **over 400 species**. It's an excellent way for kids to learn about wildlife conservation while having fun.

**Dublinia:** Step back in time to the **Viking and medieval eras** at this interactive museum. Kids can explore historical exhibits, try on Viking costumes, and even experience what it was like to live in **medieval Dublin**.

**Imaginosity, Dublin's Children's Museum:** A hands-on museum designed for children under 9, it encourages imaginative play and learning through interactive exhibits on science, art, and design.

**St. Stephen's Green:** A central park perfect for families, with a playground, ponds, and plenty of space for a picnic or leisurely stroll.

**Travel Tip: Public transport in Dublin** is family-friendly, and buses offer a **free ride for children** under 5.

### The Isle of Skye, Scotland – Nature at Its Best

**Top Family-Friendly Activities:**

**Fairy Pools:** A magical spot for families to explore, the **Fairy Pools** are crystal-clear waters surrounded by breathtaking landscapes. Kids will enjoy paddling and splashing in the pools or simply exploring the **picturesque surroundings**.

**Skye Museum of Island Life:** Perfect for a rainy day, this museum gives families insight into **Skye's past**, with recreated cottages and exhibits on the island's **history and culture**.

**Eilean Donan Castle:** A stunning **Scottish castle** located on an island in the middle of a lock. Families can explore the castle's **rooms and exhibits**, and the view from the bridge is breathtaking.

**Hiking and Wildlife Watching:** The Isle of Skye is known for its **wildlife**, including **seals**, **eagles**, and **red deer**. Kids can enjoy easy walks and hikes in nature while spotting animals.

**Travel Tip:** Dress in **layers** and be prepared for changeable weather, especially on the **Isle of Skye**, where conditions can shift rapidly.

### The Lake District, England – Outdoor Adventures for Families

**Top Family-Friendly Activities:**

**Lake Windermere:** The largest lake in England offers a variety of activities for families, including **boating**, **swimming**, and **fishing**. Take a scenic boat ride or enjoy a peaceful lakeside walk with the kids.

**Beatrix Potter's House:** A great visit for families with young children, this **museum and garden** is dedicated to the author of *Peter Rabbit*. Kids will love exploring the garden and learning about Potter's life.

**Aira Force Waterfall:** A beautiful, family-friendly walk through the woods that leads to a stunning waterfall. The route is accessible for children and provides plenty of opportunities for exploration.

**The World of Beatrix Potter:** An interactive attraction in **Bowness-on-Windermere**, bringing Potter's famous characters to life. Kids can enjoy hands-on exhibits and immersive displays.

**Travel Tip:** The **Lake District** can be busy during peak tourist season, so plan excursions early in the day for a more relaxed experience.

# CULTURAL INSIGHTS

## Cultural Insights: Enriching Your Travel Experience

Travel isn't just about visiting new places—it's about **immersing yourself in different cultures**, understanding local traditions, and connecting with people whose lives may differ greatly from your own. Whether you're exploring bustling cities, quiet villages, or remote islands, gaining cultural insights adds **depth and meaning** to your journey. It allows you to appreciate the **history, customs, and values** that shape a destination's identity, turning a simple trip into an unforgettable experience.

Here's how cultural insights can enhance your travels and what to look for when exploring new destinations.

### Understanding Local Traditions and Customs

Every culture has its own set of **traditions, etiquette, and social norms** that reflect its history and way of life. Learning about these customs not only shows respect but also helps you engage more meaningfully with local communities.

**Key Areas to Explore:**

**Greetings:** In Japan, a bow is customary, while in parts of Europe, cheek kisses are common. In contrast, a firm handshake might be the norm in the U.S.

**Table Manners:** In Ethiopia, meals are often shared from a communal plate, and using your right hand is traditional. In Thailand, it's polite to eat with a spoon rather than a fork.

**Dress Codes:** Modest attire is required when visiting religious sites like **mosques in the Middle East** or **temples in Southeast Asia**.

By observing these practices, you'll not only avoid unintentional faux pas but also show genuine appreciation for the local culture.

## Language and Communication

While you don't need to be fluent in the local language, learning a few basic phrases can go a long way. Simple greetings like **"hello," "thank you," and "please"** in the native language often bring smiles and create instant connections.

**Helpful Tips:**

**Use translation apps** for quick assistance.

**Listen actively**—body language, gestures, and tone can convey meaning even when words don't.

**Practice cultural sensitivity:** Some cultures value indirect communication, while others are more direct. Understanding these nuances can help avoid misunderstandings.

## Festivals and Celebrations

Attending local festivals is one of the best ways to experience a culture's **vibrant traditions, music, dance, and food**. Festivals often reflect a region's history, religious beliefs, or agricultural cycles.

**Notable Festivals Around the World:**

**Carnival in Brazil:** A dazzling display of parades, costumes, and samba music.

**Diwali in India:** The Festival of Lights, symbolizing the victory of light over darkness.

**Oktoberfest in Germany:** A celebration of Bavarian culture, complete with beer, pretzels, and folk music.

**Up Helly Aa in Scotland:** A Viking fire festival in the Shetland Islands, featuring torch-lit processions and traditional Norse costumes.

Participating in these events provides a **firsthand look at local customs and community spirit**.

### Art, Architecture, and Heritage Sites

Exploring a destination's **art, architecture, and historical landmarks** offers valuable insights into its past and present. Museums, galleries, and ancient ruins often tell stories of a region's evolution over centuries.

**Examples of Cultural Heritage:**

**The Acropolis in Athens:** A symbol of ancient Greek civilization.

**The Louvre in Paris:** Home to masterpieces from different eras and cultures.

**Machu Picchu in Peru:** An Incan citadel that reflects the ingenuity of ancient engineering.

**Harris Tweed Weaving in Scotland:** A living tradition that showcases Scottish craftsmanship and heritage.

Engaging with these sites allows you to **connect with history** in a tangible, meaningful way.

### Cuisine as a Cultural Window

Food is a universal language that reflects a region's **history, geography, and identity**. Tasting local dishes introduces you to **traditional flavors, cooking methods, and ingredients** unique to that culture.

**Culinary Experiences to Try:**

**Street food tours** in cities like Bangkok, Mexico City, or Istanbul.

**Cooking classes** that teach traditional recipes.

**Dining with local families** through cultural exchange programs.

Each meal tells a story, from the spices used to the way food is prepared and shared.

### Responsible and Respectful Travel

When exploring different cultures, it's important to practice **responsible tourism**:

**Support local businesses** by buying from artisans and eating at family-run restaurants.

**Ask permission before taking photos**, especially of people.

**Respect sacred sites**—follow rules regarding dress codes and behavior.

Traveling with **an open mind and a respectful attitude** not only enriches your experience but also fosters positive connections between visitors and local communities.

## British Isles History and Heritage: A Journey Through Time

The **British Isles**, encompassing **England, Scotland, Wales, Ireland, and hundreds of smaller islands,** boast a rich tapestry of history and heritage that spans thousands of years. From **ancient stone circles and Roman conquests** to **medieval castles and the rise of global empires**, the story of the British Isles is one of conquest, cultural fusion, and resilience. This region's historical depth is reflected in its **monuments, traditions, languages, and landscapes**, offering travelers an immersive journey through time.

### Prehistoric Beginnings: The Dawn of Civilization

The history of the British Isles begins with its earliest inhabitants, dating back to the **Mesolithic period (around 8000 BC)**. Evidence of prehistoric life can be found in ancient monuments and archaeological sites scattered across the region.

**Key Sites:**

**Stonehenge (England):** One of the world's most iconic prehistoric monuments, built around **3000 BC**, its purpose remains a mystery, though it likely held ceremonial significance.

**Callanish Stones (Scotland):** Located on the Isle of Lewis, these standing stones date back to **2900 BC** and were likely used for **rituals and astronomical observations**.

**Newgrange (Ireland):** A **Neolithic passage tomb**, older than the Egyptian pyramids, known for its winter solstice alignment, flooding the inner chamber with sunlight.

These sites reflect the **sophistication of early societies**, their spiritual beliefs, and their connection to the natural world.

### Celtic Influence and the Iron Age

By **600 BC**, the British Isles were dominated by **Celtic tribes**, whose influence remains strong today in the form of languages like **Welsh, Irish Gaelic, and Scots Gaelic**. The Celts brought with them:

**Complex social structures**, including tribal kings and warriors.

**Intricate art**, characterized by **spiral motifs and metalwork**.

**Druidic religious practices**, focusing on nature worship and sacred sites.

The legacy of the Celts is visible in cultural festivals, folklore, and place names throughout the British Isles.

## Roman Britain (43 AD – 410 AD)

The **Romans** invaded Britain in **43 AD**, leaving an indelible mark on its history. They introduced:

**Advanced infrastructure**, including roads, baths, aqueducts, and cities like **Londinium** (modern-day London).

**Hadrian's Wall:** A monumental fortification in northern England, built to defend the empire's frontier.

**Latin language and Roman law**, influencing the development of British governance.

Although the Romans never fully conquered Scotland or Ireland, their presence significantly shaped Britain's cultural and urban landscape.

## The Medieval Era: Kings, Castles, and Conquests

Following the Roman withdrawal, the British Isles entered a period marked by **Viking raids, Anglo-Saxon settlements, and Norman conquests**.

**Key Events:**

**Anglo-Saxon Period:** Germanic tribes settled in England, establishing kingdoms like **Wessex** and **Mercia**.

**Viking Invasions:** From the 8th century, Norse warriors raided and settled in parts of **Scotland, Ireland, and England**, leaving a lasting impact on language and culture.

**Norman Conquest (1066):** Led by **William the Conqueror**, the Normans introduced **feudalism**, **stone castles**, and significant architectural changes, including the **Tower of London**.

Medieval Britain also saw the rise of **chivalry, cathedrals, and literary works** like **Beowulf** and the **Arthurian legends**.

### The Renaissance and the British Empire

The **Tudor period (1485–1603)** marked a time of political and religious upheaval, with figures like **Henry VIII** and **Elizabeth I** shaping Britain's future. The **Protestant**

**Reformation** transformed religious life, while maritime exploration expanded British influence globally.

The subsequent rise of the **British Empire** in the 17th and 18th centuries made Britain a dominant world power. This era saw:

The establishment of colonies across **Africa, Asia, and the Americas**.

The **Industrial Revolution**, which began in Britain, revolutionizing industry, transportation, and society.

Cultural advancements in **science, art, and literature**, with figures like **Shakespeare**, **Newton**, and **Darwin**.

### Modern Britain: Wars, Unity, and Change

The **20th century** brought profound changes:

**World Wars I & II** tested Britain's resilience, with landmarks like the **Churchill War Rooms** in London serving as historical reminders.

The decline of the empire led to the formation of the **Commonwealth of Nations**.

The **Good Friday Agreement (1998)** marked a milestone in the peace process between **Northern Ireland** and the **Republic of Ireland**.

Today, the United Kingdom and the Republic of Ireland thrive as diverse, dynamic nations, embracing both tradition and modernity.

### Cultural Heritage: A Living Legacy

The British Isles' heritage isn't confined to museums and monuments. It lives on through:

**Languages:** Gaelic, Welsh, and Scots continue to be spoken.

**Traditions:** Highland games, Irish music, Morri's dancing, and medieval festivals.

**Landmarks:** From **Edinburgh Castle** to the **Giant's Causeway**, historical sites connect past to present.

## Local Customs and Etiquette in the British Isles: A Guide for Travelers

The **British Isles**, including **England, Scotland, Wales, Northern Ireland**, and the **Republic of Ireland**, are rich in **tradition, history, and cultural diversity**. While these regions share many customs, each has its own unique quirks and social norms. Understanding local etiquette and customs can help travelers navigate everyday interactions smoothly, avoid misunderstandings, and foster positive connections with the locals. Here's a guide to **help you blend in** and make the most of your trip to the British Isles.

## Greetings and Social Interactions

### Polite and Reserved

In the British Isles, **politeness and respect for personal space** are paramount. People tend to be **more reserved** when compared to other cultures, especially in initial encounters. When meeting someone for the first time:

**Handshakes** are the most common form of greeting, often firm but not overly strong.

In **Ireland** and parts of **Scotland**, it's not uncommon to receive a **warm hug** from close friends or family. However, in more formal settings, a handshake remains the standard.

**Titles** such as **Mr., Mrs., or Dr.** are used until you're invited to use first names, particularly in more formal contexts.

**Politeness is key**—you'll often hear "**please**," "**thank you**," and "**sorry**" used frequently. Saying "sorry" is a sign of empathy in the UK, even if you're not at fault, especially when passing someone on the street.

## Small Talk and Conversation

**Conversations** often revolve around neutral topics like the weather (which is a classic British standby). Asking about someone's **day, their work**, or **travel plans** are safe starting points.

**Avoid controversial topics** such as politics or religion unless you know the person well. Instead, stick to **cultural topics**, like local events, music, or food.

**Public displays of affection** are generally understated. Holding hands is common among couples, but excessive public displays of affection may be considered inappropriate.

## Dining Etiquette

**Punctuality**

Being **on time** is a sign of respect in the British Isles, especially in **business or formal dining settings**. In social gatherings, arriving a little late (around 15 minutes) is typically acceptable, but **being excessively late** without prior notice is considered rude.

**At the Table**

**Napkins** should be placed on your lap as soon as you sit down.

**Table manners** are formal, and eating with your **knife and fork** is the norm. Use the **European style of eating**—fork in the left hand, knife in the right.

**Tipping** is customary, though not obligatory. In restaurants, **10–15%** is typical, unless a **service charge** is already included in the bill. Tipping for taxis or other services is generally round up to the nearest pound.

## Meal Etiquette

**Tea** is a huge part of British culture, often enjoyed in the afternoon with **biscuits (cookies)** or cakes. When you're invited to a **"cuppa"** (cup of tea), it's a sign of hospitality.

**Alcohol** is a common part of social life, especially in **pubs** or **bars**. The practice of **"rounds"** means that when one person buys a drink, they'll often buy drinks for the whole group, and the group takes turns.

## Personal Space and Behavior

### Respecting Personal Space

British people generally value their **personal space**. Stand about **an arm's length apart** when talking to someone you don't know well, and be mindful of personal boundaries. **Queueing (standing in line)** is an essential part of British culture, and cutting in line is considered very rude.

### Modesty and Humility

In the British Isles, **modesty** is highly valued. Boasting or showing off is frowned upon. It's common for British people to downplay their successes, and conversely, a great deal of modesty is expected if someone compliments you. Accept compliments with a simple "**thank you**," rather than offering a boastful response.

## Dressing Appropriately

### Dress Codes

The British Isles have a **wide variety of dress codes** depending on the occasion:

**Formal occasions** (such as weddings, dinners, or ceremonies) often call for **smart attire**. For men, a **suit and tie** is typical, and women may wear **dresses or smart separates**.

**Casual clothing** is widely accepted in many public settings, but it's important to look **neat and well-groomed**. Wearing **trainers (sneakers)** to a **fancy restaurant or theater** might be frowned upon.

**Rain gear** is essential—**umbrellas** and **waterproof jackets** are common, as the weather in the British Isles can be unpredictable, especially in the winter and spring months.

## Punctuality and Timekeeping

**Being on Time**

In the British Isles, **punctuality is highly regarded**, and arriving **on time for meetings, dinners, or social events** is a sign of respect. If you're running late, it's polite to call ahead and let the host know.

**Public Transport**

The British are generally **good at following timetables**. **Trains, buses**, and **public transport** usually run on time. However, always check the **timetable** for any potential delays or changes. If you're using the **London Underground** (Tube), remember to stand on the **right side of the escalators**, leaving room for people in a rush to pass on the left.

## Festivals and Events to Experience in the British Isles: Celebrating Culture and Tradition

The **British Isles** are renowned for their rich cultural heritage, and there's no better way to immerse yourself in this vibrant history than by attending one of the many

**festivals and events** held throughout the year. From lively music festivals and traditional celebrations to historic commemorations and quirky local events, the British Isles offer a festival for every interest. Here's a guide to some of the **most iconic festivals and events** you should consider experiencing during your visit.

### Edinburgh Festival Fringe – Scotland

**Why Experience It?**

The **Edinburgh Festival Fringe** is the world's largest arts festival, held every August in **Scotland's capital**. With **thousands of performances** across a variety of venues, including theaters, street corners, and outdoor spaces, the Fringe is a celebration of creativity and innovation.

**Highlights:**

The festival features an incredible range of **theater, comedy, dance, and music**, with performances from both **established artists** and **emerging talent**.

**Street performers** and impromptu shows can be found throughout the city, adding to the dynamic atmosphere.

Don't miss the **Edinburgh International Book Festival** and **Edinburgh Art Festival**, which run alongside the Fringe.

**Travel Tip: Book tickets and accommodations early, as the city gets crowded during this popular event.**

### Glastonbury Festival – England

**Why Experience It?**

**Glastonbury Festival**, held annually in **Somerset**, is one of the most iconic music festivals in the world. It attracts **thousands of music fans** from across the globe to its sprawling site for several days of live music, dancing, and revelry.

**Highlights:**

Expect performances from **legendary artists, emerging bands**, and **specialty genres** ranging from rock and pop to electronic and folk.

The festival is known for its **art installations, sustainability efforts**, and **family-friendly activities**.

Beyond the music, the festival features **theater, circus acts**, and **alternative wellness activities**, making it a full cultural experience.

**Travel Tip: Be prepared for muddy conditions (it's famous for its rain), and pack comfortable, durable clothing.**

## St. Patrick's Day – Ireland

**Why Experience It?**

**St. Patrick's Day**, celebrated on **March 17th**, is **Ireland's national holiday,** marking the **patron saint's feast day**. It's a vibrant celebration of Irish culture, music, and heritage, celebrated across the country, but especially in **Dublin**, where the festivities are on full display.

**Highlights:**

The **St. Patrick's Day Parade** in **Dublin** is a colorful and lively procession featuring **music, dancing**, and **traditional costumes**.

Expect to see **street parties, pub crawls,** and **live music sessions** throughout the city.

The celebration is a great way to experience **Irish culture**, from **traditional Irish dancing** to hearty **Irish food** and, of course, **pints of Guinness**.

**Travel Tip: Wear something green and arrive early to get a good view of the parade!**

## The Proms – England

**Why Experience It?**

For classical music lovers, the **BBC Proms** is a must-see. Held annually in **London** at the **Royal Albert Hall**, this **eight-week festival** features a series of classical concerts, culminating in the spectacular **Last Night of the Proms**.

**Highlights:**

The festival includes performances from top orchestras, including the **London Symphony Orchestra** and the **Royal Liverpool Philharmonic**.

Expect an eclectic mix of **classical music, contemporary composers**, and even **popular music** interpreted by orchestras.

The **Last Night of the Proms** is a joyous, patriotic celebration with audience participation, waving flags, and singing along to traditional British tunes.

**Travel Tip: If you're visiting during the festival, try to get tickets for a Promming session—these are standing tickets available at an affordable price.**

### Notting Hill Carnival – London, England

**Why Experience It?**

Held every August in the heart of **Notting Hill**, the **Notting Hill Carnival** is one of the largest street festivals in Europe and a vibrant celebration of **Caribbean culture**. It features colorful parades, energetic music, and delicious food, drawing crowds from around the world.

**Highlights:**

The **Carnival Parade** showcases elaborately designed costumes and floats as **steel bands**, **calypso music**, and **soca rhythms** fill the streets.

**Caribbean food stalls** offer mouthwatering dishes such as **jerk chicken**, **rice and peas**, and **plantains**.

The event also includes **dance performances, sound systems**, and **family-friendly activities**, making it a lively and inclusive festival for all ages.

**Travel Tip: Wear comfortable shoes and prepare for large crowds; the streets can get very busy.**

### The Changing of the Guard – London, England

**Why Experience It?**

The **Changing of the Guard** ceremony at **Buckingham Palace** is a quintessential British experience, drawing visitors from around the world who want to witness this **historic, highly choreographed ritual**.

**Highlights:**

The ceremony takes place daily in the summer and every other day in winter at **11:00 AM**.

The **Guards** march from **Wellington Barracks** to Buckingham Palace, accompanied by a military band.

It's a beautiful display of British **pageantry** and **tradition**.

**Travel Tip: Arrive early to secure a good spot, as this is a popular event.**

## Tasting the Best of British Cuisine: A Culinary Journey Through the Isles

When people think of British cuisine, traditional dishes like **fish and chips** or **afternoon tea** might come to mind. However, the culinary landscape of the British Isles is far richer and more diverse than its global stereotypes suggest. Rooted in **centuries of history**, influenced by **global cultures**, and enhanced by a focus on **fresh, local ingredients**, British cuisine offers something for every palate. Whether you're dining in a cozy countryside pub, a bustling city market, or a Michelin-starred restaurant, the UK's food scene is a delightful blend of tradition and innovation.

### Traditional British Dishes You Must Try

**Full English Breakfast**

A hearty way to start the day, the **Full English Breakfast** is a beloved staple. It typically includes:

**Bacon, sausages, and eggs** (fried, scrambled, or poached)

**Grilled tomatoes, mushrooms, baked beans, and hash browns**

**Black pudding** (a type of blood sausage)

Served with **toast and tea or coffee**

Regional variations exist, such as the **Full Scottish**, which might include **haggis** and **tattie scones**, or the **Ulster Fry** in Northern Ireland, featuring **soda bread** and **potato farls**.

### Fish and Chips

Arguably Britain's most iconic dish, **fish and chips** features **crispy battered fish** (usually cod or haddock) served with thick-cut **chips (fries)**, often accompanied by:

**Mushy peas**

**Tartar sauce**

A sprinkle of **malt vinegar**

For an authentic experience, enjoy it from a seaside **"chippy"** wrapped in paper, fresh from the fryer.

**Shepherd's Pie & Cottage Pie**

These comforting classics are made with a savory base of **minced meat** (lamb for shepherd's pie, beef for cottage pie) cooked with **onions, carrots, and peas**, topped with creamy **mashed potatoes** and baked until golden.

### Roast Dinner with Yorkshire Pudding

A staple of **Sunday lunches**, the British **roast dinner** includes:

**Roast beef, lamb, pork, or chicken**

**Roasted potatoes** and seasonal vegetables

**Yorkshire pudding** (a light, airy batter pudding)

Served with rich **gravy** and sometimes **horseradish or mint sauce**

**Afternoon Tea**

Introduced in the 19th century, **afternoon tea** is a quintessential British tradition. It features:

**Finger sandwiches** (cucumber, smoked salmon, egg mayo)

**Scones with clotted cream and jam**

A selection of **cakes and pastries**

Served with a pot of **freshly brewed tea**

Enjoy it at elegant establishments like **The Ritz in London** or quaint countryside tea rooms.

### Regional Specialties Across the British Isles

**Scotland:**

**Haggis:** A savory dish made from sheep's offal mixed with oats and spices, traditionally served with **"neeps and tatties"** (turnips and potatoes).

**Cullen Skink:** A creamy smoked haddock soup with potatoes and onions.

**Wales:**

**Welsh Rarebit:** A rich, cheesy sauce made with ale, mustard, and spices, served over toasted bread.

**Bara Brith:** A traditional tea loaf made with dried fruits and spices.

**Ireland:**

**Irish Stew:** A hearty dish featuring **lamb or beef**, potatoes, carrots, and onions.

**Boxty:** A traditional potato pancake, often served with a savory filling.

**Cornwall:**

**Cornish Pasty:** A pastry filled with **beef, potatoes, turnips, and onions**, originally made for miners as a portable meal.

## British Desserts You Can't Miss

### Sticky Toffee Pudding

A moist sponge cake made with dates, drenched in **toffee sauce**, and served with **custard or cream**.

### Victoria Sponge

Named after Queen Victoria, this light sponge cake is layered with **jam and whipped cream**.

### Marmalade & Jams

Perfect with **toast or scones**, British marmalade is made from **Seville oranges**, offering a tangy, bittersweet flavor.

## British Beverages to Complement Your Meal

**Tea:** The national beverage, enjoyed throughout the day with a dash of milk.

**Pimm's:** A refreshing summer drink mixed with lemonade and garnished with fruits and mint.

**Cider:** Especially popular in the West Country, known for its **crisp apple flavor**.

**Ales and Stouts:** Try a pint of **real ale** or a creamy **Guinness** in a traditional pub.

**Whisky:** Particularly in Scotland, where **single malts** are world-renowned.

## The Modern British Food Scene

In recent years, Britain has embraced a **vibrant culinary renaissance**. Cities like **London, Manchester, and Edinburgh** boast **Michelin-starred restaurants, global fusion cuisine,** and **thriving street food markets**.

Farmers' markets showcase **local, organic produce**, and sustainability is at the heart of many new dining concepts.

Diverse cultural influences from around the world have shaped the modern British palate, blending traditional dishes with bold new flavors. Indian curries, Caribbean jerk chicken, Middle Eastern mezze, and Southeast Asian Street food are as much a part of the British food landscape as classic pub fare.

## English Breakfast, Fish and Chips, Haggis, and More: Iconic Dishes of the British Isles

The **British Isles** boast a rich culinary heritage, blending hearty, traditional fare with flavors influenced by centuries of cultural exchange. From the comforting **English Breakfast** to the bold flavors of **Scottish haggis**, these dishes are more than just meals—they're a reflection of the region's history, landscapes, and local produce. Whether you're savoring a seaside portion of **fish and chips** or digging into a warming **shepherd's pie**, each dish tells a story of tradition and taste.

Here's a closer look at some of the most iconic dishes you must try when exploring the British Isles.

### The Full English Breakfast: A Hearty Start to the Day

Often referred to simply as a **"Full English,"** this traditional breakfast has been a staple of British cuisine since the Victorian era. Designed to be filling and energizing, it's a hearty meal that combines a variety of savory items:

**Bacon and Sausages:** Usually grilled or fried, offering a smoky, savory flavor.

**Eggs:** Fried, scrambled, or poached to your preference.

**Baked Beans:** A sweet and tangy accompaniment in tomato sauce.

**Grilled Tomatoes and Mushrooms:** Adding a fresh, earthy balance to the richness of the meats.

**Black Pudding:** A type of blood sausage, popular in many parts of the UK.

**Hash Browns or Fried Bread:** For a crispy, golden texture.

Served with **toast** and a strong cup of **English breakfast tea** or coffee, this meal is a must-try for those looking to experience a true British morning ritual. Variations exist across the Isles, including the **Full Scottish** (with haggis and tattie scones) and the **Ulster Fry** in Northern Ireland.

### Fish and Chips: A Seaside Classic

No trip to the UK is complete without indulging in a plate of **fish and chips**. This beloved dish became popular in the 19th century and remains a British culinary icon today.

**Key Components:**

**Fish:** Typically, **cod** or **haddock**, coated in a crispy, golden batter and deep-fried to perfection.

**Chips:** Thick-cut fries, fluffy on the inside and crunchy on the outside.

**Accompaniments:** Traditionally served with **mushy peas**, **tartar sauce**, and a generous splash of **malt vinegar**.

For the most authentic experience, enjoy fish and chips wrapped in paper from a seaside **"chippy"** (fish and chip shop), preferably overlooking the ocean with a cool breeze in the air.

### Haggis: Scotland's National Dish

A dish steeped in tradition; **haggis** is often described as Scotland's national food. Though its ingredients may seem unconventional to some, it's beloved for its rich, savory flavor.

### What's in Haggis?

Haggis is made from a mixture of **sheep's heart, liver, and lungs**, minced with **onion, oatmeal, suet, spices, and stock**, all encased in a sheep's stomach (though synthetic casings are commonly used today).

### How Is It Served?

Traditionally served with **"neeps and tatties"** (mashed turnips and potatoes) and a dram of **Scotch whisky**. It's especially popular during **Burns Night** celebrations, honoring Scottish poet Robert Burns, who famously penned an ode to the dish.

Despite its reputation, haggis has a **nutty, spicy flavor** and a texture that's both crumbly and moist—definitely worth trying when visiting Scotland.

## More British Classics to Savor

### Shepherd's Pie & Cottage Pie:

These comforting, savory pies are made with a layer of minced meat (lamb for shepherd's pie, beef for cottage pie), mixed with vegetables like carrots and peas, and topped with creamy mashed potatoes before being baked until golden.

### Bangers and Mash:

A simple yet satisfying dish of **sausages ("bangers")** served with **creamy mashed potatoes ("mash")**, often accompanied by rich **onion gravy** and a side of **peas**.

### Cornish Pasty:

Originating from Cornwall, this handheld pastry is filled with **beef, potatoes, swede (rutabaga), and onions**, wrapped in a flaky, golden crust. It was historically a portable lunch for miners and remains a beloved British snack.

**Ploughman's Lunch:**

A traditional **cold meal** typically featuring **chunky bread, sharp cheddar cheese, pickles (like Branston pickle), apple slices, and cold cuts**. It's a popular pub dish, often enjoyed with a pint of local ale.

### British Desserts Worth Saving Room For

**Sticky Toffee Pudding:**

A rich, moist sponge cake made with dates, drenched in **butterscotch toffee sauce**, and served warm with a dollop of **clotted cream** or **custard**.

**Eton Mess:**

A refreshing dessert made with **crushed meringue, whipped cream, and fresh strawberries**, believed to have originated from Eton College.

**Treacle Tart:**

A traditional pastry filled with **golden syrup (light treacle), breadcrumbs, and lemon juice**, offering a perfect balance of sweet and tangy flavors.

## Regional Wines, Beers, and Spirits of the British Isles

The **British Isles** boast a rich and diverse heritage when it comes to **wines, beers, and spirits**, reflecting centuries of tradition, local ingredients, and evolving craftsmanship. From the **peaty whiskies of Scotland** to the **crisp ciders of Somerset** and the **emerging English wine scene**, each region offers unique beverages that tell the story of its landscape and culture. Whether you're a connoisseur or simply curious, exploring these regional drinks is a flavorful journey through British and Irish history.

## Whisky (Scotland and Ireland): The Spirit of Heritage

### Scottish Whisky (Scotch)

Scotland is world-renowned for its whisky, commonly referred to as **"Scotch"**. Its production is deeply tied to the land, using local **barley, pure water, and peat** to create complex flavors. There are five main whisky regions, each with distinct characteristics:

**Speyside:** Known for **rich, fruity, and sweet single malts** like **Glenfiddich** and **Macallan**.

**Islay:** Famous for **peaty, smoky whiskies** such as **Laphroaig** and **Ardbeg**, with bold maritime flavors.

**Highlands:** Diverse in style, from the **robust Glenmorangie** to the delicate **Dalwhinnie**.

**Lowlands:** Lighter, floral whiskies, often triple-distilled, like **Auchentoshan**.

**Campbeltown:** Once the whisky capital of the world, known for its **salty, briny character**.

### Irish Whiskey

Irish whiskey tends to be **smoother and triple-distilled**, with a **lighter, fruitier profile** compared to Scotch. Popular brands include:

**Jameson:** A globally recognized blend with **hints of vanilla and spice**.

**Redbreast:** A rich, **pot still whiskey** with notes of dried fruit and sherry.

**Bushmills:** Distilled in Northern Ireland, offering both blends and single malts.

Irish whiskey is often enjoyed neat, in cocktails like the **Irish Coffee**, or simply with a splash of water to open up the flavors.

### English Wines: A Growing Reputation

While the British Isles aren't traditionally known for wine, the **southern regions of England**—particularly **Kent, Sussex, and Hampshire**—are now celebrated for producing exceptional **sparkling wines**.

**English Sparkling Wine**

Made using the same method as **Champagne**, English sparkling wines are praised for their **crisp acidity** and **fine bubbles**.

Notable vineyards include **Nyetimber**, **Chapel Down**, and **Ridgeview**, which produce wines with notes of **green apple, citrus, and brioche**.

The cool climate and chalky soils (similar to France's Champagne region) create ideal conditions for **Chardonnay, Pinot Noir, and Pinot Meunier** grapes.

### Regional Beers and Ales: Britain's Brewing Legacy

**Traditional Ales**

The UK has a rich brewing heritage, with styles that reflect regional tastes:

**Bitter:** A well-balanced ale with **malty and hoppy notes**, served at cellar temperature. Popular brands include **London Pride** and **Timothy Taylor's Landlord**.

**Pale Ale:** Originating in England, this style is characterized by its **golden hue** and **crisp bitterness**.

**Porter and Stout:** Dark, roasted beers with flavors of **coffee, chocolate, and caramel**. The most famous example is Ireland's **Guinness**, known for its creamy texture and iconic dark color.

**Craft Beer Movement**

The UK's **craft beer scene** has exploded in recent years, with innovative breweries like **BrewDog (Scotland)** and **Beavertown (London)** experimenting with **IPAs, sours, and barrel-aged brews**.

### Cider and Perry: A Taste of the Countryside

**Cider (England and Wales)**

The West Country, particularly **Somerset, Herefordshire, and Devon**, is famous for its traditional ciders, made from **fermented apple juice**.

**Traditional Farmhouse Ciders:** Often dry, unfiltered, and full of bold, tannic flavors.

**Modern Ciders:** Crisp and refreshing, with both sweet and dry varieties available. Brands like **Thatchers** and **Westons** are widely popular.

**Perry:**

Made from pears instead of apples, perry has a **lighter, more delicate flavor** and is produced primarily in the same regions as cider.

## Iconic British and Irish Spirits

**Gin (England and Wales)**

The UK has experienced a **gin renaissance** in recent years, with a surge of **craft distilleries** producing both traditional and experimental gins.

**London Dry Gin:** Classic, juniper-forward style. Famous brands include **Tanqueray**, **Beefeater**, and **Bombay Sapphire**.

**Flavored and Botanical Gins:** Distilleries like **Hendrick's (Scotland)** have popularized gins infused with **cucumber, rose, and exotic botanicals**.

Enjoyed in a classic **G&T (gin and tonic)**, garnished with fresh herbs or citrus for added flavor.

**Pimm's No.1 Cup (England)**

A quintessential British summer drink, **Pimm's** is a gin-based liqueur infused with **herbs and citrus**. Often mixed with lemonade and garnished with **cucumber, mint, strawberries, and orange**, it's refreshing and light—perfect for garden parties.

**Mead and Liqueurs: Traditional Flavors Reimagined**

**Mead:**

An ancient drink made from **fermented honey**, water, and sometimes fruit or spices. Mead has seen a resurgence, with modern producers offering both sweet and dry varieties.

**Local Liqueurs:**

**Drambuie (Scotland):** A sweet, whisky-based liqueur flavored with honey, herbs, and spices.

**Baileys Irish Cream (Ireland):** A rich, creamy liqueur blending **Irish whiskey, cream, and cocoa**, often enjoyed over ice or in coffee.

# SHORE EXCURSION AND LOCAL ADVENTURES

## Active Adventures: Hiking, Cycling, and Water Sports in the British Isles

The **British Isles** offer a paradise for outdoor enthusiasts seeking **active adventures** amidst diverse landscapes. From rugged mountain trails and scenic coastal paths to thrilling water sports, the region provides countless opportunities to connect with nature while enjoying physical challenges. Whether you're a seasoned adventurer or a casual explorer, activities like **hiking, cycling, and water sports** allow you to experience the natural beauty and rich history of the British Isles from an exciting, immersive perspective.

**Hiking: Exploring Iconic Trails and Natural Wonders**

**Best Hiking Destinations**

**The Lake District (England):** A UNESCO World Heritage site, the Lake District offers dramatic mountain scenery, glacial lakes, and charming villages. Popular hikes include **Scafell Pike**, the highest peak in England, and the picturesque trails around **Derwentwater**.

**Snowdonia National Park (Wales):** Home to **Mount Snowdon**, the highest mountain in Wales, with multiple routes like the **Pyg Track** and **Miners' Track** leading to breathtaking summit views.

**The Scottish Highlands:** Offering rugged beauty with trails such as the **West Highland Way**, a 96-mile route from Milngavie to Fort William, passing through stunning lochs, glens, and mountain landscapes.

**The Causeway Coast (Northern Ireland):** Hike along the **Giant's Causeway Coastal Path**, with its dramatic cliffs, basalt columns, and panoramic views of the North Atlantic.

**South West Coast Path (England):** Stretching over 600 miles, this coastal trail takes you through **Cornwall**, **Devon**, and **Dorset**, offering sea views, sandy coves, and quaint fishing villages.

**Hiking Tips:**

**Weather:** Be prepared for sudden changes, especially in mountainous areas.

**Gear:** Sturdy hiking boots, waterproof clothing, and a map or GPS are essential.

**Safety:** Inform someone of your route, especially when hiking in remote areas.

### Cycling: Scenic Routes for Every Level

**Top Cycling Routes**

**Camel Trail (Cornwall):** A family-friendly, traffic-free route along a disused railway line, offering views of the **Cornish countryside** and estuaries.

**Loch Ness 360° Trail (Scotland):** A circular cycling route around the famous **Loch Ness**, with a mix of quiet roads and forest paths.

**Hadrian's Cycleway (England):** Stretching from the **Solway Coast** to the **North Sea**, this 174-mile route follows the historic line of **Hadrian's Wall**, blending Roman heritage with scenic landscapes.

**Great Western Greenway (Ireland):** A beautiful, off-road trail in **County Mayo**, following the old Westport to Achill railway line along the stunning **Clew Bay** coastline.

**Isle of Wight Cycle Routes:** Known as a **cycling paradise**, the Isle of Wight offers routes through rolling hills, coastal cliffs, and charming villages.

**Cycling Tips:**

**Rentals:** Many destinations offer bike rentals, including e-bikes for challenging routes.

**Traffic Awareness:** While many routes are off-road, always be cautious when sharing roads with vehicles.

**Fitness Level:** Choose routes suitable for your experience, whether flat trails or steep climbs.

## Water Sports: Thrills on Lakes, Rivers, and the Sea

**Popular Water Sports Destinations**

**Surfing (Cornwall, England):** The beaches of **Newquay**, especially **Fistral Beach**, are considered the surfing capital of the UK, offering waves for beginners and pros alike.

**Kayaking and Canoeing (Loch Lomond, Scotland):** Paddle through **Scotland's largest loch**, surrounded by forested hills and islands.

**Coasteering (Pembrokeshire, Wales):** A thrilling adventure that involves **climbing, swimming, and cliff-jumping** along rugged coastal terrain.

**Sailing (Isle of Wight, England):** Known for its world-famous **Cowes Week regatta**, the Isle of Wight offers excellent sailing conditions and picturesque harbors.

**Stand-Up Paddleboarding (Jurassic Coast, England):** Paddle along the stunning cliffs and rock formations of this UNESCO World Heritage site.

**Water Sports Tips:**

**Safety First:** Always wear a life jacket and check local conditions, especially tides and weather.

**Lessons:** Beginners can book lessons with certified instructors to ensure safety and build confidence.

**Gear:** Many coastal towns offer equipment rentals, from surfboards to kayaks.

### Combining Adventures: Multi-Activity Experiences

For those who crave variety, many locations in the British Isles offer **multi-activity adventures**:

**Adventure Centers (Snowdonia, Wales):** Combine rock climbing, zip-lining, mountain biking, and white-water rafting in one trip.

**Isle of Skye (Scotland):** Hike the **Quiraing**, kayak along dramatic coastlines, and cycle through rugged landscapes—all in a single destination.

**The Wild Atlantic Way (Ireland):** This scenic coastal route offers opportunities for **hiking, surfing, cycling**, and **whale watching**.

## Scenic Day Trips: Castles, Gardens, and National Parks in the British Isles

The **British Isles** are a treasure trove of scenic landscapes, rich history, and breathtaking architecture. Whether you're drawn to the **romantic ruins of ancient castles**, the **manicured elegance of historic gardens**, or the **untamed beauty of national parks**, there's no shortage of incredible day trips to explore. These destinations offer the perfect escape from bustling cities, allowing travelers to immerse themselves in the natural and cultural heritage of the region. Here's a guide to some of the most **memorable scenic day trips** across the British Isles.

### Castles: Witnesses to History and Legends

The British Isles are dotted with thousands of castles, each telling stories of **medieval battles, royal intrigues, and ancient legends**.

### Windsor Castle (England)

Located just outside London, **Windsor Castle** is the **oldest and largest occupied castle in the world**.

A favorite residence of the British monarchy, it showcases **opulent State Apartments, St. George's Chapel**, and the impressive **Changing of the Guard** ceremony.

Explore the castle grounds with panoramic views of the **Thames River** and surrounding countryside.

### Edinburgh Castle (Scotland)

Perched atop an extinct volcano, **Edinburgh Castle** dominates the city skyline.

Discover the **Crown Jewels of Scotland**, the historic **Stone of Destiny**, and sweeping views of the city from the **castle ramparts**.

Its rich history includes royal residences, military strongholds, and tales of sieges and intrigue.

### Caernarfon Castle (Wales)

A UNESCO World Heritage Site, **Caernarfon Castle** in North Wales is an imposing medieval fortress built by **King Edward I**.

Its **polygonal towers** and massive walls reflect the grandeur of medieval military architecture.

The castle also played a role in modern history, hosting the **investiture of Prince Charles** as Prince of Wales in 1969.

## Gardens: Tranquil Escapes Full of Beauty

The British Isles boast some of the world's most beautiful gardens, ranging from formal Victorian landscapes to wild, naturalistic designs.

### Kew Gardens (England)

Officially known as the **Royal Botanic Gardens, Kew**, this UNESCO World Heritage Site is located in southwest London.

Home to over **50,000 plant species**, including exotic plants in the iconic **Victorian glasshouses**.

Explore the **Treetop Walkway** for a bird's-eye view or relax in the peaceful **Japanese Garden**.

### Bodnant Garden (Wales)

Located in **Conwy**, Bodnant Garden offers stunning views of **Snowdonia National Park**.

Famous for its **Laburnum Arch**, a breathtaking golden tunnel of flowering laburnum trees that blooms in late spring.

Features **terraced gardens**, lush woodlands, and a rich collection of rare plants from around the world.

**Powerscourt Gardens (Ireland)**

Situated in **County Wicklow**, Powerscourt Gardens are considered among the finest in Europe.

The estate features **Italian and Japanese gardens**, cascading terraces, **ornamental lakes**, and **sweeping mountain views**.

The nearby **Powerscourt Waterfall**, Ireland's tallest, makes for an excellent addition to your visit

## National Parks: Natural Wonders to Explore

For nature lovers, the British Isles offer a diverse range of **national parks** filled with rugged mountains, serene lakes, and dramatic coastlines.

**Lake District National Park (England)**

A UNESCO World Heritage Site in **Cumbria**, known for its **glacial lakes, forested valleys, and towering peaks**.

Perfect for **hiking, boating, and scenic drives**, with highlights like **Lake Windermere**, **Scafell Pike**, and the charming town of **Keswick**.

Literature enthusiasts can visit **Dove Cottage**, once home to poet **William Wordsworth**.

Snowdonia National Park (Wales)

Home to **Mount Snowdon**, the highest peak in Wales, accessible via hiking trails or the **Snowdon Mountain Railway**.

The park offers breathtaking views of **rugged cliffs, deep glacial valleys, and picturesque villages** like **Beddgelert**.

Ideal for **hiking, rock climbing, zip-lining**, and even **surfing** at an inland surf lagoon.

The Cairngorms National Park (Scotland)

The **largest national park in the UK**, featuring the **Cairngorms Mountain range**, **ancient Caledonian pine forests**, and abundant wildlife, including **red deer and golden eagles**.

Popular activities include **hiking, skiing, mountain biking**, and visiting traditional Highland villages like **Aviemore**.

Explore the **whisky distilleries** along the **Malt Whisky Trail** within the park's boundaries.

### Coastal Escapes and Hidden Gems

For those who love the sea, the coastlines of the British Isles are filled with scenic spots:

**Giant's Causeway (Northern Ireland):** A UNESCO World Heritage Site with **40,000 interlocking basalt columns** formed by ancient volcanic activity.

**Jurassic Coast (England):** Stretching along **Dorset and East Devon**, famous for its **dramatic cliffs, fossil-rich beaches**, and natural landmarks like **Durdle Door**.

**Isle of Skye (Scotland):** Known for its rugged beauty, with highlights like the **Old Man of Storr, Fairy Pools**, and **Quiraing**.

## Cultural Experiences in the British Isles: Museums, Music, and Arts

The **British Isles** are a cultural mosaic, shaped by **thousands of years of history, artistic expression, and musical innovation**. From the world-renowned museums of London to the lively traditional music of Ireland and Scotland, the region offers an array of experiences that celebrate its rich heritage. Whether you're an art enthusiast, a history buff, or a music lover, exploring the **museums, music, and arts** of the British Isles provides a deeper connection to its diverse cultures and timeless traditions.

### Museums: Gateways to History and Heritage

The British Isles are home to some of the **world's most prestigious museums**, offering insights into everything from **ancient civilizations** to **modern art**.

### The British Museum (London, England)

One of the most visited museums globally, the **British Museum** houses over **8 million artifacts** spanning human history.

Highlights include the **Rosetta Stone**, the **Elgin Marbles** from the Parthenon, and **Egyptian mummies**.

Admission is **free**, making it an accessible cultural gem in the heart of London.

### The National Gallery (London, England)

Located in **Trafalgar Square**, the National Gallery showcases over **2,300 paintings** from the **13th to the 20th century**.

Masterpieces by artists such as **Van Gogh, Monet, Rembrandt, and Leonardo da Vinci** are on display.

Free entry with optional paid exhibitions.

### The National Museum of Scotland (Edinburgh, Scotland)

A fascinating blend of **Scottish history, culture, and science**.

Exhibits range from **prehistoric artifacts** to the **famous Lewis Chessmen** and **Dolly the Sheep**, the first cloned mammal.

Located near the historic **Royal Mile**, it's perfect for combining with a stroll through Edinburgh's Old Town.

**Titanic Belfast (Belfast, Northern Ireland)**

A striking, modern museum built on the site where the **RMS Titanic** was constructed.

Interactive exhibits tell the story of the Titanic's creation, maiden voyage, and tragic sinking.

A must-visit for maritime history enthusiasts.

## Music: A Vibrant Soundtrack of the Isles

Music is deeply woven into the cultural fabric of the British Isles, from ancient folk traditions to contemporary global icons.

**The Beatles Story (Liverpool, England)**

Dedicated to **The Beatles**, this immersive museum in Liverpool's **Albert Dock** celebrates the band's legacy with memorabilia, interactive exhibits, and recreated venues like the **Cavern Club**.

**Traditional Irish and Scottish Folk Music**

Experience the lively energy of **traditional music sessions** in pubs across Ireland and Scotland.

Instruments like the **fiddle, bodhrán, tin whistle, and bagpipes** create an authentic soundscape.

Cities like **Galway, Dublin, and Edinburgh** are renowned for their vibrant live music scenes.

**Glastonbury Festival (England)**

One of the world's largest music festivals, held annually in Somerset.

Features a diverse lineup of **rock, pop, folk, electronic, and world music**.

A cultural phenomenon that attracts music lovers from around the globe.

## Arts: From Historic Masterpieces to Contemporary Creativity

The British Isles have long been a center for the arts, fostering talents from **Shakespeare** to **Banksy**.

**The Globe Theatre (London, England)**

A faithful reconstruction of **Shakespeare's original Globe Theatre** on the banks of the Thames.

Experience **live performances** of Shakespeare's plays in an authentic, open-air setting.

Guided tours offer insights into **Elizabethan theater** and the life of the Bard.

**Tate Modern (London, England)**

Housed in a former power station, the Tate Modern is the UK's premier museum of **modern and contemporary art**.

Features works by **Picasso, Warhol, Rothko**, and **Damien Hirst**.

Free entry, with some special exhibitions requiring tickets.

**Edinburgh Festival Fringe (Scotland)**

The **world's largest arts festival**, held every August in Edinburgh.

Showcases thousands of performances, from **theater and comedy** to **dance, circus, and spoken word**.

A dynamic celebration of **creativity and diversity**, attracting artists and audiences worldwide.

**Street Art (Bristol, England)**

Home to the world-famous street artist **Banksy**, Bristol's streets are adorned with thought-provoking murals.

Take a **street art tour** to discover the city's vibrant urban art scene, blending **political commentary** with bold visuals.

## Unique Cultural Experiences

**Poetry and Literature Tours:** Explore the literary heritage of authors like **William Wordsworth** in the Lake District, **James Joyce** in Dublin, and **Dylan Thomas** in Wales.

**Gaelic Language and Culture (Scotland & Ireland):** Visit the **Outer Hebrides** or the **Gaeltacht regions** of Ireland to experience traditional **Gaelic language, music, and storytelling**.

**Artisan Workshops:** Participate in craft workshops such as **Harris Tweed weaving** in Scotland, **pottery in Cornwall**, or **glassblowing in Waterford, Ireland**.

## Hidden Gems: Off-the-Beaten-Path Destinations in the British Isles

While iconic landmarks like **London's Tower Bridge**, **Edinburgh Castle**, and the **Cliffs of Moher** often steal the spotlight, the **British Isles** are brimming with lesser-known destinations that offer equally breathtaking beauty and rich cultural experiences. These **hidden gems**—from remote islands and ancient ruins to quaint villages and secret gardens—provide travelers with the chance to escape the crowds and discover the authentic charm of the region.

Here's a guide to some of the most captivating **off-the-beaten-path destinations** across the British Isles.

### The Isle of Lundy (England)

**Where: Off the coast of Devon, in the Bristol Channel.**

**Why Visit:**

Known as the "**island that time forgot**," **Lundy** is a remote, rugged paradise ideal for nature lovers and adventurers. With no cars and limited modern distractions, it's the perfect escape for those seeking tranquility.

**Wildlife Watching:** Home to colonies of **Atlantic puffins**, **seals**, and even **wild ponies**.

**Outdoor Adventures:** Enjoy **hiking** along dramatic cliffs, **rock climbing**, and **snorkeling** in clear waters teeming with marine life.

**Historical Sites:** Explore ancient ruins, including **Bronze Age settlements**, and the **Victorian-era Marisco Castle**.

**Travel Tip:** Access Lundy by ferry from **Ilfracombe** or **Bideford**—the journey itself offers stunning sea views.

### St. Kilda (Scotland)

**Where: A remote archipelago in the Outer Hebrides, west of mainland Scotland.**

**Why Visit:**

**St. Kilda** is a UNESCO World Heritage Site, known for its **dramatic cliffs, seabird colonies**, and fascinating human history. Once home to a resilient community that lived off the harsh land until their evacuation in 1930, the islands now stand as a haunting testament to human endurance.

**Wildlife Haven:** The world's largest colony of **northern gannets** and rare species like the **St. Kilda wren**.

**Rugged Landscapes:** Towering sea stacks, rugged cliffs, and **crystal-clear waters** perfect for kayaking and photography.

**Cultural Heritage:** Ruins of ancient stone houses and evidence of a unique way of life, isolated from the modern world for centuries.

**Travel Tip:** Reachable via boat tours from the Isle of Harris—**ideal for experienced travelers** seeking raw, untouched beauty.

**Portmeirion (Wales)**

**Where: In Gwynedd, North Wales, along the estuary of the River Dwyryd.**

**Why Visit:**

**Portmeirion** is a colorful, whimsical village designed in the style of an Italian Riviera town, complete with **Mediterranean architecture**, vibrant gardens, and artistic flair.

**Architectural Marvel:** Built by Sir **Clough Williams-Ellis** in the 20th century, blending Italian elegance with Welsh landscapes.

**Tropical Gardens:** Thanks to its mild climate, exotic plants flourish here, creating lush, vibrant spaces.

**Pop Culture Fame:** Known as the filming location for the cult classic TV series **"The Prisoner"**.

**Travel Tip:** Stay overnight in one of Portmeirion's boutique hotels for a magical, after-hours experience when day visitors have left.

## Dingle Peninsula (Ireland)

**Where:** In County Kerry, on Ireland's scenic southwest coast.

**Why Visit:**

Less crowded than the famous **Ring of Kerry**, the **Dingle Peninsula** offers **stunning coastal views**, rich Gaelic culture, and charming small towns.

**Wild Atlantic Way:** Dramatic cliffs, rolling hills, and pristine beaches perfect for scenic drives and photography.

**Dingle Town:** A lively harbor town with traditional Irish pubs, live folk music, and the legendary **Fungie the dolphin**.

**Ancient Sites:** Explore **Beehive huts (clocháns)**, early Christian relics, and **Ogham stones** dating back over 1,500 years.

**Travel Tip:** Rent a bike and cycle the **Slea Head Drive** for jaw-dropping views of the Atlantic Ocean.

**Dark Hedges (Northern Ireland)**

**Where: Near Ballymoney in County Antrim.**

**Why Visit:**

This eerie, atmospheric avenue of intertwined **beech trees**, planted in the 18th century, has become world-famous after appearing in **"Game of Thrones"** as the **Kingsroad**.

**Photographer's Dream:** The twisted branches create a natural tunnel with hauntingly beautiful light, perfect for dramatic photography.

**Off-the-Path Serenity:** While popular with GoT fans, visiting early in the morning or late afternoon offers a peaceful, magical experience.

**Travel Tip:** Pair your visit with a trip to the nearby **Giant's Causeway** or **Carrick-a-Rede Rope Bridge** for a full day of exploration.

### The Fairy Pools (Isle of Skye, Scotland)

**Where: At the foot of the Black Cuillin mountains on the Isle of Skye.**

**Why Visit:**

The **Fairy Pools** are a series of crystal-clear, blue-green pools connected by small waterfalls, nestled in a dramatic mountain landscape.

**Natural Swimming Pools:** Brave souls can take a dip in the **icy, refreshing waters**.

**Hiking Paradise:** Combine your visit with hikes through Skye's **rugged, otherworldly terrain**.

**Photographic Beauty:** The contrast between the clear waters, dark mountains, and moody skies makes for stunning photos.

**Travel Tip:** Visit early or late in the day to avoid crowds and catch the magical light reflecting off the water.

# Cruise Tips & Practical Information: Navigating Your Voyage with Ease

Embarking on a cruise is an exciting adventure, offering the perfect blend of **relaxation, exploration, and luxury**. Whether you're a first-time cruiser or a seasoned traveler, knowing the right tips and practical information can make your journey smoother and more enjoyable. From packing essentials to managing onboard activities, here's a comprehensive guide to help you get the most out of your cruise experience.

### Before You Sail: Planning and Preparation

**Booking Tips:**

**Choose the Right Itinerary:** Consider the destinations, cruise length, and type of ship. For scenic voyages like the **British Isles**, look for routes that include a mix of cultural cities, historic ports, and natural landscapes.

**Cabin Selection:** If you're prone to seasickness, opt for a **mid-ship cabin on a lower deck**, where there's less motion. For the best views, a **balcony cabin** is ideal.

**Travel Insurance:** Always purchase comprehensive travel insurance that covers **medical emergencies, trip cancellations, and lost luggage**.

**Documents to Prepare:**

**Passport and Visas:** Ensure your passport is valid for at least six months beyond your cruise dates. Check visa requirements for each port of call.

**Cruise Tickets and Travel Documents:** Keep printed and digital copies of your **boarding pass, itinerary, and insurance documents**.

**Health Documents:** Some cruises may require proof of vaccinations or negative health tests, especially for international routes.

### Packing Essentials: What to Bring

**Clothing:**

**Smart Casual Wear:** Perfect for daytime activities and casual dinners.

**Formal Attire:** Many cruises host **formal nights**, so pack a cocktail dress, suit, or equivalent.

**Layered Clothing:** The weather can vary, especially on cruises around the **British Isles**. Pack layers, including a **light jacket, sweaters, and rain gear**.

**Comfortable Shoes:** Bring **walking shoes** for shore excursions and **sandals** or flip-flops for the pool.

**Other Essentials:**

**Power Strip (non-surge protected):** Many cabins have limited outlets.

**Travel-Sized Toiletries:** While basics are provided, you may prefer your own products.

**Day Bag:** For excursions, pack a small backpack for **water, sunscreen, and personal items**.

**Medications:** Carry a supply of any **prescription meds**, plus over-the-counter remedies for **seasickness, headaches, and minor ailments**.

**Onboard Tips: Making the Most of Your Cruise**

**Embarkation Day:**

**Arrive Early:** Aim to arrive at the port at least **2-3 hours before departure** to avoid last-minute stress.

**Carry-On Bag:** Keep important items like **documents, medication, and valuables** with you, as your checked luggage may take time to reach your cabin.

**Maximizing Onboard Activities:**

**Daily Schedules:** Cruise lines provide a **daily bulletin or app** with activity schedules, dining options, and showtimes. Plan your day to make the most of events.

**Reservations:** Book popular activities, **specialty dining**, and **spa treatments** early, as they fill up quickly.

**Shore Excursions:** You can book tours through the cruise line or independently. Cruise-organized excursions offer convenience and guarantee you'll return on time, while independent tours often provide more flexibility and lower costs.

**Managing Expenses:**

**Onboard Account:** Cruises operate on a **cashless system** where all purchases are charged to your room key. Link a **credit card** to manage your spending easily.

**Beverage Packages:** If you plan to enjoy drinks regularly, consider purchasing a **drinks package** for cost savings.

**Wi-Fi Plans:** Onboard Wi-Fi can be pricey and slow. Check for **internet packages** or wait until you're in port for free hotspots.

### Health & Safety Tips

**Seasickness:** Even if you don't usually get motion sick, pack **seasickness bands, ginger tablets, or medication** just in case.

**Stay Hydrated:** Cruise ships can be dehydrating due to air conditioning and sun exposure. **Drink plenty of water**, especially on hot excursions.

**Hand Hygiene:** Prevent illness by using the **hand sanitizers** provided throughout the ship and washing your hands frequently.

## Disembarkation: A Smooth Farewell

**Preparing to Leave:**

**Customs Forms:** Some destinations require passengers to complete **customs declarations** before disembarking.

**Luggage Tags:** The night before your cruise ends, you'll receive **color-coded luggage tags**. Place them on your bags and leave them outside your cabin for collection.

**Final Account Check:** Review your onboard account for any discrepancies before disembarking.

**Post-Cruise Transfers:**

Arrange **transportation from the port to the airport or hotel** in advance, especially in busy cruise terminals.

### Bonus Tips for a Stress-Free Cruise

**Download Cruise Apps:** Most cruise lines have apps for checking daily schedules, making reservations, and messaging fellow passengers.

**Set a Budget:** Onboard spending can add up quickly. Set a daily budget to avoid surprises at the end of your trip.

**Be Flexible:** Weather or other factors can sometimes affect itineraries. Stay adaptable, and embrace the adventure!

## Currency and Payment Methods in the British Isles: A Traveler's Guide

When traveling through the **British Isles**, understanding the local currency and payment methods is essential to managing your finances smoothly. Whether you're exploring the **historic cities of England**, the rugged landscapes of **Scotland**, or the charming towns of **Ireland**, knowing how to pay for goods and services will ensure a stress-free travel experience. The British Isles include several countries, but their currency systems are relatively straightforward to navigate. Here's everything you need to know about **currency** and **payment methods** in the region.

### Currency in the British Isles

**The Pound Sterling (GBP)**

**England, Wales, and Northern Ireland** use the **British Pound Sterling (£)**, often referred to as the **pound**. It is the official currency of the **United Kingdom**, and its symbol is **£**.

The **Republic of Ireland** uses the **Euro (€)** as its currency. Although Ireland is geographically part of the British Isles, it is not part of the UK and has its own currency.

**Banknotes and Coins**:

In the UK, **banknotes** come in denominations of **£5, £10, £20, and £50**, and **coins** are available in **1p, 2p, 5p, 10p, 20p, 50p, £1**, and **£2**.

The **Euro** in Ireland is also available in **banknotes** of €5, €10, €20, €50, €100, €200, €500 and coins in **1c, 2c, 5c, 10c, 20c, 50c, €1, and €2**.

**Currency Exchange**

Currency exchange is widely available at **banks, currency exchange offices, and airports**. However, **airport exchange rates** are often less favorable, so it's best to exchange money at a bank or local exchange shop if possible.

**ATMs** are widely available in major cities and towns. Look for machines that are part of reputable networks like **Visa** or **Mastercard** for the best rates and lowest fees.

## Payment Methods in the British Isles

### Credit and Debit Cards

**Credit and debit cards** are widely accepted in the British Isles, especially in **shops, restaurants**, and **hotels**. **Visa, Mastercard**, and **American Express** are the most commonly used networks.

**Chip-and-PIN** cards are standard in the UK, and most merchants will require a **PIN** for purchases, even for smaller transactions. Some **contactless payment methods** are available for purchases under a certain value (typically £30).

**American Express** is not as commonly accepted in some smaller establishments, particularly in rural areas, so it's a good idea to also carry a **Visa or Mastercard** for extra convenience.

**ATM Withdrawals**: You can use your **debit or credit card** to withdraw cash from **ATMs**, but be mindful of any **foreign transaction fees** your bank may charge.

**Mobile Payments and Digital Wallets**

Mobile payment methods like **Apple Pay**, **Google Pay**, and **Samsung Pay** are becoming increasingly popular and accepted in the UK and Ireland. Many retailers, public transport systems, and restaurants now offer **contactless payment options** through mobile apps.

**PayPal** is also commonly used for **online purchases** and may be accepted at some physical stores. Ensure that your digital wallet or mobile payment app is linked to a valid **credit or debit card** for ease of use.

## Tipping and Service Charges

**Tipping in the British Isles**

**United Kingdom**: Tipping is generally **optional**, but it's appreciated for good service. In restaurants, a **10-15% tip** is customary if service is not included in the bill. In pubs, it's common to leave **small change** when paying for drinks. Taxi drivers usually receive a **tip of around 10-15%** of the fare, depending on the service.

**Republic of Ireland**: Similar to the UK, tipping is also **optional**, but a **10-15% tip** is expected in restaurants if service is not already included. For taxis, rounding up the fare is common.

**Service Charges**: Some restaurants, particularly in tourist areas, may include a **service charge** on the bill, so check before leaving an additional tip.

**Cash vs. Cards**

**Carrying Cash**

While **credit and debit cards** are widely accepted, having some **cash on hand** is still useful for:

Small purchases at **markets, street vendors**, or in rural areas where cards may not be accepted.

Tips in cash, as some small establishments may not allow tips to be added to the card payment.

**Public transport**: In certain areas, **bus fares** or **small local train stations** may only accept cash.

## ATMs and Cash Withdrawals

**ATMs** are plentiful in the British Isles, and withdrawing cash is straightforward. However, be aware that **foreign cards** may incur additional fees for withdrawals, so it's advisable to check with your bank before traveling.

Most **major cities and towns** have **cash exchange shops**, but the rates may not be as competitive as those offered by ATMs or local banks.

### Safety Tips for Handling Money

**Notify Your Bank**: If you're traveling from abroad, it's wise to **notify your bank** of your travel dates to avoid any issues with your credit or debit cards being flagged for unusual activity.

**Use Secure ATMs**: Stick to ATMs located at **bank branches** or in well-lit, busy areas to avoid fraud.

**Keep Backup**: Always have a **backup payment method**, such as a secondary card or some local currency, in case of emergencies.

# Language and Basic Phrases for Traveling the British Isles

Traveling through the **British Isles**—which includes **England, Scotland, Wales, Northern Ireland, and the Republic of Ireland**—is an enriching experience filled with diverse cultures, rich histories, and vibrant local traditions. While **English** is the predominant language spoken across these regions, you'll also encounter other languages such as **Welsh, Scots Gaelic, and Irish Gaelic**. Learning a few **basic phrases** not only helps with practical communication but also shows respect for the local culture, often earning you a friendly smile and warmer interactions.

Here's a guide to the languages you'll encounter and some essential phrases to enhance your journey.

### English: Variations Across the Isles

While English is spoken everywhere, you'll notice **regional dialects, accents, and slang** that vary significantly:

**British English (England):** Includes different accents like **Cockney (London)**, **Scouse (Liverpool)**, and **Geordie (Newcastle)**.

**Scottish English:** Often mixed with Scots words and pronounced with a distinctive Scottish lilt.

**Welsh English:** Influenced by the Welsh language, with unique vocabulary and intonation.

**Irish English:** Features charming idioms and expressions like "**grand**" (meaning good or fine) and "**craic**" (meaning fun or good times).

**Useful English Phrases:**

**Hello:** Hi / Hello

**Goodbye:** Bye / See you later

**Please:** Please

**Thank you:** Thanks / Cheers (informal)

**Excuse me:** Excuse me / Pardon me

**How much is this?**

**Where is the bathroom?** (or "toilet" in the UK)

**Can you help me?**

**Travel Tip:** In the UK and Ireland, it's common to hear **"cheers"** used not just for toasting but also as a casual way to say **"thank you"**.

**Welsh (Cymraeg) – Spoken in Wales**

**Welsh** is a Celtic language with a rich literary history, spoken alongside English in many parts of Wales. Road signs are bilingual, and Welsh is especially prevalent in **North and West Wales**.

**Basic Welsh Phrases:**

**Hello:** Helo (heh-lo)

**Goodbye:** Hwyl (hoil)

**Please:** Os gwelwch yn dda (oss gwel-ookh un thah)

**Thank you:** Diolch (dee-olch)

**Yes / No:** Ie (yeah) / Na (nah)

**Cheers (for a drink):** Iechyd da (yeah-chid dah)

**Where is...?** Ble mae...? (blay my...)

**Cultural Note:** Pronouncing **"diolch"** correctly can really impress locals, as it's a core expression of politeness.

### Scottish Gaelic (Gàidhlig) – Spoken in Scotland

While **Scottish Gaelic** is spoken by a smaller percentage of the population, especially in the **Highlands and the Western Isles**, it's an important part of Scotland's heritage. You'll see Gaelic on signs, particularly in the north and west.

**Basic Scottish Gaelic Phrases:**

**Hello:** Halò (ha-lo)

**Goodbye:** Mar sin leat (mar shin lat)

**Please:** Mas e does thoil e (mas eh do hol eh)

**Thank you:** Tapadh leat (tapa le-at)

**Yes / No:** Tha (ha) / Chan eil (chan-nyel)

**Cheers:** Slàinte (slan-juh)

**Fun Fact:** The word **"slàinte"** is commonly used for toasting across both Scotland and Ireland, meaning **"health."**

### Irish Gaelic (Gaeilge) – Spoken in Ireland

In the **Republic of Ireland, Irish Gaelic** is an official language alongside English. It's especially prominent in **Gaeltacht regions** like **Galway, Donegal,** and **Kerry.** While most people speak English daily, Irish is taught in schools and holds cultural significance.

**Basic Irish Gaelic Phrases:**

**Hello:** Dia dhuit (jee-ah ghwitch)

**Goodbye:** Slán (slawn)

**Please:** Le do thoil (leh duh hull)

**Thank you:** Go raibh maith agat (guh rev mah agut)

**Yes / No:** Tá (taw) / Níl (neel)

**Cheers:** Sláinte (slawn-cha)

**Cultural Note:** Even a simple **"Go raibh maith agat"** will be appreciated in rural areas where Irish is more commonly spoken.

### Local Slang and Expressions to Know

Each region has its own colorful expressions. Here are a few fun ones:

**"What's the craic?" (Ireland):** What's up? / How's it going?

**"I'm chuffed!" (England):** I'm very pleased or happy.

**"It's baltic!" (Scotland):** It's freezing cold.

**"Lush" (Wales):** Something really nice or delicious.

**"Mind the gap" (England):** Famous phrase in the London Underground, warning passengers about the space between the train and the platform.

### Politeness Matters: Mind Your Manners

In the British Isles, **politeness is key**. People often use phrases like:

**"Sorry"** even if you're not at fault, just as a polite interjection.

**"Would you mind…?"** instead of directly asking for something.

**"Could I have…?"** when ordering food or drinks, rather than saying, "I want."

Simple gestures of courtesy go a long way in making interactions smoother.

## Staying Connected: Wi-Fi and Communication While Traveling the British Isles

In today's digital age, staying connected while traveling is almost as important as packing your passport. Whether you need to **navigate unfamiliar streets**, **share your adventures on social media**, or simply **keep in touch with family and friends**, having reliable communication tools is key. Traveling through the **British Isles—including England, Scotland, Wales, Northern Ireland, and the Republic of Ireland**—offers numerous ways to stay online, from public Wi-Fi hotspots to local SIM cards. Here's a comprehensive guide to help you stay connected seamlessly during your trip.

## Wi-Fi Access: Where and How to Connect

**Free Public Wi-Fi**

You'll find **free Wi-Fi hotspots** widely available across the British Isles in:

**Cafés and Restaurants:** Chains like **Starbucks**, **Costa Coffee**, and **Pret A Manger** offer free Wi-Fi with a purchase.

**Hotels and Accommodations:** Most hotels, hostels, and B&Bs provide complimentary Wi-Fi, though speeds may vary depending on location.

**Transportation Hubs:** Airports like **Heathrow** (London), **Dublin Airport**, and **Edinburgh Airport** have free Wi-Fi. Train stations, including those operated by **National Rail** and **Transport for London**, often offer free access.

**Public Libraries and Tourist Information Centers:** Great spots for reliable connections, especially in smaller towns.

**Tip:** Free Wi-Fi networks often require you to sign in with an email or accept terms and conditions. Use a **VPN (Virtual Private Network)** for added security when accessing sensitive information on public networks.

## Mobile Data: Using Your Phone Abroad

**International Roaming**

If you're traveling from outside the UK or Ireland, check with your mobile provider about **international roaming packages**:

**EU Travelers:** Roaming within the **Republic of Ireland** is often included in EU mobile plans, but charges may apply in the UK post-Brexit.

**US, Canada, and Other Non-EU Travelers:** Providers like **Verizon, AT&T, and T-Mobile** offer international plans. These can be convenient but sometimes expensive compared to local options.

## Local SIM Cards

For extended stays or heavy data use, buying a **local SIM card** can be more cost-effective:

**Popular UK Providers: EE, O2, Vodafone, and Three**.

**Popular Irish Providers: Vodafone Ireland, Eir, and Three Ireland**.

**Where to Buy:** Airports, mobile shops, supermarkets, or online.

**Cost:** Prepaid SIM cards typically cost between **£10–£30 (€10–€30)** with generous data allowances.

**Tip:** Make sure your phone is **unlocked** before leaving home so it can accept foreign SIM cards.

### Portable Wi-Fi (MiFi) Devices

If you're traveling with family or a group and need to connect multiple devices, consider renting a **portable Wi-Fi hotspot (MiFi device)**:

**How It Works:** A small device that connects to local mobile networks and provides Wi-Fi for several devices simultaneously.

**Where to Rent:** Companies like **Travel WiFi UK**, **Skyroam**, or through local providers at airports.

**Benefits:** Great for road trips, remote areas, or when you need consistent connectivity without changing SIM cards.

### Communication Apps for Easy Contact

Instead of relying on traditional international calls, use **free or low-cost apps** to stay in touch:

**WhatsApp:** Popular in the UK and Ireland for **texting, voice, and video calls** over Wi-Fi or mobile data.

**Skype and Zoom:** Great for video calls with family and friends.

**Viber and Telegram:** Widely used messaging apps with strong privacy features.

**FaceTime:** Perfect for iPhone users to connect via video or audio over the internet.

**Tip:** Make sure your contacts have the same apps installed to ensure smooth communication.

### Cruise Connectivity: Staying Online at Sea

If your journey includes a **cruise around the British Isles**, staying connected can be more challenging:

**Onboard Wi-Fi:** Most cruise ships offer Wi-Fi packages, but speeds may be slow, and costs can be high.

**Port Stops:** Consider using free Wi-Fi at cafes or purchasing a local SIM card when docked.

**Satellite Internet:** Luxury cruises may offer satellite-based Wi-Fi for more consistent service.

### Emergency Communication Tips

In case of emergencies, it's essential to have reliable ways to contact local authorities:

**UK Emergency Number: 999** or **112** (for police, ambulance, fire services)

**Ireland Emergency Number: 112** or **999**

**Roaming Tip:** Even if you don't have a local SIM, emergency numbers can be dialed from any mobile phone.

### Cost-Saving Tips for Staying Connected

**Download Maps Offline:** Use apps like **Google Maps** or **Maps.me** to navigate without data.

**Preload Content:** Download movies, books, and music before your trip to save on data usage.

**Wi-Fi Calling:** Enable **Wi-Fi Calling** on your phone settings to make calls over Wi-Fi without extra charges.

## Health and Safety Tips for Traveling the British Isles

Exploring the **British Isles**—encompassing **England, Scotland, Wales, Northern Ireland, and the Republic of Ireland**—is an exciting adventure filled with rich history, stunning landscapes, and vibrant cultures. While these destinations are generally considered **safe and traveler-friendly**, being prepared with basic **health and safety tips** ensures a smooth, worry-free journey. From understanding local healthcare systems to practicing common-sense precautions, here's what you need to know to stay healthy and secure during your trip.

## Health Tips: Staying Well on the Go

### Healthcare in the British Isles

**United Kingdom (England, Scotland, Wales, Northern Ireland):** The **National Health Service (NHS)** provides public healthcare, but non-residents may need to pay for certain treatments.

**Republic of Ireland:** Healthcare is a mix of public and private services, with emergency care available to everyone.

**Travel Insurance is Essential:**

Always purchase **comprehensive travel insurance** that covers **medical emergencies, accidents, repatriation, and trip cancellations**.

Check if your insurance covers activities like **hiking, cycling, or adventure sports** if you plan to engage in them.

**Medications:**

Carry an adequate supply of any **prescription medications** you need, along with a copy of the prescription.

Keep medications in their **original packaging** to avoid issues at customs.

Over-the-counter medications like **painkillers, cold remedies, and antihistamines** are available at local pharmacies (called **"chemists"** in the UK and Ireland).

**Stay Hydrated and Eat Smart:**

Tap water is **safe to drink** throughout the British Isles.

Practice food safety by eating at reputable establishments and checking food hygiene ratings where available.

**Vaccinations and Health Precautions:**

No special vaccinations are required for travelers from most countries.

Ensure routine vaccines (like **MMR, tetanus, and influenza**) are up to date.

Use **insect repellent** in rural areas to prevent bites, although there's minimal risk of insect-borne diseases.

## Safety Tips: Keeping Yourself and Your Belongings Secure

**Personal Safety:**

The British Isles have a **low crime rate**, but **petty theft** (like pickpocketing) can occur in tourist hotspots.

Be mindful of your surroundings in crowded places like **public transport, markets, and major attractions**.

Keep valuables in a **money belt or neck pouch**, and use **anti-theft bags** with secure zippers.

**Protecting Your Belongings:**

Avoid displaying expensive jewelry, cameras, or large amounts of cash.

Lock your luggage when unattended, even in hotel rooms or cruise cabins.

Use hotel safes for important documents like **passports, travel insurance, and extra credit cards**.

**Key Reasons to Get Travel Insurance:**

**Medical Emergencies:** Covers costs for **hospital stays, doctor visits, surgeries, and medication**. Healthcare can be expensive for non-residents, even in countries with public healthcare systems like the UK and Ireland.

**Trip Cancellations or Delays:** Reimburses expenses if you have to cancel or delay your trip due to **illness, family emergencies, natural disasters, or travel disruptions**.

**Lost or Stolen Belongings:** Provides compensation for **lost luggage, theft, or damaged personal items**.

**Emergency Evacuation:** Covers the cost of **medical evacuation or repatriation** in case of serious illness or injury.

**Adventure Activities:** If you plan to go **hiking, cycling, or engage in water sports**, make sure your policy includes coverage for these activities.

**Tip:** Purchase insurance as soon as you book your trip to maximize coverage, especially for cancellation benefits.

## What to Look for in a Travel Insurance Policy

Not all policies are created equal. When comparing plans, consider the following:

**Essential Coverage to Include:**

**Medical Expenses:** Ensure coverage for at least **$100,000** for medical emergencies.

**Emergency Evacuation:** Look for coverage of **$250,000 or more** if traveling to remote areas.

**Trip Cancellation/Interruption:** Covers non-refundable expenses if your plans change unexpectedly.

**Baggage and Personal Belongings:** Protection against **loss, theft, or damage**.

**Personal Liability:** Covers legal expenses if you're held responsible for causing injury or property damage.

**Special Considerations:**

**Pre-Existing Medical Conditions:** Disclose any pre-existing conditions to avoid claim denials. Some insurers offer **waivers** for these if purchased within a certain timeframe after booking.

**Adventure Sports:** If you plan on activities like **mountaineering, scuba diving, or skiing**, confirm they're covered under your policy.

**COVID-19 Coverage:** Check if the policy covers **trip disruptions or medical care related to COVID-19**.

### Handling Emergencies While Traveling

Knowing what to do in an emergency can make all the difference.

**Medical Emergencies:**

**United Kingdom (England, Scotland, Wales, Northern Ireland):** Dial **999** or **112** for **ambulance, police, or fire services**.

**Republic of Ireland:** Dial **112** or **999** for emergency services.

**Hospital Visits:** For **non-life-threatening issues**, visit a **local pharmacy (chemist)** for advice or a walk-in clinic (urgent care center). In serious cases, go to an **Accident & Emergency (A&E)** department at the nearest hospital.

**Tip:** Keep a copy of your **insurance card** and **emergency contact numbers** with you at all times.

### How to File a Travel Insurance Claim

**Steps to Follow:**

**Contact Your Insurer Immediately:** Use the **24/7 emergency hotline** provided in your policy documents.

**Document Everything:** Keep **receipts, medical reports, police reports**, and any relevant documentation to support your claim.

**Complete the Claim Form:** Submit all required paperwork as soon as possible, following your insurer's guidelines.

**Pro Tip:** Take photos of documents with your phone in case originals are lost.

## Staying Safe to Prevent Emergencies

While insurance offers protection, prevention is always better:

**Stay Aware:** Keep an eye on your belongings, especially in crowded areas like public transport and tourist attractions.

**Emergency Contacts:** Know the location of the **nearest embassy or consulate** for your country in case you lose your passport or need assistance.

**Travel Apps:** Download apps like **Google Maps**, **offline translation tools**, and your **insurance provider's app** for quick access to help when needed.

## Emergency Contacts You Should Know

**UK Emergency Services: 999** or **112**

**Ireland Emergency Services: 112** or **999**

**US Embassy in London:** +44 20 7499 9000

**Canadian Embassy in London:** +44 20 7004 6000

**Australian High Commission in London:** +44 20 7379 4334.

## Sustainable Cruising Practices: Navigating the Seas Responsibly

As the popularity of cruising continues to rise, so does the awareness of its **environmental impact**. The cruise industry has faced scrutiny for its contribution to **carbon emissions, waste generation, and marine pollution**. However, many cruise lines are now embracing **sustainable cruising practices**, aiming to minimize their ecological footprint while promoting responsible tourism. For travelers, adopting eco-friendly habits on board and during shore excursions can also make a significant difference. Here's how cruise companies and passengers alike can support a more sustainable future for cruising.

### How Cruise Lines Are Going Green

Leading cruise companies are investing heavily in **technology and innovation** to reduce their environmental impact.

**Eco-Friendly Ship Design:**

**Eco-Friendly Itineraries:** Cruises are designing routes that reduce unnecessary fuel consumption and promote visits to destinations committed to sustainable tourism.

### Key Certifications and Organizations to Look For

**Green Marine Certification:** Recognizes cruise lines that meet rigorous environmental performance standards.

**ISO 14001:** An international standard for effective environmental management systems.

**Friends of the Earth (FOE) Report Card:** Rates cruise lines based on environmental performance in categories like air pollution, wastewater treatment, and transparency.

# PACKING FOR YOUR BRITISH ISLES CRUISE: A COMPLETE GUIDE

Embarking on a **British Isles cruise** is an exciting adventure, offering a blend of **historic cities**, **rugged coastlines**, and **breathtaking natural landscapes**. From the bustling streets of **London** to the windswept cliffs of **Scotland** and the quaint villages of **Ireland**, the region's **diverse weather** and variety of activities make smart packing essential. To help you prepare for a smooth and enjoyable journey, here's a comprehensive guide on what to pack for your British Isles cruise.

**Clothing Essentials: Layer Up for Changing Weather**

The British Isles are known for their **unpredictable weather**, often experiencing **sunshine, rain, and cool breezes** all in the same day. The key to staying comfortable is **layering**.

**Base Layers (for Comfort):**

**T-shirts and Long-Sleeved Shirts:** Lightweight, breathable fabrics for layering.

**Thermal Undershirts (for colder months):** Especially useful if cruising in early spring or late autumn.

**Outer Layers (for Warmth & Protection):**

**Waterproof Jacket or Raincoat:** A **lightweight, breathable, waterproof** jacket is a must for sudden showers.

**Fleece or Sweater:** Even in summer, evenings can be chilly, especially on deck.

**Packable Down Jacket (for colder seasons):** Compact and warm without taking up too much space.

**Bottoms:**

**Comfortable Trousers/Jeans:** Perfect for casual wear during shore excursions.

**Water-Resistant Pants:** Great for hiking or outdoor adventures.

**Dress Slacks or Skirts:** For evenings when the cruise has **smart casual or formal dress codes**.

**Evening Wear:**

**Smart Casual Outfits:** Polo shirts, blouses, dresses, or tailored pants for most dinners.

**Formal Attire (if applicable):** Check your cruise line's dress code. Some may have formal nights requiring **cocktail dresses, suits, or tuxedos**.

**Footwear:**

**Comfortable Walking Shoes:** Essential for exploring cobblestone streets and rugged terrains.

**Waterproof Hiking Boots:** If you plan on hiking in places like the **Scottish Highlands** or **Giant's Causeway**.

**Dress Shoes:** For formal nights on board.

**Flip-Flops or Sandals:** For lounging on deck or in the spa.

## Cruise Essentials: Must-Have Items for Onboard Comfort

**Travel Documents:**

**Passport & Visas:** Ensure your passport is valid for at least **six months beyond** your travel dates.

**Cruise Tickets, Travel Insurance, and Itinerary:** Keep digital and printed copies.

**Photo ID:** Some ports require an additional ID for shore excursions.

**Day Bag:**

**Small Backpack or Crossbody Bag:** Ideal for carrying essentials like water, maps, and snacks during shore excursions.

**Money Matters:**

**Credit/Debit Cards:** Widely accepted in the UK and Ireland.

**Local Currency:** Carry some **British Pounds (GBP)** and **Euros (EUR)** for small purchases, especially in rural areas.

## Tech Essentials: Stay Connected and Capturing Memories

**Gadgets:**

**Smartphone & Charger:** For photos, navigation, and communication.

**Camera (optional):** If you prefer higher-quality photos.

**Power Bank:** Keep devices charged during long excursions.

**Universal Power Adapter:** The UK and Ireland use different plug types (**Type G**), so an adapter is essential.

**Headphones:** Great for onboard relaxation or audio tours.

### Toiletries & Personal Care:

While most cruise ships provide basic toiletries, packing your personal items ensures comfort:

**Toothbrush, Toothpaste, and Floss**

**Shampoo, Conditioner, and Body Wash** (travel-sized if you prefer your own)

**Deodorant, Skincare Products, and Lip Balm** (the sea breeze can be drying)

**Sunscreen and After-Sun Lotion** (yes, even in cloudy weather, UV rays are present!)

**Motion Sickness Remedies: Seasickness bands, ginger tablets, or medication** like Dramamine if you're prone to motion sickness.

**Prescription Medications:** Bring enough for the entire trip, plus copies of prescriptions.

### Shore Excursion Essentials:

**For Outdoor Adventures:**

**Water Bottle:** Refillable to stay hydrated.

**Binoculars:** Great for wildlife spotting in places like **St. Kilda** or along **coastal cliffs**.

**Compact Umbrella:** For sudden rain showers.

**Sunglasses and Hat:** For protection from sun and wind.

**Lightweight Gloves and Scarf (seasonal):** Especially in colder regions or windy coastal spots.

### Extra Items for Convenience:

**Laundry Bag:** To separate dirty clothes.

**Ziploc Bags:** For snacks, wet clothes, or organizing small items.

**Notebook and Pen:** For jotting down travel memories or important info.

**Books, E-reader, or Magazines:** For downtime on board.

### What Not to Pack:

**Irons, Steamers, or Candles:** Prohibited on cruise ships for safety reasons.

**Excessive Cash:** Use cards when possible and carry only small amounts of local currency.

**Heavy Luggage:** Space in cabins is limited, so **pack light** and consider versatile clothing that can be mixed and matched.

## Essentials for the British Weather: How to Pack and Prepare

When planning a trip to the **British Isles**, one thing is certain: you'll encounter **unpredictable weather**. The region, which includes **England, Scotland, Wales, Northern Ireland, and the Republic of Ireland**, is known for its rapidly changing conditions. You might experience **sunshine, rain, wind, and cool breezes—all in the same day**. This variability is part of the charm of traveling through the British Isles, but it does require thoughtful preparation.

To help you stay comfortable and enjoy your trip to the fullest, here's a guide to the **essentials for navigating British weather**

**Understanding the British Climate**

The British Isles have a **temperate maritime climate**, meaning:

**Mild Temperatures:** Rarely extreme. Summers (June–August) average around **15–20°C (59–68°F)**, while winters (December–February) hover around **2–7°C (35–45°F)**.

**Frequent Rain:** Showers can occur year-round, often light but persistent, especially in **western coastal areas** like Wales and Scotland.

**Variable Weather:** A sunny morning can quickly turn into a rainy afternoon, so **layers are key**.

**Must-Have Clothing for British Weather**

**Light Layers for Flexibility:**

**T-Shirts and Long-Sleeved Tops:** Opt for **breathable fabrics** like cotton or moisture-wicking materials.

**Sweaters or Fleece Jackets:** Perfect for layering over shirts when it gets cooler.

**Lightweight, Packable Down Jacket:** Provides warmth without bulk, especially useful in spring and autumn.

**Waterproof Outerwear:**

**Rain Jacket:** A **lightweight, waterproof, and windproof jacket with a hood** is essential. Look for breathable materials like **GORE-TEX** to stay dry without overheating.

**Compact Travel Umbrella:** A sturdy, wind-resistant umbrella can be handy, though strong gusts might render it less effective in places like the Scottish Highlands.

**Bottoms:**

**Comfortable Trousers/Jeans:** For city sightseeing or casual outings.

**Water-Resistant Pants:** Ideal for hiking in wet conditions. Quick-dry fabrics are a bonus.

**Footwear:**

**Waterproof Walking Shoes or Boots:** Essential for exploring cobblestone streets, countryside trails, and rainy days.

**Comfortable Sneakers:** Great for dry weather and city strolling.

**Extra Socks:** Pack **moisture-wicking socks** to keep your feet dry and comfortable.

**Accessories to Beat the Elements**

**Sunglasses:** Yes, even in Britain! The sun does make appearances, and UV rays can be strong.

**Hat and Gloves (Seasonal):** Especially for autumn, winter, or breezy coastal regions. A **light scarf** adds warmth without bulk.

**Sun Protection: Broad-spectrum sunscreen** and **lip balm with SPF** protect against unexpected sun exposure.

**Essentials for Your Day Pack**

When venturing out, especially on **shore excursions** or countryside hikes, pack these items:

**Refillable Water Bottle:** Stay hydrated, especially during active days.

**Quick-Dry Towel:** Useful for unexpected rain or damp conditions.

**Ziploc Bags or Dry Pouch:** Protect electronics and important documents from rain.

**Map or Navigation App:** In case weather conditions affect visibility.

**Seasonal Considerations**

**Spring (March–May):**

Expect **cool breezes** and occasional rain. Light layers with a waterproof jacket are perfect.

**Summer (June–August):**

Warm days mixed with cooler evenings. **Pack shorts**, but also include a sweater for unexpected chills.

**Insect repellent** may be useful in rural areas, especially in Scotland where **midges** can be a nuisance.

**Autumn (September–November):**

Crisp air with beautiful foliage. **Layering is key**, as mornings and evenings can be chilly, with mild afternoons.

**Winter (December–February):**

Rarely extreme cold, but **damp conditions** can make it feel colder. **Thermal base layers**, a warm coat, gloves, and a hat are essential.

**Tips for Cruise Travelers**

If you're on a **British Isles cruise**, remember that weather at sea can be different from on land:

**Windproof Jackets:** Essential for standing on deck during breezy sailing days.

**Seasickness Remedies:** Choppy waters can accompany stormy weather, so pack **motion sickness bands or medication** if you're prone to seasickness.

### Final Tips for Navigating British Weather

**"There's no bad weather, only unsuitable clothing."** This British saying holds true—pack smart, and you'll enjoy your trip in any weather.

**Check the Forecast Daily:** Apps like **BBC Weather** or **Met Office** provide reliable updates.

**Embrace the Adventure:** A little rain adds to the charm of historic castles, misty landscapes, and cozy pubs with roaring fires.

# What to Pack for Excursions: A Practical Guide for Travelers

When embarking on an excursion, whether it's a shore adventure on a cruise or a day trip to explore a new destination, knowing what to pack can make a huge difference in your comfort and enjoyment. The key is to pack efficiently and thoughtfully, ensuring you have everything you need without overloading yourself. Here's a detailed guide on **what to pack for excursions** that will keep you prepared for a variety of activities and environments.

## Daypack Essentials

Your **daypack** is the most important item to pack for excursions, as it holds everything, you'll need throughout the day. It should be lightweight, durable, and large enough to hold your essentials without being cumbersome. Here's what to pack inside:

### Water Bottle

Staying hydrated is crucial, especially when you're exploring outdoor sites or walking long distances. A

**reusable water bottle** will help you avoid purchasing single-use plastic bottles, keeping your hydration needs in check while also being environmentally friendly.

## Snacks

Pack **light, non-perishable snacks** like granola bars, nuts, dried fruit, or trail mix. These snacks are perfect for keeping your energy up, especially if you're out on a longer excursion with limited food options.

## Sunscreen and Lip Balm

Regardless of the destination, protecting your skin from harmful UV rays is important. Choose a **broad-spectrum sunscreen** (SPF 30 or higher) and **lip balm with SPF** to safeguard your skin.

## Hand Sanitizer and Wet Wipes

While many destinations offer restrooms, it's a good idea to carry **hand sanitizer** and **wet wipes** to clean your hands before eating or touching your face. These are especially helpful when you're exploring more remote areas.

### Camera or Smartphone

Capture the memories by packing your **camera or smartphone** with enough storage and extra memory cards. A **portable power bank** can also be useful to keep your devices charged throughout the day.

### Clothing and Footwear

The type of clothing you pack will depend largely on your destination and the nature of your excursion. Here are some general guidelines:

### Comfortable, Weather-Appropriate Clothing

**Light Layers:** If you're traveling to a destination with varying weather conditions, pack **light layers** that can be added or removed as needed. This includes **t-shirts**, **long sleeves**, and a **light jacket**.

**Waterproof Jacket:** Always carry a **water-resistant or waterproof jacket** in case of rain. Weather can change quickly, especially if you're headed to coastal or mountainous regions.

**Hat and Sunglasses:** A **wide-brimmed hat** will protect you from the sun, while **sunglasses** help shield your eyes from UV rays.

**Appropriate Footwear**

**Comfortable Walking Shoes:** Choose shoes that provide **good support** and are comfortable for walking long distances. **Hiking boots** or **athletic shoes** are ideal if your excursion includes uneven terrain.

**Water Shoes or Sandals:** If your excursion involves water activities like **beach visits**, **kayaking**, or **river tours**, pack a pair of **waterproof sandals** or **water shoes**.

**Extra Socks and Underwear**

It's always a good idea to pack **extra socks** and **underwear** in case of unexpected changes in weather or if you get wet during your excursion.

## Miscellaneous Items

### Sunglasses and Hat

Protect your eyes from the sun with **UV-blocking sunglasses**. A **hat with a wide brim** provides shade and keeps your cool.

### First Aid Kit

A small **first aid kit** can be incredibly useful for treating blisters, cuts, or headaches on the go. Include **band-aids**, **antiseptic wipes**, **pain relievers**, and any personal medications you might need.

### Travel Documents

Carry any **necessary tickets, passports**, and **insurance documents** in a safe, easily accessible spot. A **copy of your itinerary** can also be helpful in case of emergencies.

### Bug Repellent

If you're traveling to an area known for insects, such as **rainforests** or **coastal regions**, pack a bottle of **bug repellent** to avoid bites and stings.

**Optional Items**

**Notebook and Pen**

If you enjoy documenting your travels, a **small notebook** and **pen** will allow you to jot down important notes, travel memories, or ideas.

**Local Currency and Cards**

Though **credit cards** are widely accepted, it's always good to have **cash** for smaller shops or rural destinations. Carry **local currency** for convenience, especially if you're venturing to more remote areas.

the weather brings—rain or shine.

After all, as the British often say with a smile, **"If you don't like the weather, just wait five minutes.**

## Special Considerations for Longer Cruises: What You Need to Know

Embarking on a **longer cruise**, whether it's a few weeks around the **British Isles** or an extended journey across Europe, offers an incredible opportunity to explore diverse cultures, scenic landscapes, and historic sites—all while enjoying the comforts of life at sea. However, cruising for an extended period requires **different planning** than shorter voyages. From **packing strategies** to managing health, finances, and onboard routines, here are key considerations to ensure your long cruise is smooth, enjoyable, and stress-free.

**Packing Smart for Extended Travel**

Packing for a longer cruise isn't about bringing more—it's about packing **wisely and efficiently**.

**Versatile Clothing:**

**Layered Outfits:** Choose clothes you can mix and match to create different looks. **Neutral colors** work best.

**Wrinkle-Resistant Fabrics:** These are practical since laundry facilities may be limited.

**Formal Attire:** If your cruise has multiple formal nights, pack a couple of versatile pieces that you can accessorize differently.

**Comfortable Footwear:** Include **walking shoes** for excursions, **flip-flops** for the pool, and **dress shoes** for evenings.

**Laundry Solutions:**

Check if your ship has **self-service laundry rooms** or consider **onboard laundry packages** to avoid overpacking.

Pack a **small bag of detergent** for hand-washing essentials in your cabin.

**Health and Medical Considerations**

On longer cruises, maintaining your health becomes even more important.

**Medications and Health Supplies:**

Bring an **adequate supply of prescription medications**, plus extra in case of delays.

Carry a **copy of your prescriptions** and a brief **medical history** document.

Include basic over-the-counter items like **pain relievers, motion sickness remedies, antacids, and band-aids**.

### Medical Facilities Onboard:

Most cruise ships have a **medical center**, but for complex conditions, you may need care at port.

Consider **travel insurance with medical evacuation coverage**, especially if visiting remote destinations.

### Stay Active:

Long cruises can lead to a sedentary routine. Take advantage of **onboard gyms, walking tracks, and fitness classes** to stay active.

**Stretch and move regularly** to prevent stiffness or circulation issues, especially on sea days.

### Managing Finances on a Longer Cruise

Cruising for several weeks requires planning for **expenses both onboard and ashore**.

### Budget Wisely:

**Onboard Costs:** Factor in gratuities, specialty dining, drinks, excursions, Wi-Fi, and spa treatments.

**Port Expenses:** Budget for meals, transportation, shopping, and entrance fees at attractions.

**Payment Methods:**

Carry a **credit card** with no foreign transaction fees and some **local currency** for smaller purchases in port.

Use the ship's **account management system** to track your spending in real-time.

**Staying Connected**

Extended travel often means staying in touch with family, work, or managing personal affairs.

**Wi-Fi Packages:** Long-term packages may offer better rates than daily plans.

**Communication Apps:** Use apps like **WhatsApp, Skype, or Zoom** for affordable messaging and calls.

**Mail Forwarding and Virtual Services:** Consider services that help manage **mail, bills, and banking** remotely.

### Personal Comforts and Entertainment

Spending weeks on a ship can lead to cabin fever if you're not prepared.

**Hobbies:** Bring books, e-readers, puzzles, knitting, journals, or art supplies.

**Streaming:** Download movies, shows, or podcasts in advance to enjoy during downtime.

**Personal Items:** Small comforts like **a favorite pillow, cozy blanket, or photos from home** can make your cabin feel more personal.

### Travel Documents and Visas

Longer cruises may visit multiple countries, requiring careful attention to travel documentation.

Ensure your **passport is valid for at least six months** beyond your return date.

Research **visa requirements** for all countries on your itinerary, including transit visas if applicable.

Make **copies of important documents**, both physical and digital, stored separately from the originals.

**Insurance and Emergency Planning**

For extended trips, comprehensive **travel insurance** is essential.

**Medical Coverage:** Ensure it includes international coverage, emergency evacuation, and pre-existing conditions if applicable.

**Trip Interruption Insurance:** Covers costs if you need to cut your trip short due to an emergency.

**Emergency Contacts:** Keep a list of contacts, including the cruise line's emergency numbers, local embassies, and family back home.

**Mental Health and Well-Being**

Long-term travel can be emotionally challenging.

**Routine:** Establish a daily routine to create structure.

**Social Connections:** Engage with fellow passengers, attend onboard activities, and build friendships.

**Alone Time:** Balance social activities with moments of solitude to recharge.

## Tips for Packing Light and Efficiently: Travel Smart, Travel Easy

Packing light isn't just about saving space in your suitcase—it's about **traveling with ease, reducing stress**, and allowing more freedom to enjoy your journey. Whether you're heading on a **British Isles cruise**, a city-hopping adventure, or a long-haul trip, efficient packing helps you move comfortably through airports, manage your belongings effortlessly, and avoid unnecessary baggage fees.

Here's a detailed guide on how to **pack light and efficiently** without compromising on essentials.

### Start with a Packing List

A well-thought-out **packing list** is the foundation of efficient packing.

**Categorize:** Break it down into **clothing, toiletries, tech gadgets, documents, and miscellaneous items**.

**Prioritize:** Focus on the essentials you'll actually use. Ask yourself: **"Do I really need this?"** If not, leave it behind.

**Consider Your Itinerary:** Pack according to your activities—formal dinners, outdoor excursions, or beach days require different essentials.

### Choose the Right Luggage

Your luggage can influence how much you pack.

**Carry-On Over Checked Bags:** If possible, opt for a **carry-on suitcase** or a **travel backpack**. This limits how much you bring and helps avoid checked baggage fees.

**Lightweight, Compact Bags:** Choose a suitcase made from **light materials** with **expandable compartments** for flexibility.

**Packing Cubes:** These are game-changers for organization. Use them to compress clothes and keep categories separate, making it easy to find items without unpacking everything.

**Pack Versatile Clothing (The Art of Layering)**

When packing light, **versatility is key**.

**Neutral Color Palette:** Stick to colors like **black, white, navy, and gray**. They're easy to mix and match, creating multiple outfits from fewer pieces.

**Layering Pieces:** Instead of packing bulky sweaters, layer lightweight items like **t-shirts, cardigans, and jackets**.

**Multipurpose Items:** A **scarf** can be a fashion accessory, a blanket, or even a makeshift pillow. A **sarong** can work as a beach cover-up, towel, or shawl.

**Rule of Three:** Pack **three tops for every bottom**, as tops are more noticeable in photos and easier to re-wear.

**Sample Capsule Wardrobe:**

2 pairs of pants (one casual, one dressy)

1 pair of shorts or a skirt

4-5 tops (mix of long and short sleeves)

1 versatile dress (for casual or formal settings)

Lightweight jacket or cardigan

Comfortable walking shoes + 1 pair of dress shoes

**Limit Footwear (The Bulkiest Item!)**

Shoes take up a lot of space, so choose wisely:

**Comfortable Walking Shoes:** For daily wear and excursions.

**Dress Shoes:** If needed for formal occasions, choose compact styles.

**Flip-Flops or Sandals:** Lightweight and perfect for beaches or lounging.

**Pro Tip:** Wear your bulkiest shoes during transit to save space.

**Minimize Toiletries**

Toiletries are often bulky and can leak. Simplify by:

**Travel-Sized Containers:** Use **3.4 oz (100 ml)** bottles to comply with airport liquid restrictions.

**Solid Alternatives:** Solid shampoo bars, toothpaste tablets, and soap sheets save space and avoid liquid restrictions.

**Hotel/Ship Amenities:** Check if your accommodation provides basics like shampoo, conditioner, and body wash.

**Bonus Tip:** A small **hanging toiletry bag** keeps things organized and accessible.

**Pack Tech Smartly**

Tech gear can be heavy if overpacked.

**Multipurpose Devices:** Use your smartphone for **photos, maps, reading, and communication**, reducing the need for extra gadgets.

**Universal Power Adapter:** Instead of multiple chargers, bring a universal adapter with **USB ports** to charge multiple devices simultaneously.

**Compact Power Bank:** Essential for long days exploring.

## Space-Saving Packing Techniques

**Rolling vs. Folding:**

**Roll Clothes:** Rolling reduces wrinkles and saves space. Great for casual wear.

**Bundle Packing:** Wrap outfits around a central core (like a toiletry bag) to minimize creases.

**Compression Bags:** Perfect for bulky items like jackets, as they **squeeze out air** and maximize space.

## Wear Your Heaviest Items While Traveling

To save luggage space:

**Wear your jacket, boots, or bulky sweaters** during flights or when boarding cruise ships.

**Layer up:** Planes and ships can be chilly, so you'll stay warm and save packing space simultaneously.

**Leave Room for Souvenirs**

When packing, leave some **extra space** for things you'll pick up along the way.

**Foldable Tote Bag:** Handy for extra items on the return trip.

**Vacuum-Seal Bags:** Compress dirty laundry to make room for souvenirs.

**What NOT to Pack**

**"Just in Case" Items:** If you're unsure, you likely won't need it.

**Excessive Shoes:** Stick to 2-3 pairs max.

**Bulky Towels:** Most accommodations provide towels. opt for a **microfiber travel towel** if needed.

**Books:** Use an **e-reader** or reading app to save space.

# Testimonials & Travel Stories: Memorable Experiences from the British Isles

Every journey leaves a mark, and travelers to the **British Isles** often return with stories of **breathtaking landscapes, rich history, and unforgettable encounters**. Whether cruising along the rugged coast of **Scotland**, exploring the lively streets of **Dublin**, or discovering the hidden charms of **small seaside villages**, each experience is unique. Testimonials from fellow travelers offer valuable insights, helping future visitors plan their own adventures with confidence.

Here are some **real travel stories** and testimonials that highlight the magic of cruising and exploring the British Isles.

**Exploring the Magic of Edinburgh – Sarah's Story**

*"Stepping off my cruise ship in Edinburgh, I was immediately captivated by the city's old-world charm. I joined a guided shore excursion to **Edinburgh Castle**, where I stood atop Castle Rock, gazing at panoramic*

views of the city. Our guide shared fascinating tales of Mary, Queen of Scots, and the historic Crown Jewels. Afterward, I strolled down the **Royal Mile**, stopping for a warm cup of tea at a cozy café. A visit to **Holyrood Palace** rounded out my day, making me feel as if I had stepped back in time. Edinburgh was a highlight of my cruise, and I can't wait to return!"

**Travel Tip:** Pre-book castle tickets to skip the long lines, especially during summer!

### Discovering the Isles of Scilly – Mark & Lisa's Adventure

"When we booked our British Isles cruise, we didn't expect to fall in love with the **Isles of Scilly**. This lesser-known gem off the coast of Cornwall felt like a tropical paradise. We explored **Tresco Abbey Gardens**, home to exotic plants that thrive in the islands' mild climate. The white sandy beaches were nearly empty, and the crystal-clear waters looked straight out of the Caribbean. One of the locals even invited us to a small café for fresh seafood and a chat about island life. It was an experience we'll treasure forever."

**Travel Tip:** The Isles of Scilly are best explored on foot or by bike—rent one for the day and soak in the beauty at your own pace.

## The Heart of Irish Hospitality in Dublin – James' Testimonial

*"Dublin completely stole my heart! From the moment I walked into a traditional pub, I felt at home. At **The Temple Bar**, I met a group of friendly locals who introduced me to Irish music. The lively tunes of the fiddle and bodhrán filled the air, and before I knew it, I was clapping along and learning the lyrics to an old Irish ballad. A visit to **Guinness Storehouse** was the perfect way to end the day, sipping a pint with stunning views of the city from the **Gravity Bar**. The warmth and hospitality of Dubliners made this one of my most cherished travel memories."*

**Travel Tip:** Visit smaller pubs outside of Temple Bar for a more authentic (and budget-friendly) experience.

### A Peaceful Escape to the Isle of Skye – Emily's Journey

*"The rugged beauty of **Scotland's Isle of Skye** left me speechless. My husband and I rented a car and drove along the **Trotternish Peninsula**, stopping at the breathtaking **Old Man of Storr** and the mystical **Fairy Pools**. Despite the unpredictable weather, the mist rolling over the hills added to the magic. We ended the day in **Portree**, a charming town with colorful harborfront houses, where we enjoyed a warm bowl of Cullen skink (a delicious Scottish seafood soup). This was the peaceful, nature-filled escape we had been looking for."*

**Travel Tip:** Prepare for rain and wind—bring a waterproof jacket and sturdy hiking boots!

### First-Time Cruiser's Perspective – Laura's Experience

*"As a first-time cruiser, I wasn't sure what to expect, but my **British Isles cruise** turned out to be the perfect way to explore multiple destinations without the hassle of*

*constant packing and transportation. From the towering* **Cliffs of Moher in Ireland** *to the historic streets of* **Liverpool**, *each port stop had something unique to offer. Onboard, I was amazed by the variety of activities— cooking classes, live music, and even a relaxing spa day at sea. If you're hesitant about cruising, don't be! It's a fantastic way to experience the beauty of the British Isles effortlessly."*

**Travel Tip:** Pack layers and comfortable walking shoes— you'll be exploring a lot!

## Real-Life Experiences from Fellow Cruisers: Unforgettable Journeys Through the British Isles

Cruising through the **British Isles** is an incredible way to experience its **historic cities, rugged coastlines, and charming villages**—all from the comfort of a floating hotel. Fellow travelers often return with **memorable stories**, from misty mornings in Scotland to warm pub nights in Ireland. These real-life experiences offer valuable insights for future cruisers looking to make the most of their voyage.

Here are some firsthand accounts from fellow cruisers who explored the British Isles and uncovered its hidden treasures.

**A Fairytale Day in Edinburgh – Sarah & Tom's Adventure**

*"When our cruise docked in **Leith, the port of Edinburgh**, we were eager to explore. We started with a tour of **Edinburgh Castle**, perched high above the city on Castle Rock. Standing in front of the Crown Jewels of Scotland was a surreal moment, and the view from the castle walls stretched all the way to the Firth of Forth. From there, we wandered down the **Royal Mile**, stopping at quaint shops and cozy cafés for a taste of **shortbread and Scottish tea**. Our guide even took us to the **Holyrood Palace**, where we learned about Mary, Queen of Scots. It felt like we had stepped back in time, and despite a bit of drizzle, the city's magic remained untouched."*

**Cruise Tip: Book castle tickets in advance** to avoid long queues, especially during peak summer months.

### The Soul of Ireland in Dublin – James' Story

*"One of my best cruise memories happened in **Dublin**. After a morning tour of **Trinity College and the Book of Kells**, I ventured into the heart of the city to explore its **lively pub scene**. That evening, I found myself in a small pub near Temple Bar, where a group of locals welcomed me to join them. A live band played **traditional Irish folk music**, and before I knew it, I was clapping along to **The Wild Rover** with a pint of Guinness in hand. The warmth, laughter, and music made me feel like I had truly experienced the **soul of Ireland**."*

**Cruise Tip:** Head to **smaller, less touristy pubs** for a more **authentic and budget-friendly** experience.

### The Rugged Beauty of the Isle of Skye – Emily's Journey

*"Our ship anchored near **Portree**, and we embarked on a shore excursion to the **Isle of Skye**, a place I had always dreamed of visiting. The weather was classic Scotland—**a mix of mist, sunshine, and the occasional rain shower**—but it only added to the magic. We hiked to the **Old Man*

*of Storr*, *where the landscape looked straight out of a fantasy novel. Later, we visited the* **Fairy Pools**, *a series of crystal-clear waterfalls surrounded by rolling hills. The peace and serenity of Skye were unlike anything I had ever experienced. It was the highlight of my entire cruise!"*

**Cruise Tip:** Bring **waterproof gear and sturdy hiking boots** for exploring the **Isle of Skye's rugged terrain**.

### First-Time Cruiser's Perspective – Laura's Experience

*"As a first-time cruiser, I wasn't sure what to expect, but my* **British Isles cruise** *turned out to be the perfect way to explore multiple destinations without the hassle of constant packing and transportation. From the towering* **Cliffs of Moher in Ireland** *to the historic streets of* **Liverpool**, *each port stop had something unique to offer. Onboard, I was amazed by the variety of activities—cooking classes, live music, and even a relaxing spa day at sea. If you're hesitant about cruising, don't be! It's a fantastic way to experience the beauty of the British Isles effortlessly."*

**Cruise Tip:** Pack **layers and comfortable walking shoes**—you'll be exploring a lot on foot.

## Recommended Shore Excursions from Past Travelers: Must-Do Experiences in the British Isles

Cruising through the **British Isles** offers a unique opportunity to explore **historic landmarks, breathtaking landscapes, and charming coastal towns**—all without the hassle of constant packing. Shore excursions allow travelers to **immerse themselves in local culture, history, and natural beauty**, turning brief port stops into unforgettable adventures.

Here are some **highly recommended shore excursions** from past travelers who explored the British Isles.

### Edinburgh, Scotland – Edinburgh Castle & Royal Mile Walking Tour

**Recommended by: Sarah & Tom, U.S.A.**

*"Our shore excursion in **Edinburgh** started with a guided tour of **Edinburgh Castle**, where we marveled at the **Crown Jewels of Scotland** and learned about the castle's*

*military history. The views from the castle walls stretched over the city and out toward the Firth of Forth. From there, we walked down the historic* **Royal Mile**, *stopping at* **St. Giles' Cathedral** *and charming local shops selling tartan scarves and whisky. We ended our tour with a visit to* **Holyrood Palace**, *once home to Mary, Queen of Scots. The rich history and stunning architecture made this one of our favorite days of the cruise!"*

**Travel Tip: Book castle tickets in advance** to avoid long lines, especially in the summer months.

### Dublin, Ireland – Guinness Storehouse & City Highlights Tour

**Recommended by: James, Canada**

*"I booked a shore excursion in* **Dublin** *that combined a panoramic city tour with a stop at the famous* **Guinness Storehouse**. *We started at* **Trinity College**, *where we saw the stunning* **Book of Kells** *before heading to St. Patrick's Cathedral. The highlight of the trip was the Guinness Storehouse, where we learned about the brewing process and enjoyed a complimentary pint at the* **Gravity Bar**,

*offering spectacular views over Dublin. The city's lively energy and warm hospitality made this an incredible experience!"*

**Travel Tip:** Visit **smaller local pubs outside Temple Bar** for a more authentic and budget-friendly Irish experience.

**Isle of Skye, Scotland – Fairy Pools & Old Man of Storr Hike**

**Recommended by: Emily, Australia**

*"Our ship anchored near **Portree**, and we joined an excursion to the **Fairy Pools**. These crystal-clear waterfalls, set against the dramatic backdrop of the **Cuillin Mountains**, looked like something out of a fantasy novel. After a refreshing walk, we continued to the **Old Man of Storr**, a famous rock formation with breathtaking views of the island. The mix of **misty landscapes, rolling hills, and hidden waterfalls** made this shore excursion a dream for nature lovers!"*

**Travel Tip:** Wear **waterproof clothing and sturdy hiking boots**, as Skye's weather is unpredictable.

### Belfast, Northern Ireland – Giant's Causeway & Titanic Belfast Tour

**Recommended by: Mark & Lisa, U.K.**

*"The **Giant's Causeway** is a natural wonder that must be seen to be believed! We explored the **40,000 interlocking basalt columns**, formed by volcanic activity millions of years ago. The scenery was stunning, and we even walked along the **Carrick-a-Rede Rope Bridge**, which offered thrilling views over the cliffs. Afterward, we visited **Titanic Belfast**, an interactive museum on the site where the Titanic was built. This excursion was the perfect mix of natural beauty and history!"*

**Travel Tip: Bring a windproof jacket**, as the coastal breeze at Giant's Causeway can be strong.

### Liverpool, England – The Beatles Story & Albert Dock

**Recommended by: Laura, USA**

*"As a Beatles fan, I couldn't miss this shore excursion! We visited **The Beatles Story Museum**, which took us through the band's journey from Liverpool to worldwide fame.*

*Walking down **Mathew Street**, we stopped at the **Cavern Club**, where the Beatles played in their early years. Afterward, we explored **Albert Dock**, a beautiful waterfront area filled with museums, restaurants, and lively street performances. It was the perfect way to experience the musical heart of Liverpool!"*

**Travel Tip:** Arrive early at the **Cavern Club**, as it gets crowded in the afternoons.

## Must-See Destinations and Activities in the British Isles

The **British Isles** are a treasure trove of **historic landmarks, breathtaking landscapes, and vibrant cultural experiences**. Whether you're exploring **ancient castles, dramatic coastlines, or charming villages**, there's something for every traveler. From the bustling streets of **London and Dublin** to the rugged beauty of **Scotland and Wales**, here are the **must-see destinations and activities** for an unforgettable journey through the British Isles.

**Edinburgh, Scotland – A Walk-Through History**

**Why Visit?**

Scotland's capital is **steeped in history**, with cobbled streets, grand castles, and stunning views.

**Top Activities:**

**Explore Edinburgh Castle:** Home to the **Crown Jewels of Scotland**, this fortress offers breathtaking views over the city.

**Stroll the Royal Mile:** This historic street is lined with **shops, cafés, and street performers**, leading to **Holyrood Palace**, the official Scottish residence of the British monarch.

**Hike to Arthur's Seat:** A short but rewarding climb to an ancient volcano for **panoramic city views**.

**Attend the Edinburgh Festival Fringe:** The **world's largest arts festival**, held every August, features **theater, comedy, and live performances**.

**Travel Tip:** Visit **Edinburgh Castle early** to avoid crowds, especially during summer.

## Dublin, Ireland – Culture, Pubs, and History

**Why Visit?**

Dublin combines a **rich literary heritage, lively pub culture, and historic landmarks**.

**Top Activities:**

**Visit Trinity College & The Book of Kells:** A masterpiece of medieval art housed in the stunning **Long Room Library**.

**Tour the Guinness Storehouse:** Learn about **Ireland's most famous beer**, ending with a pint at the **Gravity Bar** overlooking the city.

**Explore Temple Bar:** This area is famous for **live Irish music, cozy pubs, and vibrant nightlife**.

**Walk along the River Liffey:** Cross the iconic **Ha'penny Bridge** and admire Dublin's charming cityscape.

**Travel Tip:** Visit **smaller, local pubs outside of Temple Bar** for a more authentic experience.

**The Isle of Skye, Scotland – A Nature Lover's Dream**

**Why Visit?**

This **remote, rugged island** is home to some of the most **breathtaking landscapes** in the British Isles.

**Top Activities:**

**Hike the Old Man of Storr:** A dramatic rock formation offering **unforgettable views**.

**Explore the Fairy Pools:** Crystal-clear waterfalls surrounded by **rolling green hills**.

**Visit Dunvegan Castle:** Scotland's oldest continuously inhabited castle, home to **Clan MacLeod**.

**Drive the Trotternish Loop:** A scenic drive showcasing the **island's best landscapes**, including **Kilt Rock and Mealt Falls**.

**Travel Tip:** Pack **waterproof gear**—the weather on Skye is **unpredictable**!

### The Giant's Causeway, Northern Ireland – A Natural Wonder

**Why Visit?**

A **UNESCO World Heritage Site**, the Giant's Causeway features **40,000 basalt columns**, formed by volcanic activity.

**Top Activities:**

**Walk the Causeway Trail:** Hike along the dramatic cliffs for **panoramic coastal views**.

**Cross Carrick-a-Rede Rope Bridge:** A thrilling **suspension bridge** connecting the mainland to a small island.

**Explore the Dark Hedges:** A famous avenue of **twisted beech trees**, made famous by *Game of Thrones*.

**Visit Bushmills Distillery:** Ireland's **oldest whiskey distillery**, offering tastings and tours.

**Travel Tip:** Wear **sturdy shoes**, as the rocks can be slippery.

**London, England – A City of Endless Attractions**

**Why Visit?**

London is a **world-class city** with **iconic landmarks, diverse culture, and rich history**.

**Top Activities:**

**See Buckingham Palace:** Witness the **Changing of the Guard**, a classic British tradition.

**Tour the Tower of London:** Home to the **Crown Jewels** and steeped in royal history.

**Explore the British Museum:** A must-see for history lovers, featuring **the Rosetta Stone and Egyptian mummies**.

**Ride the London Eye:** Get a **360-degree view** of the city skyline.

**Visit Covent Garden:** A lively area with **street performances, shops, and great restaurants**.

**Travel Tip:** Use an **Oyster Card** for easy and **affordable travel on public transport**.

## The Lake District, England – England's Natural Paradise

**Why Visit?**

A **UNESCO-listed region**, the **Lake District** is England's **top destination for hiking and outdoor adventures**.

**Top Activities:**

**Boat Ride on Lake Windermere:** The largest lake in England, offering stunning views.

**Hike Scafell Pike:** England's **highest peak**, perfect for adventure seekers.

**Visit Beatrix Potter's Home:** The famous author of *Peter Rabbit* lived in this picturesque countryside.

**Explore Grasmere:** A charming village known for **Wordsworth's poetry and delicious gingerbread**.

**Travel Tip:** Visit in **spring or early autumn** for fewer crowds and **mild weather**.

## Liverpool, England – The Beatles & Maritime History

**Why Visit?**

Liverpool is famous for **The Beatles, its maritime history, and lively waterfront**.

**Top Activities:**

**Visit The Beatles Story Museum:** A must for music fans, tracing the band's journey.

**Explore Albert Dock:** Home to museums, galleries, and lively restaurants.

**Walk Along the Mersey River:** Enjoy scenic views and learn about Liverpool's **maritime heritage**.

**Catch a Football Match:** Visit **Anfield Stadium**, home of Liverpool FC.

**Travel Tip:** Visit **Mathew Street** to see the legendary **Cavern Club**, where The Beatles started their career.

Made in the USA
Las Vegas, NV
22 March 2025